The Day the King Defaulted

Moshe Arye Milevsky

The Day the King Defaulted

Financial Lessons from the Stop of the Exchequer in 1672

Moshe Arye Milevsky
Schulich School of Business
York University
Toronto, Ontario, Canada

ISBN 978-3-319-59986-1   ISBN 978-3-319-59987-8 (eBook)
DOI 10.1007/978-3-319-59987-8

Library of Congress Control Number: 2017946089

© The Editor(s) (if applicable) and The Author(s) 2017
This work is subject to copyright. All rights are solely and exclusively licensed by the Publisher, whether the whole or part of the material is concerned, specifically the rights of translation, reprinting, reuse of illustrations, recitation, broadcasting, reproduction on microfilms or in any other physical way, and transmission or information storage and retrieval, electronic adaptation, computer software, or by similar or dissimilar methodology now known or hereafter developed.
The use of general descriptive names, registered names, trademarks, service marks, etc. in this publication does not imply, even in the absence of a specific statement, that such names are exempt from the relevant protective laws and regulations and therefore free for general use.
The publisher, the authors and the editors are safe to assume that the advice and information in this book are believed to be true and accurate at the date of publication. Neither the publisher nor the authors or the editors give a warranty, express or implied, with respect to the material contained herein or for any errors or omissions that may have been made. The publisher remains neutral with regard to jurisdictional claims in published maps and institutional affiliations.

Cover image © Ian Dagnall / Alamy Stock Photo
Cover design by Henry Petrides

Printed on acid-free paper

This Palgrave Macmillan imprint is published by Springer Nature
The registered company is Springer International Publishing AG
The registered company address is: Gewerbestrasse 11, 6330 Cham, Switzerland

"The Bankers desire interest every 3 months and move that they may have assistance from the King against arrests."

**Calendar of Treasury Books
January 12, 1672**

Prologue

If you discreetly inquire about the matter—and even the finest of memories do fade over time—most folks claim they *weren't exactly surprised* by the financial difficulties experienced by Charlie. But then again hindsight is always 20/20.

What really shocked observers though was *how* his problems unfolded as well as the *severity* of the actions and reactions that followed. Early on that cold January morning when they first heard the news, most of Charlie's closest associates were completely taken aback. Given his stature in the community, the events that began to unfold—after the news reached the public—ignited a chain reaction of misery and distress. One thing is for certain, few people ever trusted Charlie with their money again.

Socking it to your creditors is not unheard of and a natural consequence of living beyond your financial means. When you think about it carefully, those who were exposed to Charlie could (probably) have seen that his lifestyle and expenditures were unsustainable. Perhaps at the time they were blinded by the glamour of it all. Either way, when the dust settled and people caught their breath again, everyone asked the same question: *For someone who appeared to be so successful, how could this have happened?* One month, the bills were being paid and the cash was flowing—and then the next month, everything came to a stop, *with a capital S.* The castle made of debt came tumbling down. Was Charlie's default predictable and as clear in advance as black on white? Or was it a rare Black Swan? And, some have pondered: was it even his fault?

To answer this question we'll need to take a step back in time. Let's start with Charlie's early years, which were by no means joyful. His adolescence in particular was stressful by any definition of the word. To begin with, Charlie lost his father under quite gruesome circumstances when he was just a teenager, surely a cause of long-term psychological trauma. Then, as the eldest son of a suddenly impoverished and homeless family, the only thing he immediately inherited was the financial and emotional responsibility of supporting a big family, including a difficult mother and some very young siblings.

Charlie spent most of his teens and twenties scavenging for his father's lost glory, his family's respect and, ultimately, his own identity. In those years, money was a constant source of anxiety. Like most Geminis—he was born at the end of May—Charlie was clever, energetic and made quite the impression on everyone he met, especially the ladies. But his charisma didn't pay the bills and the eviction notices came with dreadful regularity. To add to his worries, some of his late father's unfinished business (bills) and associates continued to haunt him.

And then—to make a long story short—one fine day, just as he was about to turn 30, Charlie's luck unexpectedly changed. Like a ray of sunshine after a decade of storms, he was bestowed with a "dream" job, returning to his family's chosen profession. Of course the first thing he did was move from his squalid digs to a much better house in a much more glamorous neighborhood, across the water. His job back in the family business paid well and the money finally flowed easily.

So, what did the charming, affable, pleasure-seeking 30-year-old with 15 difficult years behind him, do? Well, you guessed it: he started spending freely. Yes, at first, he was careful with budgets, mostly because a distant relative (nicknamed grumpy Uncle Eddie) kept a close eye on him. Soon after his good fortune was restored, Charlie felt comfortable and mature enough to marry. The courtship was quite the affair and the wedding itself was a glorious and expensive extravaganza. Charlie had (incorrectly) assumed that his wife's family was rich and therefore he could spend her (nonexistent) money as well as his own. Perhaps that was his first mistake.

Charlie went on to make other financial mistakes, especially once Uncle Eddie was gone and out of the picture. He started borrowing excessive sums of money to finance—what most people claim, but only with hindsight—an outrageous lifestyle, clothing suitable for a king, jewelry used by queens, vacations, parties (and yes, on mistresses and bastard children).

All this money was borrowed at very high rates, with little regard for whether there was enough future income to support it. You almost wonder what the lenders and bankers were thinking when they extended him the credit. It was only much later on that people learned where most of the money was really going.

And eventually it all caught up with him. Charlie stopped all payments and defaulted on his debts and obligations. He left most of these creditors high and dry. Of course, that wasn't the end of the story. In fact, it was the beginning of a chain reaction. Many of Charlie's associates had themselves borrowed money from their own creditors, thus creating a cascade of unpaid debts in the wake of the original default. In some sense, one really pities his creditors more than one does Charlie, as they were squeezed on both ends.

I'm being rather brief here, but the events were sudden, messy and complicated—and as with any financial crises, perfectly predictable to the gossipmongers and pundits *after the event transpired*. Sure, life stumbled on for Charlie after the financial crisis—walking away from debts does offer some immediate cash relief—but his family's financial reputation never recovered. Things would never be the same and few people took the time (or cared) to dig into the real reasons for his financial distress.

Do you know the Charlie of whom I write?

No? Then perhaps you might know somebody like Charlie? Practically everyone knows someone who has run into financial difficulties and has had to declare bankruptcy. Their name might not be Charlie and the circumstances are always different. But the questions are usually the same. Whose fault was it? Could anybody see it coming? How could he have been expected to pay it back? Should the lenders have been more careful?

But the Charlie I'm referring to here is England's King Charles II. He reigned from the Restoration of the English monarchy in 1660 until his death in 1685—but punctuated by one very messy bankruptcy in the very middle of his 25 years on the throne, during the cold London winter of 1672.

This book tells the fascinating but neglected story of the last time the English government formally defaulted on its debts. Make no mistake, it was a financial calamity that took decades to resolve. Yes, it was eclipsed by an even more infamous scandal called the South Sea Bubble in the second decade of the eighteenth century, which may be the reason "Charlie's" default has been lost from common memory.

But if the world's first *stock market* crash took place in London in the year 1720, then allow me to tell you about the *bond market* crash which occurred 50 years earlier in 1672. As any good financial advisor will tell you, start with bonds before stocks ....

Acknowledgments

The back page of the business section in my local newspaper the *National Post* includes a daily calendar entry, which is reprinted verbatim from the celebrated diary of Samuel Pepys. I suspect it isn't the only English-speaking newspaper around the world that participates in this rather trivial pursuit. Every weekday, the *National Post* reprints a few random paragraphs extracted from Pepys' vast entries for that particular date, which aficionados will know were written in London during the Restoration decade of the 1660s. The Pepys quotes or items are reproduced with no background, context or really any explanation at all. On any given day, the extracts might include names of individuals with whom he interacted, a description of a good meal he had enjoyed, the occasional mention of his wife Elizabeth, the Navy office where he worked or a callout to James, the Duke of York. The naughty little bits of Pepys or references to his sexual peccadilloes are selectively and very conveniently omitted—perhaps after being censored in the editions edited by the Victorians—all of which makes for some rather mundane and bland reading. I would argue that unless you are an expert in English history during the late seventeenth century, most of the activities, events or people referenced will mean little, especially to a typical business or financial audience reading this (in Canada) in the twenty-first century.

And yet, one of the largest and most influential business newspapers in Canada—or at least their executive editors—have elected to use valuable space to reprint these musings because *somebody* is enjoying it, perhaps no different from the audience for crossword puzzles and daily horoscopes. I gather there must be a dedicated group of readers who pick up the newspaper with their coffee every morning, read the accounts of what happened in financial markets the prior day, reckon the value of their stocks and bond holdings as of yesterday's 4 pm close and top it all off by musing, "Now, I wonder what Pepys wrote about this particular calendar date, 350 years ago?"

Well, those enthusiasts are the invisible—and to date very silent—group that have motivated me to continue working on this research project as my energy and intensity level intermittently sagged and I couldn't help wondering, "Why am I immersed in this trivia?" I thank these hidden supporters for implicitly inspiring me to march on when many others explicitly inquired: "1672? Who cares?"

Of course, the issue here is more than a fascination with Pepys, Evelyn or the Stuarts. Rather, for someone who has a deep and professional interest in financial markets and financial products, there is something intriguing and even hypnotic about the seventeenth century. It opened up new modes of inquiry and thinking, hand in hand with the embryonic development of capital markets and instruments. It is the century of Johannes Kepler, Francis Bacon, Galileo Galilei, Isaac Newton, Rene Descartes and John Locke. It is a century that begins with universal superstition and ignorance, a world in which the earth is believed to be the center of the universe and burning witches is the national sport and pastime. It ends with the dawn of the scientific method, laying the foundations of modern technology. In between the disparate end points is a century of religious and social turmoil. And in the middle of that transition from old to new is the age-old question of how exactly to finance and pay for society's progress. Capital and insurance markets in the twenty-first century could not function without the tools of probability and statistics, and yet their foundations as a mathematical discipline were laid in the same seventeenth century. So, how were capital-market instruments traded, valued and priced just as the new scientific paradigm was emerging? That is precisely what captivates me about the story of the *Stop of the Exchequer* or more precisely the *financial instruments* at the heart of the default. To be clear, this isn't simply a story about a king who didn't pay his debts.

Going back to the thanks and salutations, as my research writing continues to drift farther outside my technical expertise and comfort zone, I am forced to rely on a long list of very kind and knowledgeable Samaritans. With that in mind, I would like to acknowledge the following explicit individuals for providing comments, encouragement, guidance and input as well as for answering obscure questions about seventeenth-century

England and finance during the last year or two. They are Forrest Capie, Saumitra Jha, Peter Koudijs, Chris Lewin, Larry Neal, Anne Murphy, Gordon Roberts, Janette Rutterford, Margaret Schotte, Daniel Tut for research assistance and especially Barbara J. Todd from the Department of History at the University of Toronto, who carefully read the draft manuscript and provided many great comments and corrections. Also, I would like to thank Alexa Brand, Alexandra Macqueen, the wonderful staff at Palgrave Macmillan, Vinodh Kumar V and Vinoth Kuppan of SPi Global and—last but certainly not least—my wife Edna for editorial comments and assistance.

Contents

1 **Bankers Then and Now** 1
   Asset Liability Mismanagement in the Seventeenth Century 3
   A Financial Crisis in Slow Motion 7
   Outline of the Story and the Book 9
   A Brief Review of Scholarly Literature 12
   References 18

2 **Dramatis Personae** 21
   Nobility Versus Gentry 21
   King Charles II 24
   Dutch and Temple 28
   Queen Catherine of Braganza 30
   Thomas Clifford 31
   Henry Bennet: Arlington 33
   George Villiers: Buckingham 35
   Anthony Ashley Cooper: Shaftesbury 38
   John Maitland: Lauderdale 41
   George Downing 44
   Thomas Osborne: Danby 47
   References 50

3 **The Goldsmith-Bankers** 51
   From Artists to Financiers 51

    Edward Backwell   55
    Robert Viner   59
    John Banks   62
    Banking and Interest: Was It Legal?   65
    References   70

4 Personal Finances of a King   73
    Where Did the Money Go?   74
    The Cost of Plagues and Fires   81
    A Royal Allowance with Strings   84
    Customs, Excise and Hearth   85
    King's Debts Kept Growing   89
    Budget of a Modern-Day Monarch   92
    References   93

5 Paid Upon Orders from the Treasury   95
    Many Ways to Skin a Cat   101
    Valuing Collateralized Treasury Orders (CTOs)   105
    Poisson Model for the Arrival of Taxes   109
    Treat a Model Like a Gentleman   115
    Fair Compensation for Financial Risk?   115
    Position in the Queue Matters   117
    A Hint of What Went Wrong   118
    References   120

6 Diary of a Default   121
    1667: Downing Gives Orders   121
    Alliances, Duels and a Liquor Tax   131
    Selling Your Religion at Dover   136
    Prelude to the De(fault)   141
    Tuesday, January 2, 1672   150
    Danby Makes Assignments   172
    Visiting Debtors' Prison   182
    1706: Internal Rate of Return and Recovery   185
    References   190

7 Concluding Thoughts for the Twenty-First Century	193
Case Study for Business Ethics?	198
Appendix A: The Fate of a 2007 Banker	201
Appendix B: Unpacking the IRR	205
Bibliography	209
Index	215

List of Figures

Fig. 2.1   King Charles II painted by Sir Peter Lely (public domain), via Wikimedia Commons. https://commons.wikimedia.org/wiki/File%3ACharles_II_(1675).jpg   25

Fig. 2.2   Map of the Netherlands during the Anglo-Dutch wars, Source: Jan Janssonius (public domain), via Wikimedia Commons. https://commons.wikimedia.org/wiki/File%3ASeven_United_Netherlands_Janssonius_1658.jpg   29

Fig. 2.3   Queen Catherine of Braganza painted by Sir Peter Lely (public domain), via Wikimedia Commons. https://commons.wikimedia.org/wiki/File%3AQueen_Catherine_of_Braganza.jpg   31

Fig. 2.4   Clifford painted by Sir Peter Lely (public domain), via Wikimedia Commons. https://commons.wikimedia.org/wiki/File%3A1stLordClifford.jpg   32

Fig. 2.5   Arlington painted by Sir Peter Lely (public domain), via Wikimedia Commons. https://commons.wikimedia.org/wiki/File%3AHenry_Bennet.jpg   34

Fig. 2.6   Buckingham painted by Sir Peter Lely (public domain), via Wikimedia Commons. https://commons.wikimedia.org/wiki/File%3A2ndDukeOfBuckingham.jpg   36

Fig. 2.7   Shaftesbury painted by John Greenhill (public domain), via Wikimedia Commons. https://commons.wikimedia.org/wiki/File:Anthony_Ashley-Cooper,_1st_Earl_of_Shaftesbury.jpg   39

Fig. 2.8   Lauderdale painted by Jacob Huysmans (public domain), via Wikimedia Commons. https://commons.wikimedia.org/wiki/File%3AJohn_Maitland%2C_Duke_of_Lauderdale_by_Jacob_Huysmans.jpg   42

Fig. 2.9	Downing painted by Thomas Smith (harvardartmuseums.org) (public domain), via Wikimedia Commons. https://commons.wikimedia.org/wiki/File%3ASir_George_Downing_by_Thomas_Smith.jpeg	45
Fig. 2.10	Danby painted by Johann Kerseboom (public domain), via Wikimedia Commons. https://commons.wikimedia.org/wiki/File%3AThomas_Osborne%2C_1st_Duke_of_Leeds_by_Johann_Kerseboom.jpg	48
Fig. 3.1	Backwell, Likely Painted by James Granger (public domain), via Wikimedia Commons. https://en.wikipedia.org/wiki/File:Edward_Backwell.jpg	56
Fig. 3.2	Vyner, Painter unknown. https://www.geni.com/people/Sir-Robert-Vyner-1st-Baronet-Lord-Mayor-of-London/6000000028950134877	60
Fig. 3.3	Banks, Painted by Sir Peter Lely (public domain), via Wikimedia Commons. https://en.wikipedia.org/wiki/File:Sir_John_Banks,_1st_Baronet.jpg	63
Fig. 5.1	A sample treasury order (Item E407/119). Permission acquired and granted by the National Archives	96
Fig. 5.2	The masthead of the London Gazette	99
Fig. 5.3	A small corner of the gazette	100
Fig. 5.4	Exchequer and its financial relations	104
Fig. 5.5	The Tax Revenue Arrival Process	107
Fig. 6.1	Announcing the Stop of the Exchequer 1/4. Permission granted by the British Library. Item 8132.h2	152
Fig. 6.2	Announcing the Stop of the Exchequer 2/4. Permission granted by the British Library. Item 8132.h2	153
Fig. 6.3	Announcing the Stop of the Exchequer 3/4. Permission granted by the British Library. Item 8132.h2	155
Fig. 6.4	Announcing the Stop of the Exchequer 4/4. Permission granted by the British Library. Item 8132.h2	157
Fig. 7.1	Point of Optimal Debt Level (PoDeL)	194

List of Tables

Table 1.1	A basic balance sheet	5
Table 4.1	Expenses of King Charles II during the Restoration period. Twelve years of English Exchequer issues: **April 1660 to March 1672**	75
Table 4.2	Expense allocation of King Charles II during the Restoration period. Twelve years of English Exchequer issues: **April 1660 to March 1672**	76
Table 4.3	Revenue of King Charles II after the Restoration. Twelve years of English Exchequer receipts and loans: **April 1660 to March 1672**	87
Table 4.4	Total (net) banking debts of King Charles II by early 1672: at various interest rates	91
Table 5.1	How long did it take to get paid? Week in which CTO was first advertised for payment	106
Table 5.2	Valuation of a collateralized treasury order (CTO)	112
Table 6.1	Bankers' Debt created by the Stop of the Exchequer	169
Table 6.2	Cash flow from Bankers' Debt and Accrued Interest Over Time	181

CHAPTER 1

Bankers Then and Now

In the aftermath of the Great Recession of 2007–2008, despite widespread economic pain and universal public demands that "someone should pay," astonishingly *not one* of the chief executive officers (CEOs) of the 40 largest financial institutions ("the bankers") in the world was sent to prison, convicted of a crime—or even indicted by prosecutors. In fact, while the US unemployment rate actually *doubled* as a direct result of their harmful actions (and poor decisions), very few bosses lost their jobs. How ironic!

In the year prior to the financial crisis, the average salary of these 40 bankers was USD 750,000,[1] with the most successful among them earning upward of seven figures (and that's not including stock options and other ancillary financial perks). Now, you might think the Great Recession of 2007–2008 would permanently scar their careers, financial lives and monetary security—given that they caused it—but that's not what actually happened. Instead, in the years after the meltdown of mortgage-backed securities, most of these executives moved on to even-better-paying jobs; others started drawing their gold-plated pensions and retired to golf clubs, while a handful are actually still working in the exact same bank or financial institution they helped "blow up." Yes, a few got their hands slapped and there was a bit of shame (for a while), but when the dust settled,

---

[1] See Appendix A for a listing of the CEOs in 2007, their compensation and the fate of their institution, as well as how many ended up in jail or prison. Spoiler alert: none did.

they continued to prosper. According to Adair Turner[2] in his recent book *Between Debt and the Devil*, four years after the financial crisis (in 2012), more than 2500 bankers in London were earning over £1 million per year.

How did this happen? How did the bankers essentially emerge unscathed from the havoc they had wrought? With a decade of introspection the answer now is quite simple: they escaped personal financial ruin because governments around the world—effectively, the public taxpayers—*bailed out the banks*, rescued the financial system and liberated the private-sector managers from their follies. Thus, after a bit of stress and some economic drama, the bankers' financial lives continued apace. The community at large collectively "held its nose" and let them off the hook, *all for the greater good*, and the financial world moved on to other dramas.

Only time and history will tell if the financial bailout—and the lack of any major criminal prosecutions for those who caused the turmoil—was the sensible course of action. The bankers undoubtedly believe it was.

The outcome for these bankers' personal finances could not be more different than the outcome for an earlier group of bankers, some 350 years ago, during another financial crisis with debt origins that are eerily similar to those of 2007–2008. Economic historians know that episode and the particular topic of this book as *the Stop of the Exchequer of 1672*.

The events of the "stop" took place in the early dawn of bond and money markets. During the crisis of 1672, pieces of financial paper—securitized debt backed by anticipated tax revenues—became nearly worthless when England's monarchy was forced to halt the Exchequer from making any further payments of interest or principal payments on their financial obligations. I'll get to the grisly details later, but first let's start with the big picture.

The financial crisis of 1672 was not unlike other banking crises over the years, including 2007–2008. Money stopped flowing, banks froze, day-to-day commerce ground to a halt and ordinary investors suffered. But, in contrast to 2007–2008, there was no government rescue of the bankers who were (similarly) at the epicenter of the financial firestorm. Instead, the story in 1672 had a very different ending: despite bankers' pleas and petitions for what might today be called a "bailout," parliament turned a deaf ear. In the year 1672 the English bankers' only sin was not having diversified their investments—and perhaps lending (too much)

---

[2] See Turner (2016) and his forward-looking suggestions on how to avoid another financial and banking crisis, such as raising capital requirements for banks, and so on.

money to the King and Crown. They certainly didn't commit any crimes, or design securities that subsequently "blew up," as in the 2007–2008 crisis. Instead, they were just trying to efficiently manage their banking affairs in the ways that bankers always have: by lending at higher rates than they borrowed at.

As it happens, many of the successful bankers from England's post-*Restoration* period—the wealthiest financiers of the era, fêted by Samuel Pepys in his famous diary—ended up languishing in debtors' prison, some died in poverty, a few committed suicide. Still others fled the country in shame and disgrace, never returning to England during their lifetimes.

Why? Well, at the time, the bankruptcy rules could be expressed with a simple and brutal equation: no money to pay your creditors = go to jail. Unlike today's bankruptcy protection or option to reboot your finances, back in the seventeenth century, if you couldn't work out a deal to cover your debts, then you would end up being imprisoned. I'll discuss the subtle and nuanced system of debtors' prison later on, but it certainly wasn't pleasant, as Charles Dickens (and his father) could attest.

The aftermath of the financial crisis of 1672 was a tragedy of Shakespearean proportions for many of the great banking dynasties.[3] And again, it wasn't the bankers' fault. But *what exactly happened? Why did it happen? Who was to blame?*

Asset Liability Mismanagement in the Seventeenth Century

The story told in this book takes place in the aftermath of the London plague of 1665, the fire of London of 1666 and on the eve of the (third) war with the Dutch in 1672. But the tale here is not about natural disasters; rather, it is about human ones. It is about novel and poorly understood financial instruments as well as bad risk management—something equally relevant today, in the twenty-first century.

On Tuesday, January 2,[4] 1672—almost a decade after King Charles II was restored to the throne—the English Exchequer, at the time part of

---

[3] My main source for the list of London bankers of the time is Price (1970), although it seems that some of the dates (birth, death and such) are a bit off.

[4] According to the (old) Julian calendar that was still being used in England at the time, although I will take the year (1972) to begin in January and will refrain from using the cumbersome 1671–1672 for the period from January to March.

the government's Treasury department, suspended payments to depositors, investors and noteholders. By direct orders of the King, no interest, no principal and no money was to be paid out. This was an unprecedented act that ruined many prosperous goldsmith-bankers of the era who had advanced the majority of the money and held most of (what today we might call) the government bonds.

This episode—which was officially declared to be a *Temporary Stop of His Majesty's Exchequer in 1672*—is the last time the English government formally and officially defaulted[5] on its debt payments. But why did they default 350 years ago?

In a nutshell, in addition to unbearable state fiscal obligations, King Charles II had also incurred large personal debts to support his lavish lifestyle, including several mistresses and bastards. At that time the English king was responsible for expenditures and paying for government outlays that would make today's monarch howl in protest. The mid-seventeenth century was an era before reliable and efficient tax collection or proper government resources. Thus, when the King experienced what today might be labeled a "liquidity shock"—in his case, the need to prepare for a war against the Dutch—he defaulted on his financial obligations to the bankers.

Ok, you may be thinking now, *another king borrows over his head and betrays his subjects. Why is this relevant and what does it have to do with banking?*

Here's where it all started to unravel in a manner that might sound eerily familiar. The bankers (creditors) who had lent King Charles sums that amounted to years of anticipated national tax revenues were *themselves* debtors to many smaller depositors.

The king's default thus created a chain reaction of financial misery. Here's why. Think back to your basic (double-entry[6]) accounting. While the assets on the left-hand side of the bankers' balance sheets (see Table 1.1) evaporated, their obligations to depositors (on the right-hand side of their balance sheets) had not. They were borrowing money from

---

[5] Yes, there have been a few episodes of interest payment delays, especially in times of war, but never a formal default as it was declared in 1672.

[6] See Gleeson-White (2013) for the history of double-entry accounting, which was known and practiced centuries prior.

Table 1.1 A basic balance sheet

Assets (A)	Liabilities (L)
Loans to King (earning 10–30%) aka *Exchequer orders, tallies, bills, notes,* etc.	Money from depositors (paying 6%) Capped due to usury laws
	Equity (E): = A − L Banker's net worth

the public at 6%, the legal (biblical) usury[7] cap in the private market, but then lending the (borrowed) money to the King at rates that ranged from 10% to even 30%—in loans (to the monarchy) for which the commercial usury limits did not apply.

It was a classic (biblical) "spread arbitrage" gone terribly awry, and perhaps one of the first fully documented catastrophes in history. To recall the caution of Old Polonius, in Shakespeare's *Hamlet*, the bankers were both *borrowers* (from their depositors) and *lenders* (to the King and Crown), with few friends in either group! In this case though, the bankers didn't break the world—the world broke them, as you'll see.[8]

These leading bankers were able to fend off their creditors for a few months, and for some, even years—but eventually the solvency crunch caught up with them. But this wasn't just a financial accounting exercise in which *A* minus *L* was negative.

For these (primarily Anglican) bankers, it got very personal. To quote Margaret Atwood[9] in her book *Payback: Debt and the Shadow Side of Wealth,* their debts became trespasses or sins for which there was no absolution. Most of the bankers were (eventually) tossed into debtors' prison. As I said earlier and unlike today, those in debt in the seventeenth century couldn't seek bankruptcy protection, walk away from their obligations and start afresh. Nowadays well-known celebrities like Burt Reynolds, Kim Basinger, MC Hammer, Mike Tyson and 50 Cent have filed for bankruptcy protection and then moved on with their

---

[7] See Geist (2013) for a review of the history of usury laws and attitudes. I'll return to the interest rate calculations in Chaps. 5 and 6.

[8] In reference to the book *Lords of Finance: The Bankers Who Broke the World* (Ahamed, 2009) about the central bankers in the 1920s, who, the author claims, caused the Great Depression after a series of bad policies and decisions.

[9] See Atwood (2008).

glamorous life.[10] But bankruptcy is a relatively modern development[11] and deposit insurance (for banks) is an even newer concept. In an era before limited liability and these legal remedies, debtors in the late seventeenth century faced a miserable existence in the bowels of the Marshalsea and other prisons in London if they couldn't work out a proper deal with their creditors. Daniel Defoe—writing in the late seventeenth century—called these places "an emblem of hell." Charles Dickens was scarred for life after his father ended up in prison for debt. Now, whether Defoe's or Dickens' description was an exaggeration or not—and I'll discuss this matter in greater detail in Chap. 6—the fact remains that it was almost impossible to escape your personal debts. Of course, the King himself couldn't be locked up. The buck stopped at the bankers. What was their (only) sin? Mismanaging the duration of assets and liabilities on their balance sheet.

Now, to be clear, these were no ordinary bills or notes on which the government or Crown defaulted in 1672. Instead, these treasury orders were (loosely) backed by tax revenue and were some of the earliest known precursors to modern securitized debt. (I'll discuss this in great detail in Chap. 5.)

Most interestingly though, when after many years of "closure" the Exchequer was "opened" and interest payments resumed (for a while at least) to the noteholders, English parliament stipulated that the bankers had to *assign* or flow through any interest payment they received directly to the individual depositors and investors (on the right-hand side of the balance sheet). That is, in contrast to the year 2007–2008, the newly flowing money from the so-called government bailout had to *go directly to the small investor or depositor* and could not be hoarded by the bankers or paid out in bonuses.

Now perhaps there is a lesson or solution[12] to the next banking crisis to develop. After ten years, a financial crunch might now be overdue. Next time give the money directly to the people and bypass the bankers. To me

---

[10] See the research by White (2007) for more information about the (astonishing) number of people who declare personal bankruptcy in the United States every year. It is higher than the number of people who graduate from college, get divorced or are diagnosed with cancer.

[11] See Hoppit (1987) for a starting reference.

[12] For more reasonable and serious recommendations, see Admati and Hellwig (2013) or Turner (2016).

this is one of the most enduring and lasting lessons from the *Stop of the Exchequer*. I'm sure it would resonate today.

I'll discuss these *bankers' assignments* and how that process worked and were enforced later on. In fact, the assignments created an interesting secondary market in their own right. But by the time the money arrived—and keep in mind it only was a resumption of interest payments—the bankers had other pressing concerns on their mind, such as holding off their creditors and staying out of debtors' prison.

A Financial Crisis in Slow Motion

Now I should emphasize at this point that although only a few readers might have heard of *The Stop*—and very few financial economists have given it much attention[13]—it wasn't a minor episode of financial misery in the aftermath of plagues, fires and wars. Indeed, some historians claim that the instability generated by the events of 1672 and the Crown's default directly led to the creation of the Bank of England in 1694, because "kings cannot be trusted." But don't take my word for it: allow me to quote from authors far older (and more notable).

Writing in his celebrated book *The History of England* about this event, the eighteenth-century philosopher and economist David Hume[14] described: "The measure was so suddenly taken, that none had warning of the danger. A general confusion prevailed in the city, followed by the ruin of many. The bankers stopped payment and merchants could answer no bills." The prominent diarist John Evelyn, contemporary of Samuel Pepys, wrote in his entry for that date[15]: "An action which not only lost the hearts of his subjects, but ruined many widows and orphans and the reputation

---

[13] For example, there is no mention of the "stop" in Reinhart and Rogoff (2009), although they do mention (on p. 87) English defaults in the year 1340, 1472 and 1594. Likewise, Kindleberger and Aliber (2005) pay the "stop" no attention in their review and discussion of major historical financial crises. Even the great Adam Smith in his landmark *The Wealth of Nations* appears to make no reference to the event. See Smith (2000). In their historical compendium of interest rates, Sidney Homer and Richard Sylla devote a few sentences to the "stop" in the context of seventeenth-century interest rates. See Homer and Sylla (2005).

[14] See Hume (1778) Volume VI, Chap. LXV, p. 253.

[15] See entry for March 12, p. 606 (Evelyn, 1955). I should note that evoking the cliché of "widows and orphans" to justify or criticize any action should be treated with skepticism. It is often used in a polemic manner when direct evidence of harm is lacking. Evelyn's accounts in particular must be read and treated with caution, according to historians.

of the Exchequer for ever. Never did his majesties affairs prosper to any purpose after it."

It set back the development of retail banking industry (in England) for decades and I'll provide contemporary (1670s and 1680s) evidence and material as I progress through the story. Three centuries later the verdict on *The Stop* is pretty clear: "The effect was largely destructive and it figures in English history as a catastrophe little less scandalous than the South Sea Bubble," according to Henry Roseveare,[16] one of the most prominent (mid-twentieth-century) economic historians and the foremost expert on English government finances during the seventeenth century.

In other words, if you have heard of the South Sea Bubble,[17] then *you should know the story of the stop.*

It's not only the *consequences*[18] of *the Stop of the Exchequer* that are important, however: the *causes* are equally important. In particular, the financial instruments at the heart of the episode were *treasury orders*—which were very novel at the time (and which I will address in Chap. 5). Some scholars go so far as to claim that the treasury orders were the origin of paper money, or that money itself—as we know it today—was invented[19] during the regime of King Charles II.

I believe this fascinating (but mostly neglected[20]) episode also serves as a launching pad into modern-day problems; that is, the stresses and risks associated with too much debt. My plan is to tell the complete story of the financial default of the Merry Monarch (as King Charles II was known), but through the lens and using the language of twenty-first-century financial markets—a modern retelling.

---

[16] See Roseveare (1991) and p. 22 in particular.

[17] I should note that the current view among leading historians, see, for example, Hoppit (2002), is that that scandal and tragedy of the South Sea Company in 1702 has been exaggerated in terms of both its impact on the real economy and the magnitude of financial loss. In the words of Julian Hoppit, the Bubble has itself been bubbled.

[18] This affected not only bank depositors but even pensioners and retirees in unrelated schemes. See, for example, Lewin (2003). Mentions of *The Stop* appear in the social and literary references of the 1670s; see, for example, Spurr (2000).

[19] I suspect that Italian and Chinese scholars have a different view on the origins of paper money.

[20] The "stop" gets a token mention in Niall Ferguson's book, *The Ascent of Money* (Ferguson, 2008), on p. 76, or in the book by Robert Wright, *One Nation Under Debt* (Wright, 2008), on p. 22. So, modern historians and writers certainly know about this episode.

The story covers the precarious history leading up to the infamous day in 1672, the intrigue surrounding *The Stop*—including the details of those who traded on inside information beforehand—as well as the various attempts by distressed creditors to gain financial restitution. For example, in the aftermath of the default, one banker tried to seize Queen Catherine's Portuguese dowry. Another creditor quickly attempted to outrun the "speed of information" and rush to Amsterdam to sell his bonds before markets received the news. I'll get to all these anecdotes; those who succeeded and those who didn't, in due time.

But most English commoners at the time had little sympathy for the plight of these (wealthy) bankers. One of the complaints proclaimed in the (popular) perception of the event is that the bankers "got what they deserved" because they were charging the King "too much" in interest (e.g. from 10% to 30% per year) relative to the interest rate they were paying their depositors (6%). Others, who probably weren't big fans of the monarchy and the royal Stuart line, took the bankers' side in the arguments.

But what is a fair *default risk premium* when you are lending to a King (or country) that can default and when the cash flows are backed by tax revenues? These are questions that are as relevant today—think of Argentina or Venezuela or Greece—as they were 350 years ago in England. So, I'll be discussing how to "think about" risk premiums for such novel instruments.

OUTLINE OF THE STORY AND THE BOOK

This story will unfold over a total of seven (7) relatively self-contained chapters.

In Chap. 2, I will introduce the environment and political players in the drama, or the *dramatis personae*, if you will. In this chapter the reader will have the opportunity to refresh his or her knowledge of English history, with a focus on King Charles II and his close advisors. The chapter will introduce all the major political players in the drama: the King; his brother James, the Duke of York; the King's (illegitimate) son, the Duke of Monmouth; and even the King's cousin, the great cavalier Prince Rupert, all make an appearance in the story. Many famous figures in English history, well known to British schoolchildren for other reasons, were in the room during the moments of high financial drama in early January 1672.

In dealing with all matters, King Charles II relied on advisors known as the "Cabal Ministry" of colorful (and notorious) characters. And while the full cast of *The Stop* could fill a late-seventeenth-century *Who's Who*, I'll make sure to limit my introduction to the most critical and most interesting individuals. So, if you don't know much about Clifford and Arlington, or Buckingham, Ashley and Lauderdale—names that appear in all the literature and writings about *The Stop*—then Chap. 2 is where to catch up (and refresh) your English history.

In Chap. 3, I will introduce the other set of characters in the story, the bankers themselves. Many of them actually started their careers as goldsmiths. And how goldsmiths, like Backwell and Viner, became bankers is another interesting, even alchemical part of the story. From the point of view of some of the fortunate and farsighted bankers of the day, *The Stop* shouldn't have been a complete surprise. Some bankers avoided that financial asset (i.e. the debt obligations) entirely. Did they know something the others didn't? Chapter 3 will cover all you need (or want) to know about mid-seventeenth-century English bankers. I'll shed some (more) light on the plight of the people and families themselves and others, not only bankers, who invested in these instruments and who, through no fault of their own, found themselves in severe financial distress a few years later.

In Chap. 4, it's time to roll up our sleeves and work on some accounting and budgeting numbers, like revenues, expenses and deficits. This chapter will examine the finances of King Charles II in the years leading up to the default. For those of you who are curious about how he spent his money, Chap. 4 provides the answer. It's a good opportunity to compare household budgets with the King (so, how much do you spend on heating bills? How about on mistresses?).

Chapter 5 then moves from budgets and biographies to financial instruments, where I launch into a full description of the method by which the monarchy borrowed in the years of the Restoration. In particular, I will focus on the market microstructure of the *treasury orders*, tallies and so on. In addition to describing the instruments, I'll argue that from a modern financial risk management perspective, the goldsmith-bankers were *entirely justified* in charging and earning this credit spread, in the modern sense of the term. But did they overcharge? Can they be blamed or accused of causing the "stop" by demanding too much interest? I'll discuss the details and offer some valuation models. One noted historian, writing in the mid-twentieth century, claimed that by the end of the episode, when interest payments were finally resumed after decades of waiting, the total yield on the debt was 1.5%—(or a recovery rate of 101.5%) and therefore not a bad investment with ex post hindsight. I will (beg to) differ ex ante.

For those (few) readers who are (very) familiar with the "stop," this chapter is where I believe you will find the contribution to the literature. Indeed, the system was quite ingenious and orderly for its time. As tax revenues were received at the Exchequer, the bills and notes were paid off. Officials would place an announcement in the *London Gazette* that a particular loan or note was ready to be paid and then the bankers would promptly go to the Exchequer and get their principal and interest payments. I'll provide some unique data and valuation techniques that help "think about" and appreciate these instruments.

Moving on, Chap. 6 is where the drama unfolds. I'll describe the lead-up to the crises, starting in April 1667, where you will see why that particular date is important. I'll review the major financial milestones in the lead-up to the default—although I'm not trying to compete with Samuel Pepys. I'll slow down to cover the weeks and days prior to the announcement in early 1672 and then speed up again to cover the aftermath of the story, which only really ends 34 years later in late 1705.

As readers might know, Samuel Pepys stopped his own diary writing due to poor eyesight[21] a few years prior to the "stop." So, that event was obviously not mentioned in the diary, but many of the relevant characters and instruments did make an appearance on his pages. I'll make sure to note where appropriate.

Either way, and with much deference to the diarists, I'll provide a day-by-day account (or at least a reasonable conjecture) of what happened during the vital weekend of January 5, 1672.

Chapter 6 is also where I'll discuss the aftermath of the "stop," including the fate of the bankers and the unsuccessful attempts to bail them out. I'll talk about the resumption of interest payments (for a while) and the follow-up default (yes, again) a few years after that.

In the same chapter, I'll examine the *assignments* wherein the bankers had to pledge their payments to the original depositors and investors. In fact, there was yet another move by parliament (after the Revolution of 1688) to stop the payments again, which led to lawsuits in the Court of Exchequer and then the Court of Appeals. As I said earlier, it took almost 34 years to clean up the mess!

---

[21] See Tomalin (2002) for a wonderful overview and analysis of Samuel Pepys, his life and times. She also makes an interesting claim that Pepys (also) knew about The Stop in advance and managed to get his treasury orders paid before the default.

But in the end, the (at least) £1,200,000 of bankers' debt—which today would be worth hundreds of millions—was "written down" and then rolled into England's national debt in 1706. The descendants of the bankers, who themselves were long gone from the scene, and their depositors (finally) reached financial closure: they owned government bonds backed by parliament and not by the monarch's whim.

But, hold on. In the final irony, the annuities and perpetuities that came into existence from the bankers' debt were exchanged by their holders into—yes, wait for it—common stock in the South Sea Company in the second decade of the eighteenth century, thus linking the stock and bond crashes in one long 50-year arc!

Finally, Chap. 7 concludes with some brief modern-day lessons or take-aways—positioned and presented as ethical dilemmas—that should be relevant to highly indebted individuals in the twenty-first century. There is something to be learned from a King's misfortune which perhaps can be used as the template for a lesson in a modern business school.

A Brief Review of Scholarly Literature

England's King Charles II wasn't the first, last or even the most notorious monarch to default on his debts. During the Middle Ages, the most infamous defaulter was Spain's King Philip II (b. 1527, d. 1598), nicknamed the "borrower from hell" by the historians and Genoese bankers who lent him the money for his wars (including the attempted Armada invasion of England in 1588). The sixteenth-century Spanish and similar cases of default were quite different from that of Charles II. For starters, those bankers didn't languish in prison. The financial instruments were interesting in and of themselves, but (again) different. Moreover, if recent scholarship is to be seriously considered,[22] it appears that the financial implications of Spain King Philip II's default were expected and anticipated, and thus benign compared to (the unexpected events in) 1672 England.

---

[22] See the related and readable book by Drelichman and Voth (2014), in which they make the argument that King Philip's bankers actually expected these defaults and were jointly sharing the risks of the loan by charting suitable interest rates. There are many important differences between the Spanish and English cases. For example, the Genoese bankers certainly did not end up in prison or disgraced.

On the same note, to be very clear, this book does not break any new historical research ground, nor does it uncover previously unknown archival material. Instead, think of this as a literature review of the material known to a small group of specialists, but with an interesting contemporary twist and from the perspective of modern risk and return. My pedagogical intention is to tell (what I think is) an intriguing story and make the details accessible to a much wider audience than graduate students of financial history.

My intended audience is a student, but in the very broad sense of the word: that is, a reader with an interest in banking, finance and economics who is curious about the origin of systems that today we take for granted— including the rocky path of financial and banking innovation. In writing this tale I am inspired by popular accounts of financial history[23] such as the infamous South Sea Bubble[24]—the mention of which leads to widespread nods of recognition—or the lesser-known (American) financial disasters such as the panic[25] of 1907, the monetary crises[26] of 1914 and of course the notorious market crash[27] of 1929 (*more nods*).

As for what I *won't* be covering in this book, I plan to refrain from weighty reflections about the history of borrowing or the sociological impact of debt[28] or the philosophical development[29] of credit markets and so on. I'm neither a philosopher nor a sociologist (and not even a proper historian) but obviously respect that these are fertile areas of scholarship.

I will (also) *not* wade into the contentious debate about whether the credible and trustworthy financial institutions that came into existence in the aftermath of the Revolution of 1688, such as the Bank of England in the spring of 1694, reduced the risk of further government defaults and thus lowered market interest rates (or maybe they didn't).

---

[23] See the very entertaining book *Devil Take the Hindmost* by Chancellor (1999), as well as the recent book *Money Changes Everything* by Goetzmann (2016).

[24] For example, see the very entertaining book by Balen (2002), as well as Dale (2004) or Carswell (1960) or Kindleberger and Aliber (2005). Note that the meltdown or deflating of the stock price bubble took place during the years 1720–1722.

[25] See Bruner and Carr (2007).

[26] See Silber (2007).

[27] The most entertaining and enduring account is provided by Galbraith (1997). See also Bernstein (1996) for a captivating story of risk over the ages.

[28] See Graeber (2011) for an excellent and perhaps overwhelming account of the origins and development of debt and debt instruments over the last 5000 years.

[29] For that angle, see Wennerlind (2011) and his intriguing claim that threats and fear of violence were an important ingredient in establishing credit markets.

Indeed, there is a lively and ongoing debate among economic historians on exactly this topic and the role of financial institutions,[30] under the rubric of *credible commitment*. The (big) theory in that field can be stated as follows: because of the royal Stuart's dismal track record in paying back their debts, the most prominent example of which is *the Stop of the Exchequer*, rational lenders would never trust any English monarch (again). Debatable—as you will learn the details—but let's work with this idea for a moment.

If a country wanted to borrow money at a reasonable interest rate, parliament itself (*not* the King) would have to take the financial reins in hand—set up a proper and reliable system of taxation—and guarantee or stand behind the debt payments. Of course, parliament needed power to be able to make these sorts of guarantees, and in the seventeenth century, kings weren't in the habit of giving sovereignty away voluntarily. But—get this—a rational monarch would actually be willing to transfer this authority willingly to the third party (i.e. parliament) to signal *credible commitment*. Think of this in a *game theoretic* way as an equilibrium outcome for all players. The benefit (to the King) of this handover of power would be lower interest rates, financial prosperity and good times for all. Well, at least that's the theory. It's all somewhat controversial, especially since interest rates didn't quite melt away in 1688 after the Glorious Revolution.

Either way, the credible commitment debate is above my historical credentials and academic pay grade. Nevertheless, and although it isn't directly relevant, it's an undercurrent to our story. Namely, the worse the impact of the *Stop of the Exchequer*—and the more blame that can be attached to King Charles II—the greater is the need for a remedy against fiscally naughty kings and monarchs. So, as you read the details and learn the specifics, remember that the narrator (of any story) might have a party-political agenda. I'll try to stay away from the political. Rather, my objectives in these pages are to

1. tell an important (forgotten) financial story in an interesting way;
2. make it accessible—introducing the relevant characters—without getting bogged down in the archival minutia;

---

[30] See, for example, the best-selling book by Acemoglu and Robinson (2012), the widely cited article by the Nobel Prize-winning economist Douglas North (North & Weingast, 1989), as well as Quinn (2001) and Neal (1990).

3. discuss the financial instruments involved (the *treasury orders*) from the perspective of a modern borrower, thinking in terms of risk and return;
4. highlight the consequences of bad financial decisions, too much debt, the inability to raise revenues and poor risk management in the seventeenth century—I'll touch upon some of the ethical dilemmas that should resonate in the twenty-first century; and
5. perhaps most importantly, inspire readers to go back to the original sources and learn more about *the Stop of the Exchequer*.

That said, given the importance of this episode, I'm not the first to write about this story. I am indebted to many scholars (both living and deceased) upon whose work I am relying, quoting (and hopefully not distorting). Indeed, over the last 350 years, many historians and even lay writers have tackled the story of the "stop" from a variety of angles and with different levels of scholarly detail. In fact, when I discussed the idea of this book with a well-known scholar and historian of the period, the reaction I received was: "It has been 350 years. What else is there left to say[31]?"

So, to give credit where it's due, in addition to the earlier-mentioned popular references to the philosopher David Hume or the diarist John Evelyn, a number of academic-based and scholarly authors in the twentieth century have indeed written about and discussed the episode and surrounding consequences in very great detail. In fact, the research is ongoing—as old documents in the archives are analyzed in a new light—and new insights have emerged even after 350 years have passed. Indeed, I'll reference and mention their work where appropriate. Here I will give brief credit to the early ones (aka giants), from whom I learned the details of this story and began my own journey.

For starters, all historians with an interest in government finance in the late seventeenth century owe an enormous debt of gratitude to the monumental work of Dr. William A. Shaw,[32] who, in the early years of the twentieth century, carefully compiled records of the Exchequer and provided one of the earliest lists of revenues and expenditures during the regime of King Charles II.

---

[31] My response was: "Yes, but only a handful of people alive today—outside of academics—have heard of the story."

[32] See Shaw (1904), and in particular the introductions to the many volumes of Treasury records that he edited. Another important source is Chandaman (1975), who corrects many of the errors and inconsistencies in the work of Shaw (1904), and whose numbers I use for some of King Charles II's expenditures.

Now, I know that subsequent researchers have questioned the accuracy of (some of) his numbers—and perhaps his motives—but as a data collection exercise his work was unparalleled. Dr. Shaw's work enabled scholars such as A. Browning[33] and R. D. Richards,[34] writing in the 1920s, to properly analyze the "stop" and differentiate facts—how big was the economic impact?—from fiction and rumors. These scholars focused on the event itself and were less concerned with the aftermath or the bankers. The errors and omissions in Shaw's work were corrected by C. D. Chandaman in the book published in 1970s. He too discussed the "stop" and is the source for many of my numbers and figures.

This work was then followed by a capstone piece by K. Horsefield[35] in the 1980s. In that article, which is the main academic reference at this point, he also examined the aftermath of the "stop" and shed additional light on the personal implications for the bankers involved. Finally, the book by Henry Roseveare,[36] based on a series of lectures in the late 1980s, provides a comprehensive list of references and is a must-read for scholars. And that was it on the "stop" for a while.

More broadly than the "stop," there are hundreds of books, scholarly articles and diaries on economic life during the Restoration, perhaps even starting with Samuel Pepys and his diary. Also, as I alluded to earlier, the finances of the monarchy during the late seventeenth century is one of the most scrutinized topics in English history, given its inevitable connection to the Glorious Revolution of 1688. So, it can be a bit tricky at times to decide who is "in" and who is "out" when it comes to references. My criterion on inclusion was whether a particular book or article helped shed light or illuminate the story itself.

Chronologically speaking though, there are more recent accounts of the "stop." One is a book by B. G. Carruthers called *City of Capital*,[37] published in 1996. In addition to very briefly telling the story, Carruthers documents the social rank, location and occupation of the individual investors (depositors) affected by *The Stop*, which confirms earlier claims that the sums involved were not trivial, although the total number of depositors affected were on the order of 2000, comprising both men and women.

---

[33] See Browning (1929, 1966).
[34] See Richards (1927, 1929), important sources and authors I'll return to later on.
[35] See Horsefield (1982), who expands the analysis to the "community at large" but with ample reference to Richards (1929) as the "fullest record available."
[36] See Roseveare (1991), as well as the earlier Roseveare (1973).
[37] See Chap. 3, and in particular pp. 60–70.

Another (very) recent reference worth noting early on is the book by C. Desan on the *history of money*, published in 2014, which contains an entire chapter on treasury orders and the financial environment during the 1660s and 1670s. She also (briefly) mentions the "stop." So *the Stop of the Exchequer* isn't a secret—to people who study these things.

In fact, there are many other (obscure) references to the "stop" itself over the years, especially as it relates to the legal precedent set by the bankers' debt, which I'll get to in Chap. 6. Here is the bottom line. Although I might not be able to expand and elaborate on every historical reference or mention of the "stop," I'll be sure to footnote most of them at some point in the narrative.[38]

I should however point out that some of the secondary stories I have stumbled across in my research contain inaccuracies and outright falsehoods, possibly motivated by political considerations and leanings. For example, one author[39] claims that King Charles II physically raided the Exchequer, (as his father, King Charles I, did before him), forcefully took the bankers' gold and coins for himself and used them to buy jewels for his (favorite) mistress, Nell Gwyn. Well, that never actually happened at any time during the Restoration. Authors with republican leanings (aka Whigs) tended to "trash talk" the King. The loyal royalists (aka Tories) defended him. The battle continues in the twenty-first century.

In sum, my objective is a modern retelling of *The Stop* and surrounding events from a twenty-first-century perspective. This book differs from the meticulous academic work of others by focusing (much more) attention on the valuation and perception of risk. Indeed, if I bring any special toolkits to this task, it's the ability to use the *valuation models of risk and return* to analyze the securities involved. But before I get into the minutia of securitizing the Crown's tax revenues, or the difference between "tallies of pro" versus "tallies of sol," it's time for some English history[40] in the mid-seventeenth century.

---

[38] See also the book by Brewer (1988) on the relation between financial matters and England's power in the eighteenth century, as well as the records collected by Dickson (1967), which is another classic.

[39] See Iddesleigh (1887) as an example of a highly exaggerated (aka "Whig") version of events. More on the Whigs versus the Tories and how an eighteenth- and nineteenth-century author's political affiliation might have affected the telling of the story of "The Stop" will come in Chap. 6.

[40] For those (English) readers who had enough of this in grade school, feel free to skip ahead to Chap. 3.

References

Acemoglu, D., & Robinson, J. A. (2012). *Why Nations Fail: The Origins of Power, Prosperity and Poverty*. New York: Crown Business, a division of Random House.

Admati, A., & Hellwig, M. (2013). *The Bankers' New Clothes: What's Wrong with Banking and What to Do About It*. Princeton: Princeton University Press.

Ahamed, L. (2009). *Lords of Finance: The Bankers Who Broke the World*. London: Penguin Books Ltd.

Atwood, M. (2008). *Payback: Debt and the Shadow Side of Wealth*. Toronto: House of Anansi Press.

Balen, M. (2002). *The King, the Crook and the Gambler: The True Story of the South Sea Bubble and the Greatest Finacial Scandal in History*. New York: Harper Collins.

Bernstein, P. L. (1996). *Against the Gods*. New York: John Wiley and Sons.

Brewer, J. (1988). *The Sinews of Power*. Cambridge: Harvard University Press.

Browning, A. (1929). The Stop of the Exchequer. *History, 14*(56), 333–337.

Browning, A. (1966). Settlement of the Banker's Debt Created by the Stop of the Exchequer. *English Historical Documents, Volume VI c. 1660–1714*. Routledge.

Bruner, R. F., & Carr, S. D. (2007). *The Panic of 1907: Lessons Learned from the Market's Perfect Storm*. Hoboken, NJ: John Wiley & Sons, Inc.

Carswell, J. (1960). *The South Sea Bubble*. Stanford, CA: Stanford University Press.

Chancellor, E. (1999). *Devil Take the Hindmost: A History of Financial Speculation*. New York: Farrar, Straus and Giroux.

Chandaman, C. (1975). *The English Public Revenue 1660–1688*. Oxford: Clarendon Press.

Dale, R. (2004). *The First Crash: Lessons from the South Sea Bubble*. Princeton: Princeton University Press.

Dickson, P. G. (1967). *The Financial Revolution in England*. London: Macmillan.

Drelichman, M., & Voth, H. J. (2014). *Lending to the Borrower from Hell: Debt, Taxes and Default in the Age of Philip II*. Princeton: Princeton University Press.

Evelyn, J. (1955). *The Diary of John Evelyn*. In E. de Beer (Ed.), *Six Volumes*. Oxford: The Clarendon Press.

Ferguson, N. (2008). *The Ascent of Money: A Financial History of the World*. New York: Penguin Books.

Galbraith, J. K. (1997). *The Great Crash 1929*. New York: Houghton Mifflin Company.

Geist, C. R. (2013). *Beggar Thy Neighbour*. Philadelphia: University of Pennsylvania Press.

Gleeson-White, J. (2013). *Double Entry: How the Merchants of Venice Created Modern Finance*. New York: W.W. Norton and Company.

Goetzmann, W. N. (2016). *Money Changes Everything: How Finance Made Civilization Possible*. Princeton: Princeton University Press.

Graeber, D. (2011). *DEBT: The First 5,000 Years*. Brooklyn, NY: Melville House Publishing.
Homer, S., & Sylla, R. (2005). *A History of Interest Rates* (4th ed.). New York: John Wiley & Sons, Inc.
Hoppit, J. (1987). *Risk and Failure in English Business 1700–1800*. Cambridge: Cambridge University Press.
Hoppit, J. (2002). The Myths of the South Sea Bubble. *Transactions of the Royal Historical Society, 12*, 141–165.
Horsefield, J. K. (1982). The Stop of the Exchequer Revisited. *The Economic History Review, 35*(4), 511–528.
Hume, D. (1778). *The History of England: From the Invasion of Julius Caesar to the Revolution in 1688*. Indianapolis, IN: Liberty Fund (1983).
Iddesleigh, S. H. (1887). The Closing of the Exchequer by Charles II in 1672. *Lectures and Essays of the Earl of Northcote*, 244–285.
Kindleberger, C. P., & Aliber, R. (2005). *Manias, Panics and Crashes: A History of Financial Crises* (5th ed.). Hoboken, NJ: John, Wiley & Sons, Inc.
Lewin, C. G. (2003). *Pensions and Insurance Before 1800: A Social History*. East Lothian, Scotland: Tuckwell Press Ltd.
Neal, L. (1990). *The Rise of Financial Capitalism*. Cambridge: Cambridge University Press.
North, D. C., & Weingast, B. R. (1989). Constitutions and Commitment: Evolution of Institutions Governing Public Choice in 17th Century England. *Journal of Economic History, 49*, 803–832.
Price, F. G. (1970). *Handbook of Goldsmith Bankers*. New York: Burt Franklin.
Quinn, S. (2001). The Glorious Revolution's Effect on English Private Finance: A Microhistory 1680–1705. *The Journal of Economic History, 61*(3), 593–615.
Reinhart, C. M., & Rogoff, K. S. (2009). *This Time Is Different: Eight Centuries of Financial Folly*. Princeton: Princeton University Press.
Richards, R. D. (1927). The Evolution of Paper Money in England. *The Quarterly Journal of Economics, 41*(3), 361–404.
Richards, R. D. (1929). *The Early History of Banking in England*. London: P.S. King & Sons, Ltd.
Roseveare, H. (1973). *The Treasury 1660–1807: The Foundations of Control*. London: George Allen & Unwin Ltd.
Roseveare, H. (1991). *The Financial Revolution 1660–1760*. London and New York: Longman.
Shaw, W. (1904). *Introduction to the Calendar of Treasury Books*. London: His Majesty's Stationary Office.
Silber, W. L. (2007). *When Washington Shut Down Wall Street: The Great Financial Crisis of 1914 and the Origins of America's Monetary Supremacy*. Princeton: Princeton University Press.
Smith, A. (2000). *The Wealth of Nations*. Toronto: Random House, Inc.

Spurr, J. (2000). *England in the 1670s: The Masquerading Age.* Malden: Blackwell Publishers.
Tomalin, C. (2002). *Samuel Pepys: The Unequalled Self.* New York: Vintage Books.
Turner, A. (2016). *Between Debt and the Devil: Money, Credit and Fixing Global Finance.* Princeton: Princeton University Press.
Wennerlind, C. (2011). *Casualties of Credit: The English Financial Revolution 1620–1720.* Cambridge: Harvard University Press.
White, M. J. (2007). Bankruptcy Reform and Credit Cards. *Journal of Economic Perspectives, 21*(4), 175–199.
Wright, R. E. (2008). *One Nation Under Debt: Hamilton, Jefferson and the History of What We Owe.* New York: McGraw Hill.

CHAPTER 2

Dramatis Personae

NOBILITY VERSUS GENTRY

To appreciate *who's who* as the financial saga unfolds, as well as much of what motivated the actors in this drama, I begin with a brief overview of English titles and peerage classification in the seventeenth century. Obviously, at the very top of the social hierarchy sat the immediate royal family and the monarch himself, King Charles II, to whom I will return in a moment. Just under the royals in social importance, and the highest rank within the peerage universe, was a *Duke*. There were very few Dukes and most had a very close historical connection to the royal family. In fact, some Dukes were actually members of the royal family. For example, King Charles II's younger and only surviving brother James was known as the Duke of York, and upon the death of King Charles II (much later, in 1685), James inherited the crown (at least for a short while).

One step below the level of Duke in the social hierarchy was the title *Marquess*, which is in fact properly spelled as listed here but does occasionally appear as Marquis. This title was rank number two in the peerage. And, although you might not have heard of any Marquesses—and it isn't easy to pronounce—they were very close to the title of Duke in importance. According to Queen Victoria, writing in her own journal two centuries after our period, the title Marquess was to be granted "when it was not our wishes that they be made Dukes."

© The Author(s) 2017
M.A. Milevsky, *The Day the King Defaulted*,
DOI 10.1007/978-3-319-59987-8_2

The next one down was the *Earl*; the third rank in the peerage system. Famous Earls would include the 4th Earl of Sandwich, patron saint of the paired bread bearing his name.[1] He actually died in the third Anglo-Dutch war, which is part of our story. Another was the racy and flamboyant Earl of Rochester,[2] quite possibly the greatest English poet of the seventeenth century, who died of syphilis at the age of 33 and whose writing was (quite naturally) censored during the prudish Victorian era.

Both these well-known Earls were alive during the Restoration but played little, if any, role in the financial crisis of 1672.

Moving on down, beneath the Earl was a *Viscount*, aka the fourth of five ranks in the peerage. The Viscount title was also quite rare and, to confuse matters, was occasionally used in reference to the heir of an Earl or Marquess, but only before the father (Earl) himself had died and the son inherited the title.

Finally, rounding out the five titles of English nobility was the *Baron*. So, the Barons, Earls and Dukes were the main ones, in between 5th and 3rd were Viscounts and in between 3rd and 1st were Marquesses.

More importantly, these five classes of nobility would all be referred to as Lords and they had the right, although certainly not the obligation, to attend and sit in the English House of Lords. The King at his own discretion could decide at any time to elevate someone to any one of the stairs on the ladder of nobility. Once you were promoted, you and your first-born son and his first-born son, and so on, were there for life. Think of it as a type of academic tenure in perpetuity (for males only).

Of course being a member of the nobility and a Lord didn't necessarily protect you from the king's wrath—especially if you inherited your title—and many Lords found themselves on the wrong side of the political fence and imprisoned in the Tower of London at one point or another.

For casual fans of the totally fictitious and yet very popular (from 2010 to 2015) TV show *Downton Abbey*, one of the main characters is Robert Crawley, the 7th Earl of Grantham, which you will note is rank number three in the nobility.

His (fictitious) father would have been the 6th Earl of Grantham, his grandfather 5th, and so on. Robert Crawley would have been a member of (and sitting in) the House of Lords even though he lived in Yorkshire, a few hours away from London by train.

---

[1] In fact, the fast-food chain popular in the United States (but for whatever reason unsuccessful in England) was founded by a direct descendant of said Earl.

[2] Played by Johnny Depp in the 2004 movie *The Libertine*.

Now, for the record, but not to confuse matters any more than necessary for our financial tale, England and Scotland had slightly different rules for nobility. What this means is that a Lord might have a few distinct titles within the nobility, some English and some Scottish. For example, the more fanatical fans of *Downton Abbey* will know that Robert Crawley was also called *Viscount of Downton*, which, recall, is one level under an Earl. (Personally, I would take Earl over Viscount if given the choice.) In addition to the English versus Scottish matter, the two distinct titles were possible because of various inheritances and properties associated with each. In general though, members of nobility were usually referred to by their higher title (a practice I will follow), although there are exceptions.

As a rough assessment for the size and scope of the nobility, it has been estimated[3] that there were approximately 160 families, or 6400 persons, within the ranks of the peerage in England and Wales in the late seventeenth century. Note that Bishops were also allowed to sit in the House of Lords, but they aren't included in the above numbers. Also, those figures were estimated in the late 1690s, but the size couldn't have been much smaller in the 1660s. According to Ian Mortimer—writing in his renowned time traveler's guide—in 1676 there were 11 English dukes, 3 marquesses, 66 earls, 11 viscounts and 65 barons.

Finally, and for the sake of social completeness, just under the pyramid of nobility were the gentry, then yeomen (perhaps with land) and then the poor. The gentry consisted of *baronets* (not to be confused with the noble barons) as well as *knights*, both of whom were entitled to various social privileges, including the use of the appellation "Sir" before their name. Again, all these titles were bestowed directly by the King.[4] To round out the gentry, if you weren't a baronet or a knight, you could take solace in being an *esquire* or, at the very least, a country *gentleman*. In addition, there were also urban artisans and merchants who were important actors (depositors) in our financial drama. In sum, in the late seventeenth century, the gentry of England and Wales—in other words, the baronets, knights, esquires and gentlemen—consisted of over 16,000 families or almost 150,000 persons.

I certainly don't want to drown you in social minutia, but as far as our main story is concerned, the reason for introducing this trivia around titles is to better understand the personal drive of the characters or *dramatis personae* in our story. Beyond financial greed, or fear of physically losing

---

[3] See Gregory and Stevenson (2007, p. 246), as well as the encyclopedic (Schofield & Wrigley, 1981).

[4] In fact, King James I (grandfather of our King Charles II) invented the title of baronet to raise much-needed funds.

their head, one of the important motivators in English society in the seventeenth century, similar to Jane Austen's nineteenth century, was the desire to enter and move up the nobility, mainly by engaging in activities that would earn the king's favor. A title might be more valuable than gold and was just as powerful an incentive.

It would have been a great social honor for a basic member of the gentry to be elevated to the rank of Baron or Viscount or Earl. And, although being a member of the nobility was correlated with wealth, it wasn't a prerequisite for the honor. You couldn't just bribe your way into the club. It wasn't the English way. In fact, there were many landowning gentry who were wealthier than the Barons and Earls. Perhaps one can think of this social pyramid as the seventeenth-century version of Maslow's hierarchy of (social climbing) needs, where at the very top sat King Charles II and the royal family. Unlike today, all political life was rooted and based in the Royal Court and self-advancement.

Here is the bottom line. When you read about some of the actors or players in the drama—who were making some bad financial decisions—you might wonder, "why would they do this?" Well, the answer might also have to do with the prospect of finding favor in the king's eyes.

With the social background out of the way, we are now ready for the main characters in our (financial) story.

KING CHARLES II

"The Merry Monarch"

Born in May 1630 and died in February 1685, and was King of England from 1660 until his death. In this story[5] he will be referred to simply as Charles, or King Charles II when formality dictates. He certainly should not be confused with his father Charles I, who was King of England until January 1649 when Oliver Cromwell and his colleagues chopped off his head (Fig. 2.1).[6]

---

[5] My source for the life of King Charles II is based mostly on Fraser (2002), Uglow (2009), Coote (1999), Harris (2006) and, of course, the references in Pepys (1997).

[6] In my mind, the best telling of the story of his trial and then execution is in Wedgewood (2011).

Fig. 2.1 King Charles II painted by Sir Peter Lely (public domain), via Wikimedia Commons. https://commons.wikimedia.org/wiki/File%3ACharles_II_(1675).jpg

He should also not be confused with the soon-to-be[7] King Charles III, who is not really a descendant of King Charles II. Although—in one of those odd historical coincidences—Lady Diana Spencer was a direct descendant of one of the illegitimate children of King Charles II. This of course implies that if and when the current Prince William, Duke of Cambridge, accedes to the throne, he will be the first direct descendant of King Charles II to rule England (and Great Britain).

Charles Stuart became[8] king at the age of 30, waiting 11 years after his father was killed and spending the decade of his 20s wandering around Europe, although certainly not by choice.[9] His life story is quite fascinating and the popular biographies by Antonia Fraser,[10] Jenny Uglow[11] or

---

[7] It is unknown what name he might adopt. Long live the Queen!

[8] Technically, he became king in 1649, the moment his father died, and the records of his reign are noted from that point onward.

[9] There are many (many) sources for the history of England under the Stuarts, but Trevelyan (1960) first published in 1904 is a good place to start.

[10] *King Charles II*, by Antonia Fraser (Phoenix, 2002).

[11] *A Gambling Man: Charles II and the Restoration*, by Jenny Uglow (Faber and Faber Ltd, 2009).

Stephen Coote[12] are just a few of the hundreds of books, articles,[13] stories and poems written about the man. There is absolutely no way I can do him justice in a few hundred words.

King Charles II is remembered in the popular[14] imagination as fun-loving, charming and gallant, but with a devastating weakness for (strong-willed) women. His mistresses—whom he flaunted and paraded at court without any hint of embarrassment—have become household legends in England. They include Barbara Palmer (Duchess of Cleveland), Louise de Kérouaille (Duchess of Portsmouth), Hortense Mancini, Moll Davis and the legendary Nell Gwyn. He is known to have fathered (at least) 14 illegitimate (aka natural) children, but not one legitimate[15] heir—which is why, upon his death in 1685, the crown passed to his younger (and very unpopular) brother King James II—which in turn led to the Revolution[16] in 1688.

The poet John Dryden in his poem *Absalom and Achitophel,* which was composed and published a few years before the death of King Charles II, compared Charles II to the biblical king David: both men had big hearts and a strong libido. In fact, it is alleged that Queen Victoria herself, two centuries later, had a special fondness for King Charles II over all her royal predecessors. This is quite odd, given her prudish reputation and how social norms in the Victorian era were the complete opposite of the Restoration.

Others have portrayed King Charles II in less flattering terms, describing him as lazy, uninterested in making any difficult decisions, deeply cynical and overall not worthy of the monarchy, none of which really contradicts the above descriptions. For the first few years of the Restoration (until 1667), most government business was managed by Lord Chancellor Clarendon (Edward[17] Hyde), a man who never missed the opportunity to admonish the King about his loose morals and lifestyle.

---

[12] *Royal Survivor: The Life of Charles II,* by Stephen Coote (Hodder and Stoughton, 1999).

[13] For the more academic biographies, see Hutton (1989) and Miller (1991).

[14] See, for example, the historical fiction book Plaidy (2005) for a popular portrayal.

[15] See the interesting work by Holmes (2003) on some of the health issues faced by the Stuarts.

[16] See Pincus (2009).

[17] Aka "Uncle Eddie" in the prologue.

Like his father, the beheaded King Charles I, he probably believed in the *divine right of kings*—or at least his divine right to do as he pleased. Remember that Thomas Hobbes' *Leviathan*, justifying the existence of a monarch with absolute powers, was published[18] in 1651 and revised in 1668.

Charles II's leanings toward Catholicism, the religion of his mother (Queen Henrietta Maria), brother (James, Duke of York, who eventually became King James II) and his French cousin King Louis XIV, had more to do with a desire for absolute (Catholic style) power as opposed to any deep religious convictions. He tolerated parliament and the (limited) democracy it represented only because he needed parliament taxes. So, despite his personal attempt occasionally to accommodate (non-Anglican) dissenters, paragons of liberty and freedom he and his advisors were not. This background also helps set the stage for the continuing migration of Quakers and other persecuted minorities in the late 1670s and early 1680s to North America, including William Penn (1681), who founded and was given (what King Charles II called) Pennsylvania.

As far as my story is concerned, and as you will read repeatedly, King Charles II and his administration were constantly short of money. The systematic financial difficulties are echoed repeatedly in the diaries of Samuel Pepys and John Evelyn, and we will take a careful look into his personal finances—but using slightly more reliable sources—in Chap. 4.

As just one example and implication of his financial difficulties—since I mentioned William Penn—I'll note that he (the junior one) received Pennsylvania (land) in exchange for forgiving debts of thousands of pounds owed to his father as a Navy victualler, also called William Penn, who happened to be the next-door neighbor of Samuel Pepys. The major land grant (and minor anecdote) is just one example of the desperate measures implemented by the King and his advisors to satisfy creditors during this period. Of course one can't really blame the Quakers of Pennsylvania for the financial crises of 1672. If you need to blame it on a particular country other than England, that honor will have to go to the French and perhaps the Dutch.

---

[18] See Hobbes (2013).

Dutch and Temple

"Better, Faster, Richer"

During the three decades from the years 1650 to 1680, the English fought three separate wars against the Dutch; sometimes joining with the French, who were their main rivals in trade. The first Anglo-Dutch war took place under Oliver Cromwell's rule of the Commonwealth and lasted a little over two years, from 1652 to 1654. By all accounts England won that particular skirmish (Battle of Scheveningen), with the main striker being the English Navy, helping England gain full control of the seas and a monopoly over trade with the American colonies. The English champion was General Monk, who will actually make a minor appearance in our financial story. The rematch took place ten years later, from 1665 to 1667, after King Charles II had been restored to the throne and Oliver Cromwell was long dead. During this period, the English captured New Amsterdam and named it New York, in honor of the king's brother, the Duke of York—who will also make an occasional appearance. The second Anglo-Dutch war was once again fought over trade routes and control over the seas, but this time, despite a good showing by the English in the first part of the encounter, the Dutch prevailed and the final set piece in the spring of 1667 (i.e. the penalty shoot-out?) was quite embarrassing for the English. The chronic lack of English funding was to blame and is a critical financial ingredient in our story. I'll return to the (post-game) analysis later on (Fig. 2.2).

The third (and final in the seventeenth century) Anglo-Dutch war was somewhat of a draw, all things considered. The hostilities started in March 1672, just two months after *the Stop of the Exchequer* and the (financial) preparations for the war were the main impetus for default. I'll examine this claim in very great detail in Chap. 6. That final match came to halt with the Treaty of Westminster in 1674—which was the end of hostilities between the two countries for the remainder of the seventeenth century—and a point at which New York became fully and indisputably an English possession (well, at least for another century).

On a not-unrelated note, the Dutch prime minister during this entire period was Jan de Witt, who has been described (even by the English) as a great statesman with fineness, tact and personal charm. In fact, his official

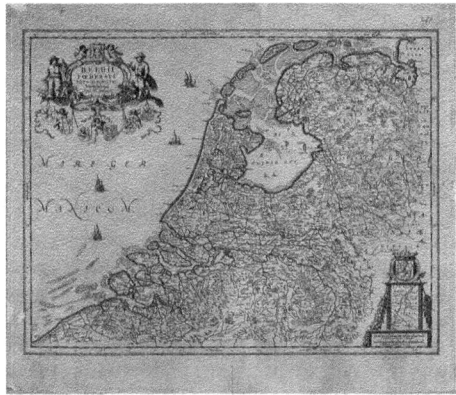

Fig. 2.2 Map of the Netherlands during the Anglo-Dutch wars, Source: Jan Janssonius (public domain), via Wikimedia Commons. https://commons.wikimedia.org/wiki/File%3ASeven_United_Netherlands_Janssonius_1658.jpg

title was *Grand Pensionary of Holland*, and oddly enough, he was one of the first people (scholars, really) to work and write about the proper valuation of pension annuities. Prime Minister de Witt put in place a remarkable and efficient system of public finances. And, while this takes us far away from our main story, it's worth noting that one of the reasons the Dutch were superior in many areas of trade and commerce—and thus the envy of the English, the French and the Spanish—was their financial efficiency. You don't hear much about Dutch financial defaults, although the year 1672 is known (even today) in the Netherlands as a disaster year for a variety of not-unrelated reasons. I'll mention that when the time comes.

Now, given the significance of the Anglo-Dutch wars, a key player in the diplomatic relations between England and the Dutch was Sir William Temple[19] (b. 1628, d. 1699), who served as the on-and-off ambassador in The Hague and tried very hard to avoid the third Anglo-Dutch war. It is quite likely that had William Temple succeeded, there might not have been a big default to write about—at least not in the year 1672, to assuage those who think it was inevitable. Temple was recalled to

---

[19] Fans of the book *Gulliver's Travels* might be interested to know that Jonathan Swift (the author) worked as personal assistant and secretary to Sir William Temple.

England (and subsequently ignored) just as King Charles' advisors prepared for war.

His link to our story is more than superficial or as a failed mediator. His career and personal finances epitomized the financial stress of the period. According to his biographer,[20] he faced immense difficulty getting paid from the Exchequer for his services during his ambassadorship. He was living in The Hague, which, he complained in letters he sent home, was 35% more expensive than living in Paris or London. Apparently, the ambassador's wife, Dorothy Osborne (coincidentally, cousin of Thomas Osborne, another name to come), had to conduct her own intense and sensitive diplomatic negotiations to get paid from Charles' ministers: thoroughly embarrassing and yet another snapshot into those financial times. Although eventually Temple (and his wife) managed to get some expenses covered, but when the Exchequer shut down in January 1672, they still owed him for ten years' worth of rent he'd paid in The Hague—none of which he recovered, according to his wife. To make matters worse, he had a cash account at one of the bankers (Edward Backwell), who froze payments after *The Stop*. Sir William Temple, the Dutch ambassador, suffered on two accounts.

QUEEN CATHERINE OF BRAGANZA

"The Portuguese Queen"

Queen and wife of King Charles II, born in Portugal in November 1638 and died almost two decades after her husband, in December 1705, back in her home country of Portugal. She was a visibly devout Catholic for her entire life, never quite fitting into the promiscuous court of Restoration England, and was always regarded with some suspicion by a large segment of the Protestant population. Her relevance to our story though, other than being married to our main protagonist, is the money from her dowry. This dowry was supposed to have included two million Portuguese cruzados, which is approximately 32 tonnes of gold, plus the garrison of Tangiers. This would have been enough to bankroll the King (and all his mistresses) for quite a while. This sizeable dowry was likely the main reason King Charles II and his advisors brokered the marriage (Fig. 2.3).

---

[20] *Sir William Temple: The Man and His Work*, by H. E. Woodbridge (1940).

Fig. 2.3 Queen Catherine of Braganza painted by Sir Peter Lely (public domain), via Wikimedia Commons. https://commons.wikimedia.org/wiki/File%3AQueen_Catherine_of_Braganza.jpg

In fact, when Catherine arrived in England in 1661 to marry Charles, she came with much less than the two million cruzados and Charles, who was stuck with her, spent the next 15 years of his regime trying to slowly recover the money from the Portuguese with the help of some Jewish merchants who had Dutch and Portuguese connections. Also, some of the goldsmith-bankers—who I'll get to—also took part in the "dowry rescue" operations.

THOMAS CLIFFORD

"The Impulsive Papist"

Counselor to the King, Sir Thomas Clifford was born a member of the gentry in August 1630 but moved up the social ranks and died a member of the nobility in October 1673. He served his country in naval campaigns against the Dutch in the 1660s, and then as a member of the House of Commons. He was described by contemporaries, such the diarists Samuel Pepys and John Evelyn, as having remarkable energy and being very productive. During the years he served in the House of Commons, he was a

Fig. 2.4 Clifford painted by Sir Peter Lely (public domain), via Wikimedia Commons. https://commons.wikimedia.org/wiki/File%3A1stLordClifford.jpg

member of almost 300 committees. He was also known for being impulsive and hot-headed, ready for "extreme measures," and for the "rudeness of his tongue," according to Pepys. He was also said to be generous with the bribes he made to others as part of his responsibilities for the secret service budget (Fig. 2.4).

More importantly and much more relevant to our story, Thomas Clifford is likely the person who made the suggestion to King Charles II to default in early 1672. Defaults and bankruptcies can always be traced to decisions, and this one likely was Clifford's. He proposed it, argued in favor of it and convinced his fellow Privy Council members that there was no alternative. (Of course the bankers probably would not have seen things in the same light.)

It's not surprising to hear biographers[21] describe Clifford as having a "shallow knowledge of financial affairs." But at the time, the King obviously accepted the idea (or there wouldn't be a book in your hands) and Sir Thomas Clifford—who was only a member of the gentry at that point—was rewarded with peerage and became Baron (ok, lowest rank, but still a Lord[22]) Clifford of Chudleigh a few months after the "Stop,"

---

[21] See, for example, the chapter on Clifford in Lee (1965), which is the source for most of the material in this section.

[22] There was an element of strategy here as well, in that the King needed men such as Clifford to move (from the House of Commons) to help manage the House of Lords.

just as the bankers and their depositors started their long (34-year) march for justice and compensation.

One final point about Clifford: in the seventeenth century, religion was ever present in all dramas and our story is no different. In contrast to the official Anglican religion, Thomas Clifford was a practicing Catholic or, in the words of John Evelyn, "a little warped to Rome." In his active political career, he took "Catholic views," such as opposing any relaxation on eating meat during Lent, as just one example from the early 1660s. This strident position (not just about Lent)—which manifested itself in a variety of actions, including toleration for dissenters—led to his eventual downfall. I'll get to the wretched details on the religious persecution later on, but he eventually had to resign from his role as chief advisor to the King. English history doesn't remember him kindly and he died under mysterious circumstances. For the record, no banker has ever been accused or charged in his death.

Henry Bennet: Arlington

"The Smooth Diplomat"

He was known and is referred to in this book as Earl of Arlington, or simply Arlington. He was born in January 1618 and died in the month of July 1685, just a few months after the death of his boss and commander in chief, King Charles II. Like the previously mentioned Thomas Clifford, Arlington was a member of the king's inner circle of advisors and was "in the room" during the financial events of late 1671 and early 1672 (Fig. 2.5).

Although he was originally destined for the Church, the social upheaval of the 1640s disrupted those lofty plans. He and his family were firmly on the royalist's side, taking up arms for King Charles I. In 1643, during one of the military clashes for which he volunteered, he was severely injured and permanently scarred on his nose. This became a badge of honor he wore prominently, and boasted about repeatedly—and explains the black mark in the accompanying picture. Like other royalists who were persona non grata in England during Cromwell's rule of the Commonwealth, Arlington wandered Europe with the royal party and became a member of their (mostly poor and ragged) entourage. He served (then) Prince Charles, his brother James and their mother Queen Henrietta Maria in a variety of roles, and eventually was posted for a few years as a "pseudo ambassador" to Spain, where he assimilated the skills and Persona of a true diplomat.

Like others in the royal circle, Arlington gained his position of power during the Restoration, eventually becoming a privy councilor, Secretary

Fig. 2.5 Arlington painted by Sir Peter Lely (public domain), via Wikimedia Commons. https://commons.wikimedia.org/wiki/File%3AHenry_Bennet.jpg

of State as well as postmaster-general. His governmental responsibilities included diplomacy—for which he was reputed to have great skill and an ambassador's natural etiquette—as well as procuring mistresses for the King (the "royal pimp"?), another task in which he apparently excelled. It is presumed that he acquired most of these skills during his time at the royal court of Spain. Although compared to the licentious undertakings of King Charles II, it seems Arlington himself was faithful to his wife and didn't participate in the Court's promiscuity (or perhaps he managed to hide it well). Arlington was also known and admired for organizing dazzling parties and was an impeccable host. His connection to the royal family was fortified further when Arlington's only daughter married one of the many illegitimate sons King Charles II sired with his primary mistress, Barbara Villiers.

Unlike his fellow minister Clifford, Arlington was known as cautious, levelheaded, diplomatic and more likely to operate behind the scenes, preferring to exert his influence in private with the King. However, he did share a trait with Clifford, namely their religion. Like King Charles II himself, Arlington also "leaned toward Rome" but managed to hide his religious views from the public (like the King) and lie (under oath) when necessary to avoid disclosing this fact to a largely Protestant and Anglican parliament. In the end though, on his deathbed, he openly proclaimed himself to be a Roman Catholic—and some claim that early in life he was a (proper) Anglican.

Now this religious business is relevant to our story for a variety of reasons. First, if he was Catholic (in 1672)—and this would apply to Clifford as well—then he was more likely to take a jaundiced view of usury and the (high) interest rates charged by the goldsmith-bankers. I will argue that part of *the Stop of the Exchequer* and the default of 1672 was a concerted war on interest and usury grounded in scripture.

Second, and perhaps more importantly, in 1670, King Charles II signed an accord known as the Treaty of Dover[23] with his French Catholic (cousin) King Louis XIV, aka the Sun King. The controversial provisions of the treaty—with details that only Clifford and Arlington knew about—promised the King much-needed financial support (aka bribes) in exchange for some rather unpalatable conditions and requests. I'll get to that story in Chap. 6, since it is directly relevant to the "Stop." But it's worth noting that only Clifford and Arlington knew of this (bizarre) deal, and I suspect they were (more) trusted because of their religious leanings. Again, the newfound flow of money from France to England negotiated by Clifford and Arlington might have been a factor in the overall complacency in the lead-up to the default. More to come. One final trivia fact worth mentioning[24] is that the Earl of Arlington lived in (suitably enough) Arlington House, which was expanded in the early eighteenth century and eventually became known as (the Southern Wing of) Buckingham Palace.

George Villiers: Buckingham

"The Rake and Libertine"

Known as the 2nd Duke of Buckingham, or simply Buckingham (and occasionally Bucks), Villiers was born in Westminster in January 1628 and died in April 1687. His father, the eminent 1st Duke of Buckingham, was a confidant, courtier and close friend of King Charles I, but was assassinated when George was an infant. The child subsequently moved into the royal nursery and developed a sibling-like relationship (and rivalry) with the future King Charles II, who was two years younger (Fig. 2.6).

---

[23] See Hutton, *The Making of the Secret Treaty of Dover* (1986).

[24] The source for the historical material in this biography is the relevant chapter in Lee (1965), as well as Henry Bennet's entry in the *Oxford Dictionary of National Biography*, written by Alan Marshall.

Fig. 2.6 Buckingham painted by Sir Peter Lely (public domain), via Wikimedia Commons. https://commons.wikimedia.org/wiki/File%3A2ndDukeOfBuckingham.jpg

After some time at Cambridge University, Villiers participated in the (second) Civil War in the same brigade as Prince Rupert of the Rhine, unsurprisingly on the royalist side and against the parliament. As that cause was lost and his "surrogate dad" King Charles I was beheaded by Oliver Cromwell in January 1649, he joined the (exiled) royal family in wandering the continent. But he then had a falling out with the royal court and in a stunning change of heart and sides—perhaps motivated by an attempt to recover his family's lost lands—he returned to England during the Commonwealth. Some say he actually spied for Oliver Cromwell while in Europe, others claim he was a double agent. Either way, he ended up in London marrying the daughter of Lord Thomas Fairfax, a leading general of the parliament army and noteworthy figure during the Civil War. It was a rocky return, but one that cast a cloud of suspicion over George's true loyalties.

Upon the Restoration and the king's return to London in 1660, his royalist *bona fides* were hard to rehabilitate and Buckingham never truly regained the trust he had lost, although Oliver Cromwell hadn't seemed to trust him either.

Buckingham was tolerated, and even welcomed, by the King because plain and simple he was great fun—the "coolest kid at the party." Indeed, Buckingham was one of the most renowned and notorious characters of the Restoration court.[25] The title of the biography by J. H. Wilson[26] (published in 1954), *A Rake and His Times,* captures the essence of his Persona. One could also use the terms *libertine* and *debauchee.* During the 1660s and 1670s Buckingham was a close friend of his fellow hell-raiser, poet and womanizer the Earl of Dorset, as well the notorious Earl of Rochester (recall, the one played by Johnny Depp). The well-known series of paintings by William Hogarth entitled *The Rake's Progress,* although a product of the early eighteenth century and a storyboard of another rake's life, were nevertheless a reflection of Buckingham's persona, especially the orgies, debt and prison time. The common denominator of most Restoration rakes is that they served as an entourage of courtiers or personal comedians to King Charles II, occasionally stepping across the line and incurring His Majesty's wrath.

In fact, Buckingham landed in the Tower of London—for the second or possibly third time—after he was accused of "commissioning a horoscope of the king's birth," which was a treasonous offense 350 years ago, as it could apparently predict the king's date of death. He is also known as a duelist and got himself into a spot of trouble when he fell in love with the Countess of Shrewsbury while her husband (and his wife) were both still alive. The cuckolded and enraged husband then challenged the Duke of Buckingham to a duel, but ironically lost his life to the sword, leaving the path to his widow's home wide open for Bucks.

Now, lest you leave with the impression that Bucks was a frivolous and romantic buffoon, note that the Duke was also a Fellow of the Royal Society and a great connoisseur of the sciences. He experimented with various forms of glass and apparently asked for a laboratory to be built in the Tower of London so his experimentation could continue during his many stays there. He was also known to have a great singing voice and composed a number of plays that continue to be staged in the twenty-first century. Basically, he was a Restoration wit.

Buckingham's role in *the Stop of the Exchequer* is more than comic relief or entertainment, since he too was a privy councilor and party to the deliberations around the time of the default—and his wife makes a brief

---

[25] The source for most of the material is Bruce Yardley, 'Villiers, George, second duke of Buckingham (1628–1687)', *Oxford Dictionary of National Biography,* Oxford University Press, 2004, as well as the recent book, *The Mistresses of Cliveden: Three Centuries of Scandal, Power and Intrigue in an English Stately Home,* by Natalie Livingstone, cited as Livingstone (2015).

[26] Cited as Wilson (1954).

appearance in our story as well. Buckingham obviously lacked administrative experience, and his connection to the King was more of a casual semi-trusted advisor (and Master of the Horse), compared to, say, that of Clifford or Arlington. Charles II was quoted as saying that Buckingham was useless "in power," but dangerous when "out of it."

Nevertheless, Buckingham did have political and parliament connections, commercial interests and a wide network of peers. Moreover, his cousin Barbara Villiers (aka the Countess of Castlemaine) was the king's powerful, much reviled and very expensive primary mistress; another connection which didn't hurt (for a while). In the end, although he was never involved in the nuts and bolts of government debt management, fiscal policy or tax revenues, Buckingham was intimately familiar with the crushing power of personal debts. Around the time the Exchequer defaulted in 1672, he too had to be bailed out of his financial liabilities. In other words, and in some sense, his personal financial life paralleled the national one.

ANTHONY ASHLEY COOPER: SHAFTESBURY

"The Two-Faced Achitophel"

Born in July 1621 in Dorset (England), died in January 1683 in Amsterdam (Dutch Provinces) and married three times in between, Anthony Ashley Cooper is also known to history as the Earl of Shaftesbury—a title he received later in life—and I'll simply call him Shaftesbury from this point forward. Interestingly, he is also known in the annals of Colonial America, or at least to the historians of that period, as the constitutional father of the Carolinas, where he had pursued commercial interests. As a young man, following the requisite education at Oxford with Puritan and Calvinist leanings, he sat for a while in the House of Commons, representing the county of Dorset. During the Civil War, he took up arms *against* King Charles I and actually became a member of Oliver Cromwell's council of state during the Commonwealth. Eventually, Shaftesbury fell out with the parliament and saw the royalist light, just in time for the Restoration of King Charles II, who courted him after he switched sides. Convenient timing! (Fig. 2.7).

As with the previously mentioned Clifford, Arlington and Buckingham, Shaftesbury was a member of the Privy Council to King Charles II. His relationship with the King soured toward the late 1670s, however (mostly

Fig. 2.7 Shaftesbury painted by John Greenhill (public domain), via Wikimedia Commons. https://commons.wikimedia.org/wiki/File:Anthony_Ashley-Cooper,_1st_Earl_of_Shaftesbury.jpg

after the events depicted in our financial story), and he became one of the king's greatest antagonists and fierce opponents in parliament.

Overall, he was a very complicated and controversial figure,[27] and featured prominently in a number of critical episodes of English history. Some refer to him as the political founder of the Whig party.[28] Shaftesbury's character has been widely savaged over the 350 years that have since elapsed. Even his biographer K. H. D. Haley started his grand tome of 750 pages by stating, in the very first line, "Shaftesbury stands pilloried for all time" after duly quoting the poet John Dryden, who wrote (about Shaftesbury): "A name to all succeeding ages, cursed."

---

[27] The source for this material is Tim Harris, 'Cooper, Anthony Ashley, first earl of Shaftesbury (1621–1683)', *Oxford Dictionary of National Biography*, Oxford University Press, 2004, as well as the more detailed biography by K. H. Haley, *The First Earl of Shaftesbury*, cited as Haley (1968). See also the book by Isenberg (2016) for a fascinating discussion of Shaftesbury's connection to the history of The Carolinas.

[28] He is also closely linked to the infamous Popish Plot, in which a certain Titus Oates created (from whole cloth) a plot in which Catholic Jesuits were planning to assassinate King Charles II in the fall of 1678. The details of that disgrace would needlessly raise the hair on the back of your neck and take us far adrift from our story at this early stage.

Why the bad reputation? Well, even in an era of rapidly shifting alliances (remember Buckingham), nefarious dealings and fickle politicians, it seems Shaftesbury's greatest offense was switching sides much too often. Among his many about-faces was the suggestion that the royal line of succession be modified by parliament. Recall that King Charles II had no legitimate children with Queen Catherine. By the late 1670s it became clear that Charles' brother James would (eventually) succeed him to the throne. The problem with this was, as usual, religion: James was an overtly practicing Catholic, in contrast to his brother Charles, who managed to hold the public in suspense. Either way, an openly Catholic king was anathema to the majority of the Protestant country and brought back memories and fears of Queen (Bloody) Mary, or Guy Fawkes and the Gunpowder Plot to blow up parliament during the reign of their grandfather King James I.

For a very long time Catholics were blamed for the Fire of London in 1666, and only recently (in the nineteenth century) was the "claim" removed from the memorial. Well, Lord Shaftesbury's solution to a potential Catholic monarch, formed in cahoots with the Duke of Buckingham, was to suggest that the King ship his wife Catherine to the Carolinas in North America. Then, after she "abandoned" him, he could marry someone younger (and fertile). When that plan didn't find royal favor, Lord Shaftesbury encouraged the idea that King Charles II select one of his many (at least 14) illegitimate children—the oldest actually—who was indeed Protestant and pick him as his heir. How does one legitimize a bastard son, you ask? Well, by claiming that (a very young) King Charles II had in fact married his first (teenage) love, the mother of said illegitimate son (who was long dead), but had simply not bothered to inform anyone about the nuptials.

Anyway, without getting into the soap operatic details (the King, for his part, vehemently objected to all of this scheming and, to his credit, would never tolerate any maltreatment of his wife, the queen), Lord Shaftesbury didn't succeed in any of this. He did of course manage to get himself on the wrong side of King Charles II and was very politely encouraged to leave the country.

All of this might seem ahead of our time—and somewhat tangential—but despite Lord Shaftesbury's historical reputation as one of the king's greatest opponents, during the late 1660s and early 1670s (our period), he was in fact one of his main financial advisors. At that relevant time, he was with the "in" crowd. All this political flip-flopping is why he is often compared to the biblical figure of Achitophel, who transitioned from King David's close advisor to supporter of the rebellion led by his son Absalom.

In the late 1670s the Absalom in question was the above-alluded-to Duke of Monmouth, King Charles II's eldest (illegitimate) son.[29]

Now, back to the money trail. Shaftesbury was the Chancellor of the Exchequer from 1667 to 1672 and had a ringside seat to *the Stop of the Exchequer*. He was quite familiar with the business community in the City of London (who were most affected by the default); much more so than Clifford or Arlington, both of whom lacked commercial insight. He actually opposed the entire measure of *The Stop* (i.e. default of debt to City bankers) and tried to prevent it. More on the chronology will appear in Chap. 6. In sum, Shaftesbury was a central character in English political life during the 1660s, 1670s and early 1680s, until he was accused of High Treason and forced to leave the country and die (with debts and) in exile.

One final factoid worth noting about Shaftesbury was that his close friend and houseguest (and for a while personal physician) for many years was none other than John Locke, the philosopher, with whom he remained quite close during his knotty and volatile political life story—and another name that will make an occasional appearance in our own story.

JOHN MAITLAND: LAUDERDALE

"The Zealous Scotsman"

John Maitland, who is known to history as the Duke of Lauderdale after the honor he received in the spring of 1672, was born in Scotland in May 1616 and died in England in August 1682. Together with the four previously mentioned advisors, Clifford, Arlington, Buckingham and Ashley, he (Lauderdale) was the fifth and final member of the king's inner circle of counselors during the period of *the Stop of the Exchequer*. Coincidentally, the initials of these five spell out the word CABAL, and now you have the origin of the phrase within the political context of a clique or governing ministry. Officially, the five of them were known as the Committee of Foreign Affairs, part of the Privy Council, a group that gained power after the "fall" of Lord Clarendon in the spring of 1667, which is when our story begins in Chap. 6 (Fig. 2.8).

---

[29] For those interested in this fascinating story, see the book by Anna Keay, *The Last Rebel*, cited as Keay (2016). For all non-British readers, who might not have been force-fed this story in grade school, the Duke of Monmouth rebelled after his uncle James became king in 1685, and the tragic Duke lost his head (literally). All this might have never happened if Shaftesbury had **not** put delusions of grandeur in the Duke's head.

Fig. 2.8 Lauderdale painted by Jacob Huysmans (public domain), via Wikimedia Commons. https://commons.wikimedia.org/wiki/File%3AJohn_Maitland%2C_Duke_of_Lauderdale_by_Jacob_Huysmans.jpg

Very generally speaking, in political and religious matters, Clifford and Arlington tended to one side or faction of the cabal, while Buckingham, Shaftesbury and Lauderdale were bound on the other side, although their membership in these factions didn't stop them from snipping at or trying to one-up one another. (Abraham Lincoln's *team of rivals* comes to mind.) Contemporary historians[30] claim that this factious group of five might not have been as influential as commonly thought, and that Arlington (previously introduced) really pulled the strings. Who knows? But the public (at the time) certainly believed the cabal to be in charge—and it makes for a great part of the story!

The term cabal and these five advisors were popularized and mythologized by another Charles, the great Victorian writer Charles Dickens, in his 1850s book: *A Child's History of England*. The book became part of the school curriculum and might explain the term's endurance (in England) long after the five members themselves have been forgotten. Of course the word "cabal" precedes Dickens and the Restoration, and can be traced back to *kabbalah*, esoteric Jewish mysticism, hidden meanings and secret agendas, which is fittingly *apropos*.

---

[30] See Hutton (1989, p. 305), for example.

Lauderdale was the oldest and most senior member of the cabal, being in his mid-50s during the events described in our story. Before he became a close advisor and member of King Charles' inner circle, he spent almost ten years of his life in various jails, including the Tower of London and Windsor Castle. This is because in the decade after the English Civil Wars (1650s), he was incarcerated by the Lord Protector Oliver Cromwell for the prevailing political and religious sins of the times, namely being a monarchist, a Presbyterian and a Covenanter (an adherent of the National Covenant in 1638 or of the Solemn League and Covenant in 1643, upholding the organization of the Scottish Presbyterian Church).

Upon his release from jail, just as King Charles II was returning to England from exile, Lauderdale was made Secretary of State for Scotland. Naturally, he spent most of his time preoccupied with Scottish affairs and as an advocate for Scottish interests in England. He was instrumental and the key person in the political negotiations taking place in the late 1660s and early 1670s attempting to unify England and Scotland. Indeed, King Charles (initially) favored and encouraged the union with his ancestral homeland Scotland—recall that his grandfather King James was Scottish—although Charles' motives were less nationalistic than financial. (It was all about money, really. More in Chap. 6.)

Lauderdale worked tirelessly to win commercial concessions from the English for Scotland. These concessions were sorely needed because his countrymen were treated as foreigners in most international trade matters. In fact, the Scottish were not allowed to trade directly with the colonies and instead had to reroute their boats and ships via England (and thus pay more tax) under the so-called Navigation Act.

Lauderdale's advocacy for Scottish interests within England and his powerful political influence made him the envy of another dejected group, the Irish, who wished they had a similar advocate close to the King (which they never got). Samuel Pepys, never lacking for an opinion on anything or anyone, described Lauderdale as a "cunning fellow" who had "the power of Scotland in his hand." Although it appears Pepys didn't like Lauderdale's (lack of) taste in music, according to another entry in his diary.

In addition to the justifiable jealousy of the Irish, Lauderdale's advocacy also gained him the enmity of the English, not unlike most Scottish (politicians) in seventeenth-century England. Historians have also described him as licentious and impatient, with a tendency toward brutality and violence, which apparently became worse during the 1670s as his health deteriorated. He was labeled the king's evil counselor—although I suspect that could apply equally to any member of the cabal—and an anonymous contemporary poet referred to him in a widely circulated poem as a "haughty monster" and "rampant villain."

Lauderdale definitely wasn't popular, especially after he suggested during one of the many episodes of parliament dissent that Scottish forces should be called down and used to suppress anyone who disagreed with his boss. Lauderdale's name is often associated with the factions of advisors encouraging King Charles to employ arbitrary and unaccountable government. This of course is an accusation that had been made repeatedly against the Stuart dynasty, from the days of James to Charles and back.

Lauderdale was in the room during the fateful events around January 1672 and tended to side with Shaftesbury and Buckingham (pro commerce) in financial matters. He might also have been somewhat distracted in early 1672, as he was also concerned with personal matters. His wife had recently died and he was about to marry his longtime mistress (and soon-to-be second wife) Elizabeth Murray, known to history as the witty and beautiful Duchess of Lauderdale.[31] She in turn wrote a series of letters to Gilbert Burnett—a contemporary historian of sorts, who will make an occasional appearance—describing the causes and aftermath of the "Stop."

And, like his boss the King, and despite two marriages, Lauderdale left no male heirs. So, upon his death in 1682, his dukedom and the English title Duke of Lauderdale died with him. Fort Lauderdale in Florida has no relation.

George Downing

"The Puritanical and Efficient Administrator"

George Downing was born in the year 1623 in Dublin (Ireland) and died in July 1684 in Cambridge (England). He is indeed the person after whom (10) Downing Street in London is named. When George was 15 years old, his family made the hazardous 70-day journey across the Atlantic and immigrated to New England in 1638, where his uncle John Winthrop was the first governor of the Massachusetts Bay Colony (Fig. 2.9).

The Downing family settled in Salem—the city upon a hill—where they were respected and active members of the local church. A few years after arriving in New England, the 19-year-old George enrolled in the

---

[31] See the relevant chapter in Lee (1965) on Lauderdale, as well as the recent (historical fiction) novel *Royalist Rebel* (Seymour, 2013) for more on Elizabeth Murray, the Duchess of Lauderdale.

Fig. 2.9 Downing painted by Thomas Smith (harvardartmuseums.org) (public domain), via Wikimedia Commons. https://commons.wikimedia.org/wiki/File%3ASir_George_Downing_by_Thomas_Smith.jpeg

newly established Harvard University and was (apparently) a member of the first-ever graduating class. Upon completing his studies at Harvard in 1642, he did some ad hoc tutoring for a while, and then, like many young graduates, he took some time off to travel and sightsee from Barbados in the Caribbean to Newfoundland. His mother, the sister of John Winthrop, wrote that her son "really liked to travel."

His relation to our story,[32] and the reason the current Prime Minister of the United Kingdom lives on a street with his name, is that in the year 1646 he decided to leave America and return to England. (Perhaps that is why the English admired him.) Yes, the reverse immigration pattern did take place occasionally!

Once back in England he became a roaming Puritan preacher and then chaplain in a dragoon regiment. At some point he attracted the attention of Oliver Cromwell himself, who offered George a position as a spy and eventually as the scoutmaster-general in 1649, in charge of intelligence

---

[32] The source for the material in this biography is the book by John Beresford, *The Godfather of Downing Street*, cited as Beresford (1925), as well as Jonathan Scott, 'Downing, Sir George, first baronet (1623–1684)', *Oxford Dictionary of National Biography*, Oxford University Press, 2004. See also Lehman (2016) for more on Puritans, New England and money.

gathering. Eventually, George pivoted away from preaching and more toward diplomacy and politics. By November 1657, a decade after leaving Salem, he was appointed ambassador and moved to The Hague, where he directed spying operations for Cromwell, including keeping tabs on (the future) King Charles II and his royal entourage.

More than a geographical footnote (as his mother said, he liked to travel), while in The Hague, he also had the opportunity to learn and imbibe the methods of "Dutch finance" from a world-class group of merchants whose innovative methods were copied by many nations. His Dutch contacts and knowledge were critical in the lead-up to the commercially motivated Anglo-Dutch wars of the 1660s and 1670s. It's also worth noting that he wasn't very popular or liked as an ambassador in The Hague and was eventually expelled by the Dutch, returning (permanently) to London. Perhaps they didn't like his puritan brand of Calvinism.

In yet another change of sides, similar to Lord Shaftesbury's conversion, during the restoration of the monarchy in 1660, George was able to ingratiate himself with King Charles II. He did this by openly admitting (and writing about) the "error of his prior ways," perhaps by groveling, and by blaming his New England upbringing for his earlier misguided puritanical leanings. (Perhaps it was something in Salem's water supply.) In fact, he received more than simply a pardon: he was knighted in May 1660, and then in July 1663, he was created a Baronet (not a Baron, nor a member of the peerage) and was henceforth known as Sir George Downing. One can describe his position and role at the Exchequer, which I'll get to in Chap. 6, as a type of tollbooth collector. Every time someone entered to conduct any business, he got a small entrance fee. Not everyone was convinced, however, of his newfound loyalty, and the ever-gossipy Samuel Pepys called him a "perfidious rogue" in one of his diary entries. Although entries at later dates indicate a certain begrudging respect and admiration for his skill,[33] so it's unclear what Pepys really thought about him. The (other) diarist John Evelyn commented: "From a fanatic preacher not worth a groat, he has become excessive rich." In fact, for a while during the seventeenth and eighteenth centuries, his name was even nominalized (turned into a noun), and the phrase "A George Downing" was used as a term of contempt for a man who looks out for his own interests and is miserly with others, especially fellow countrymen.

---

[33] Downing at one point boasted to Pepys (December 27, 1668) that his Dutch spies were able to pickpocket the keys from de Witt's pockets, use them to access state documents, copy them and then return the keys to his pocket without him noticing.

More relevant to the financial aspects of the story is that Sir George was eventually appointed a secretary to the commissioners of the treasury, where—perhaps consistent with his tightfistedness and keen awareness of the value of every pound—he implemented numerous administrative improvements. His best-known work revolved around the instruments and efficiency of debt management, which were so critical during the reign of King Charles II. I'll return to Downing's bureaucratic innovations in detail later on in Chap. 6. Indeed, he features quite prominently in our story. One final introductory remark, which might quench curiosity, relates to the famous "Number Ten" (Downing). Over the course of his life, the penny-pinching treasury official managed to accumulate quite a fortune (remember the tollbooth) and died with substantial property, including a small piece of land adjacent to Saint James Park in London, which is now known as Downing Street.

THOMAS OSBORNE: DANBY

"The Anglican Fixer-in-Chief"

Born in February 1632 and died in July 1712. Despite the many diverse titles he accumulated, he is best known as the Earl of Danby, or simply Danby. Although his family had always been supporters of the monarchy (aka royalists), he himself was also an exceedingly effective social climber. Over his 80-year lifespan, much of which was spent in poor health—and early on, in poor wealth—he accumulated the entire collection of peerage titles. He started with Baron Osborne (1), then Viscount Latimer (2) in 1673 and then Earl of Danby (3) in 1674. It took a while for the next one, but he was rewarded with the Marquess of Carmarthen (4) in 1689 and finally Duke of Leeds (5) in the year 1694. His path up the social ranks of England's aristocracy was notable, but also tumultuous and rocky. He was widely detested by his peers, many of whom endeavored to erect roadblocks to his ascension at every opportunity. Politically, he was a fervent supporter of the Church of England, aka the Anglicans, and had little tolerance for dissenters and nonconformists, such as the Levelers, Puritans, and Quakers, as well Roman Catholics. In his own way he was quite the fanatic (or bigot) (Fig. 2.10).

Danby's role in our story is central, less to do with religion or politics and more in the realm of finance. For better or worse he was the official most responsible for cleaning up the financial mess created by *the Stop of*

Fig. 2.10 Danby painted by Johann Kerseboom (public domain), via Wikimedia Commons. https://commons.wikimedia.org/wiki/File%3AThomas_Osborne%2C_1st_Duke_of_Leeds_by_Johann_Kerseboom.jpg

the Exchequer. His ruthlessness and "fiery sprit" in managing affairs as Treasurer of the Navy earned him a promotion to the more challenging task of managing all the financial dealings of the Crown. And, although it took many decades for creditors (or their descendants) to receive proper compensation and final settlement from *The Stop*, none of that would have been possible without the energetic administrative work done by Danby. In the aftermath of the default, he was promoted to the exalted position of Lord Treasurer: a role that, for all intents and purposes, was the highest official post in England. I'll depict the details of Danby's actions later on in the story, but for now I'll merely say it was significant. In addition to compiling a detailed catalog of *who was owed what*, a list I'll display in Chap. 6, he negotiated financial compensation with the bankers and managed to get them some meager interest income (at least for a while).

Although he was an early ally of his patron Buckingham and in cahoots with Lauderdale, both members of the cabal introduced earlier, the animus he created over the years—even with friends and colleagues—boomeranged and, eventually, his enemies got the better of him. His list of adversaries was quite impressive, ranging from the French (Catholic) mistress of King Charles II, known as the Duchess of Portsmouth, fighting over her allowance, all the way to Lord Shaftesbury, who, by then, was an ex-member of the cabal.

It didn't help his case that Danby was widely perceived to be "corrupt and a corruptor of others" according to his biographer,[34] who you think might be more sympathetic to his subject. Lord Shaftesbury called him "proud, ambitious and false." The philosopher and historian Gilbert Burnet, author of the book *History of My Own Time,* was said to have referred to him as "one of the most hated ministers to ever serve a king." John Evelyn and Samuel Pepys weren't fans either. And, although they all had their own political and religious biases, the bottom line is that none of the contemporaries who knew him personally are on record as being supporters or close friends. King Charles II was said to have remarked that Danby had none. Family matters were no better for him, as he was estranged from his own sons and his marriage was (said to be) unhappy.

Not surprisingly, like the many fallen stars who plummeted from royal grace before him, Danby's descent eventually occurred in the year 1678 when he was impeached by parliament and was sent to the Tower of London. One of the many charges against him was embezzlement of funds from the royal treasury, in addition to a variety of other obscure political sins. And, although conditions in the Tower of London weren't anything like the debtors' prison mentioned earlier, Danby did spend five full years in those infamous quarters.

But then, consistent with his lifetime ambition and drive, upon his release from "The Tower" (in 1683), he managed to continue his climb up the social ladder. Proving that indeed there are second acts in English life, Danby made himself eternal. He is widely known (at least in England) as one of the "immortal seven" who invited William of Orange to invade and depose King James II in 1688, the year of the revolution. Indeed, that is another story and another time. Twenty years after the event depicted in this book, Danby, our esteemed financial fixer, was rewarded by King William III with the title of Marquess and then Duke, leaving the memory of the impeachment and the Tower of London far behind him. He was quite a remarkable fellow in my opinion, and likely the reason many streets and avenues around the English-speaking world have been named after Danby. In fact, I live on one such street in Toronto, Canada.

---

[34] See A. Browning, *Thomas Osborne: Earl of Danby and Duke of Leads* (Oxford University Press, 1913) for most of this information.

References

Beresford, J. (1925). *The Godfather of Downing Street*. Boston: Houghton Mifflin.
Browning, A. (1913). *Thomas Osborne: Earl of Danby and Duke of Leeds*. Oxford: Oxford University Press.
Coote, S. (1999). *Royal Survivor: The Life of Charles II*. London: Hodder and Stoughton.
Fraser, A. (2002). *King Charles II*. London: Phoenix, Imprint of Orion Books Ltd.
Gregory, J., & Stevenson, J. (2007). *Britain in the Eighteenth Century: 1688–1820*. New York: Routledge.
Haley, K. (1968). *The First Earl of Shaftsebury*. Oxford: Clarendon Press.
Harris, T. (2006). *Restoration: Charles II and His Kingdoms*. London: Penguin Books.
Hobbes, T. (2013). *Leviathan*. New York: Oxford University Press.
Holmes, F. (2003). *The Sickly Stuarts*. Gloucestershire: Thrupp, Stroud and Sutton.
Hutton, R. (1986). The Making of the Secret Treaty of Dover. *The Historical Journal, 29*(2), 297–318.
Hutton, R. (1989). *Charles the Second: King of England, Scotland and Ireland*. Oxford: Clarendon Press.
Isenberg, N. (2016). *White Trash: The 400-Year Untold History of Class in America*. New York: Viking: Penguin Random House.
Keay, A. (2016). *The Last Royal Rebel: The Life and Death of James, Duke of Monmouth*. London: Bloomsbury.
Lee, M. (1965). *The CABAL*. Urbana: University of Illinois Press.
Lehman, C. (2016). *The Money Cult: Capitalism, Christianity and the Unmaking of the American Dream*. Brooklyn, NY: Melville House Publishing.
Livingstone, N. (2015). *The Mistresses of Cliveden: Three Centuries of Scandal, Power and Intrigue in an English Stately*. Home: Ballantine Books.
Miller, J. (1991). *Charles II*. London: George Weidenfeld and Nicolson Limited.
Pepys, S. (1997). *The Concise Pepys*. (T. Griffith, Ed.) Hertfordshire: Wordsworth Classics of World Literature.
Pincus, S. (2009). *1688: The First Modern Revolution*. New Haven: Yale University Press.
Plaidy, J. (2005). *The Loves of Charles II*. New York: Crown Publishing Group.
Schofield, E. A., & Wrigley, R. S. (1981). *The Population History of England: 1541–1871*. New York: Cambridge University Press.
Seymour, A. (2013). *Royalist Rebel*. Barnsley: Pen & Sword.
Trevelyan, M. G. (1960). *England Under the Stuarts*. Middlesex: Penguin Books.
Uglow, J. (2009). *A Gambling Man: Charles II and the Restoration*. London: Faber and Faber Ltd.
Wedgewood, C. V. (2011). *A King Condemned*. London: Tauris Parke.
Wilson, J. H. (1954). *A Rake and His Times*. New York: Farrar, Straus and Young.
Woodbridge, H. E. (1940). *Sir William Temple: The Man and His Work*. New York: Oxford University Press.

CHAPTER 3

The Goldsmith-Bankers

FROM ARTISTS TO FINANCIERS

The goldsmith-bankers are the main financial protagonists in our story. So now, with the royal personae or government politicians having been introduced, this is as good a time as any to explain how a bunch of craftsmen—who basically made jewelry and ornaments from gold—became the leading financiers in England during the seventeenth century. Although students of monetary economics know the answer to this question,[1] it's worth repeating here for a more general audience, especially considering the historical link to King Charles I.

First, as you might expect, the goldsmiths were indeed artists—and great ones at that. For as long as gold has existed as a precious and highly coveted metal, goldsmiths have "worked" the gold into utensils, goblets, religious items and, of course, jewelry. They learned how to melt and cast, cut and solder, polish and engrave over centuries of experience transmitted from one generation to the next. This highly refined skill was passed down from master to apprentice—in many cases, from father to son, and, in fact, the craft of goldsmithing is still taught and practiced today.[2] The

---

[1] For example, see the article by G. Selgin, "Those Dishonest Goldsmiths" (a title which is much more inflammatory than necessary), published in the *Financial History Review*, cited as Selgin (2012). See also Quinn (1997).

[2] Full disclosure: My wife is a jeweler and has studied goldsmithing.

famous (Russian) *Faberge Easter Eggs*, the (Sumerian) *Ram in a Thicket* or the *Golden Buddha in Thailand*, which is the world's largest gold object, were all made by goldsmiths.

More importantly to our story, if you are in the goldsmith business, whether it be in the twenty-first century or the seventeenth century, you probably have large quantities of gold and silver in your workshop or workbench, which means that you must keep your premises *very safe*, secure and burglar-proof. It is not a stretch or exaggeration to claim that seventeenth-century goldsmiths had the best vaults and security systems in all of London. A vault was the safest place for a gold coin or bar. Well, perhaps the second-safest place, next to the Royal Mint in the Tower of London.

Now, in a parallel development—which is ironic considering the family connection—in the year 1640, as the decade of English civil wars and unrest was just about to begin, King Charles I found himself pressed for cash to finance his agenda and missions (does this sound familiar?). The King couldn't really ask (or even beg) parliament for the money—like his son did 30 years later—because he wasn't on speaking terms with parliament. In fact, parliament had been summarily dismissed and he was about to wage war on most of the members. That's the English[3] civil war.

So, what King Charles I decided to do was head over to the Royal Mint and simply help himself to the money, cash and coins he required. This was money that was being held or deposited in the Royal Mint by London bankers and merchants. Yes, he basically stole the money. Now, just to be clear here, this act was very different and much more egregious than—but is often confused with—the more subtle machinations behind *the Stop of the Exchequer*. The similarities in motive are uncanny, however, and I'll return to 1640 when I get to 1672.

Now, historians (Stuart apologists?) have since clarified that King Charles I didn't actually pilfer the money, but rather borrowed it, although without the merchants' permission, and had promised to return the money just as soon as possible. Needless to say, the reaction from the London business community was complete outrage. London was more of a parliament (vs. Royalist) town anyway and this move didn't help the King's popularity amongst the moneyed class. And, once again, although

---

[3] See the interesting article by Jha (2015) for a discussion of the economic aspects of the civil war and how the financial assets and investments held by parliament affected their views on the King.

the King promised to pay interest on the money he "borrowed," he was forced to return most of it soon after raiding the Tower of London.

Now, I would elaborate further if this book were called *The Day the King's Dad Pinched the Gold*, but I'm interested in events that took place 30 years later. But you are starting to get a feel for the royal Stuart's attitude to property law.

Back to the goldsmiths: after 1640, it became clear that the safest place in London for merchants' money was no longer really that safe. The memory of the seizure persisted long after the details of the event had been forgotten. The problem then was, where should merchants keep their gold and silver and coins—if even the Royal Mint was (theoretically) not safe?

Yes, you guessed it. They approached the goldsmiths—those admired craftsmen and workers—to store it for them. After all, their workshops were safe. What were another few bags? The goldsmiths, who perhaps saw this new business as a nice added revenue stream, started advertising and promoting this as one of their core services. From a legal perspective though, the operation was clearly about safekeeping and the relationship was one of "bailee" (i.e. storing property) and "bailor" (i.e. transferring of property).

Then, and around the same time—and this is key—the goldsmith-bankers also started lending or leasing some of the excess gold and silver they weren't using in their own operations to merchants and other vendors, all for a small fee of course.

Now, just to be clear,[4] the goldsmith-bankers weren't the only game in town for making small loans of gold and silver. In fact, the medieval profession of *scriveners*—that is, those who could read and write and who did much of the legal paperwork for merchants—eventually morphed from accountants into money managers and financial advisors. The scriveners took (small) deposits and paid interest but were no competition for the (new) goldsmiths, with their large vaults and volume.

In time the goldsmiths had the word "banker" attached to their name and, although many had spent 10–15 years during their youth apprenticing and learning how to "work the gold" with their hands, many of them abandoned the vocation of their fathers and grandfathers and emerged as powerful financiers.[5] Others continued to work in both finance and art.

---

[4] See, for example, the book by R. D. Richards, *The Early History of Banking in England* (1929). See also Melton (1986), as well as Bagehot (1999).

[5] See Temin and Voth (2013) for an extensive analysis of goldsmith-bankers and their activities in England during the eighteenth century.

The story is almost over, but there is one missing ingredient and that has to do with the following remaining question: How did these goldsmith-bankers—who started life as craftsmen—make *so much* (i.e. Trump-like) money? After all, storing some gold and silver for a small fee couldn't possibly make them rich. And the truth is the deposit fees didn't! Instead, what (eventually) transformed them into some of the wealthiest people in the kingdom was their discovery[6] of something mysteriously known as *fractional reserve banking*.

This concept will be familiar to anyone who has formally studied banking and economics, but it's worth repeating given its centrality to the story: as merchants in London and beyond came to place their gold, silver and coins at the various goldsmiths' safe houses—and received a "warehouse receipt" with proof of their deposit—the goldsmiths realized something important about timing. Some of the depositors claimed their valuable possessions in a few days, while others kept it in storage for much longer. The money bags sat in the goldsmiths' vaults for months.

Note that from a historical point of view, we are still in the 1640s—in the aftermath of King Charles I's raid on the mint—and the early 1650s. The goldsmith-bankers must have realized that some of the deposits would remain in their premises for quite a while. At some point the proverbial light bulb must have gone on (well, whatever the pre-electrical metaphor might be) and they realized they could lend out the (long-term) gold and silver that had been deposited in their vaults, in addition to the small amount of excess gold and silver they had from their own operations.

Mathematically, instead of lending 100 ounces of gold (which belonged to the goldsmiths) at 6% interest and earning 6 ounces of gold in yearly interest profit, for example, they could "use" another 900 ounces of gold stored in their vault and lend (to others) 1000 ounces of gold and thus earn 60 ounces in profit. That was the money machine. This is a form of what is known as leverage, when carried out by a speculator or hedge fund, but called *fractional reserve banking* when undertaken by a respectable bank. In fact, when you buy a house, you do the exact same thing: you make a down payment of £100,000 and then borrow £900,000 in the

---

[6] The word "discovery" might be pushing it, as this was probably recognized as early as the fifteenth century in Barcelona. See the article by Horsefield (1949) for a discussion of the history, and in particular the cash ratio. See also the book by Steinmetz (2015) on one of the most famous (and wealthiest) bankers, Jacob Fugger, who lived well before our protagonists.

form of a mortgage. If (hypothetically) the house appreciates by 6% in that year—ignoring any interest you might owe on the mortgage—then your profit at the end of the year is £60,000 and not £6000. Remember, the entire £1,000,000 is "going to work."

Now back to the goldsmiths who learned fractional reserve banking. Was this legal? Could they simply "use" the deposited funds in that manner? In fact, how do their actions differ from what King Charles I did when he raided the Mint? Well, this isn't the place to debate the legality of the goldsmith-bankers' activities, and indeed many contemporary writers accused them of embezzlement, in addition to being usurers. Other critiques were concerned that money (and talent) was flowing to finance instead of commerce. (Sound familiar?) But the modern verdict seems to be as follows: *the goldsmiths were conducting these operations with the full knowledge and approval of their depositors.* Everyone knew about this. What is the proof of the depositor's consent? Well, for one, the paperwork or deposit receipts made it clear that depositors had a claim to a quantity of money, not a particular bag or serial number, so to speak. More importantly, the depositors were themselves being paid interest by the goldsmith-bankers, so long as they were willing to lock up those deposits for a while. Instead of paying to safekeep their funds (at the bank)—a demand deposit—some of them received compensation. Clearly, then, they knew what the bankers were up to. Of course, the risk the bankers were taking was that the depositors would all show up on a single day and demand their money back—which is a risk present today as much as in the seventeenth century and known as a "bank run"—and I'll return to that later on. For now, it's time to be introduced to some of the goldsmith-bankers.

Edward Backwell

"From Financier, to Exploited to Bankrupt"

Born a simple yeoman in 1619 and died (bankrupt) in 1683 in the United Provinces (aka the Dutch Republic). Edward started his professional life at the age of 16 as a goldsmith apprentice to Thomas Viner—uncle to Robert Viner, another banker who features in our story—and after 16 years of interning he earned his autonomy and could strike out on his own in the year 1651 (Fig. 3.1).

Fig. 3.1 Backwell, Likely Painted by James Granger (public domain), via Wikimedia Commons. https://en.wikipedia.org/wiki/File:Edward_Backwell.jpg

Although he was financially active during Oliver Cromwell's Commonwealth, his first[7] appearance on the national stage was in the year 1662, when the hard-pressed King Charles II sold the garrison (area) of Dunkirk, in what is now modern France, to King Louis XIV. The sale of Dunkirk remains controversial fully three and a half centuries after the fact, although to be fair, its upkeep was expensive. The King tasked Backwell with transferring the French money from the sale back to England and then exchanging into local funds. Like any modern-day investment banker, Backwell did more than simply take deposits or lend money. In fact, his foreign exchange skills came in quite handy and were employed again by the King when the Queen's dowry, which was mentioned earlier, had to be (slowly) exchanged from Portuguese cruzados to English

---

[7]The source for most of the material in this section is G. E. Aylmer, "Backwell, Edward (c.1619—1683)," *Oxford Dictionary of National Biography*, Oxford University Press, 2004. See also Clark (1938).

pounds. Backwell had developed financial contacts all over the Continent which is likely why he was the agent of choice for these matters.

More than just a money-man, Edward Backwell was elected as a prestigious Alderman of the City of London, which was a group of distinguished merchants and financiers involved in the management of the City's affairs (as they still are in the twenty-first century). And although he started life as a proper goldsmith, it seems that he abandoned that line of work soon after the London fire in September 1666, which destroyed his workshop and studio. He then dedicated himself entirely to financing, which (even in modern times) appears to have higher profit margins than making jewelry—and was more lucrative, for a while.

To provide just one indication of Backwell's prominence in financial matters during the Restoration, he is the banker mentioned most often (almost 60 times) in Samuel Pepys' diary during the decade of the 1660s. Although Pepys praised him in some places, claiming to enjoy intelligent conversation and discourse with him, the references weren't always flattering. In other writings, Pepys claimed that Backwell was overcharging the King for his monetary services. Additional commentators and authors echoed similar concerns about goldsmith-bankers in general, and I'll return to some of these statements later.

Despite their admitted usefulness and valuable contacts, the negative public sentiment (especially outside the city of London, in the country) toward Backwell and his colleagues most certainly contributed to the ex post justification for their ruin. In modern terms, the management fees or *credit spreads* earned by the bankers appeared excessive to outside observers and the public felt they deserved whatever calamities might befall them.

As I will argue later on in Chap. 5, viewed through the prism of modern financial economics, Backwell's financial activities were indeed risky, both ex ante and ex post. Whether or not his fees or financial compensation was economically fair is more subjective, but he did encounter some very close calls or near-financial-death experiences even before *the Stop of the Exchequer*. For example, in the year 1665, when Backwell happened to be visiting the Continent on some official business—at the time the plague was raging in London—his bank suffered a "run" by depositors and he had to be bailed out by one of his fellow bankers.

Of course, the event that eventually sealed his fortune (actually, deleted it) was *The Stop*, and I'll get to the details in Chap. 6. But it's worth noting that, even after January 1672, he continued to serve the King in various financial capacities. For example, in the year 1674, while officials at the

Exchequer were still trying to sort out who was owned what, Backwell was sent to the United Provinces (aka the Netherlands) to collect and exchange money owed to King Charles II as a result of the settlement from the third Anglo-Dutch war. Backwell wasn't compensated (much) for this effort and the trip similarly didn't yield a lot, but he was still active well into the late 1670s. Some writers[8] have taken this as proof that *the Stop of the Exchequer* wasn't a big deal—but I will argue this view is misguided.

My point here is that the Exchequer default in 1672 didn't trigger an immediate halt to Backwell's activities or make him disappear from the national scene. In fact, he served as a councilman of London in 1676 and then as a member of parliament (MP) from 1679 to 1681. Some cynics claim that his sudden conversion to politician was a deliberate strategy on his part, since MPs could use their position to protect themselves from creditors. As I will explain in Chap. 6, he owed money to hundreds of small depositors when the left-hand side of his balance sheet, and the loans he made to the King, blew up.

So, although interest income and compensation did eventually start trickling in from the Exchequer in 1677, most of it was redirected to creditors. Backwell received little of it himself. By the year 1682, he couldn't hold on any longer and was declared officially bankrupt, although the debt that actually tipped him over the financial edge wasn't owed to the small depositors; rather, it was money owed by him to the Navy.

Whatever the exact cause of his financial demise, and like others who experience this sort of financial stress later in life (he was in his mid-60s), he died soon after. But death didn't exempt his estate and executors from financial grief and it took another 15 years to settle his affairs. Perhaps this is one of the many important lessons from a financial default: the shock takes time to propagate, and it can take decades to clean up the mess, whether in the seventeenth or the twenty-first century. (I'll return to some possible modern lessons in Chap. 7.)

Edward Backwell is well known to financial and banking historians not because of his failure, but because of his success … in keeping detailed records. During the 1660s and early 1670s, he kept voluminous ledgers of his financial dealings and depositors, which by some historical miracle were not destroyed by fires or floods over the last 350 years. After passing through a number of (corporate) hands, they recently landed in the archives of the Royal Bank of Scotland (RBS) on the outskirts of

---

[8] Source: Shaw (1904).

Edinburgh. Today, the ledgers can be viewed (by anyone, including me) on microfiche, and provide a window into personal finance and consumer banking in the seventeenth century.

The depositors and names in those ledgers constitute a virtual "who's who" of Restoration England. From the Queen Mother Henrietta Maria to Prince Rupert of the Rhine and James, the Duke of York, the list also includes the previously mentioned George Downing, Lord Shaftesbury, the Earl of Arlington, the Earl of Danby, the Prince of Orange, the Duke of Monmouth and of course Samuel Pepys. They all had financial dealings with Edward Backwell and trusted him to keep their hard-earned cash safe—as a much better alternative to burying their money in the backyard. Whether or not they were affected by *the Stop of the Exchequer* depends on whether they held those deposits with Backwell over the Christmas holiday of 1671 and early 1672, or whether they had access to and then "traded" on inside information. More on that story to follow. In sum, Edward Blackwell was one the most prominent financiers or goldsmith-bankers who took deposits, lent money and provided foreign exchange services during the lead-up to *the Stop of the Exchequer.*

ROBERT VINER

"From Goldsmith to Banker to Bankrupt"

Occasionally spelled as Vyner in older documents—including his appearances in Pepys' diary—he was born in Warwick in the year 1631 and died in Windsor in September 1688. Like his contemporary, colleague (and likely, friend) Edward Backwell, Robert Viner started life in the goldsmithing business at the age of 15 as an apprentice (in 1646) to his uncle Thomas Viner. Recall that Backwell worked there and learned his craft during the same period. Robert gained his freedom from the Goldsmiths' Company and then joined Thomas Viner as a partner in 1656. In a turn of good fortune, soon after the Restoration, Robert Viner became the King's primary goldsmith, supplying the royal household with jewelry, silver plate and silverware. He continued in this role for almost the entire 25-year reign of King Charles II, even as he branched out into finance and lending—and eventually ran into financial distress. In this, he differed from Edward Backwell, who abandoned the old craft once he transitioned into a full-fledged banker. Also, unlike Backwell—and perhaps as a result of his continued involvement in the jewelry business—Robert Viner was

60   3   THE GOLDSMITH-BANKERS

Fig. 3.2 Vyner, Painter unknown. https://www.geni.com/people/Sir-Robert-Vyner-1st-Baronet-Lord-Mayor-of-London/6000000028950134877

knighted in 1665 and created baronet in 1666. He is known as Sir Robert (Fig. 3.2).

When Robert's uncle, Thomas (actually the half-brother of his father), died—and very soon after Thomas' only son died also—Robert Viner suddenly inherited a substantial estate from both, which provided him with the capital needed to expand his banking operations. His path to becoming the largest single creditor of the monarchy within a decade of the Restoration was, however, by no means smooth. Like Edward Backwell—who Robert helped bail out of a liquidity crisis during the plague—Robert Viner experienced his own "run on the bank" during June 1667. In turn, Backwell came to his aid. Whether this was out of the goodness of a friend's heart, the return of a favor or the astute attempt to prevent a more severe banking crisis is obviously unknown.

Sadly, there are no surviving ledgers or financial statements or volumes documenting Viner's banking activities, although some fragments remain. The little evidence there is points to a banker who, like Backwell, was deeply involved in the financial plumbing of the times. He made loans and held deposits and money for peers, gentry, clergy and the middling sort of borrowers. The bankers' businesses were all intertwined. Backwell's credit was Viner's debit and vice versa: no surprise, then, that a financial shock to one would have a detrimental impact on the other.

Viner's name is mentioned almost as much as that of Backwell in Pepys' diary—his name is all over the history of the Restoration, where we also learn of Viner's odd taste in memorabilia.[9] He also appears in other areas of the Restoration and court life, where he was known as quite the entertainer (some would say clown). On a more serious note, his name is inscribed on the famous monument for the Great Fire of London, designed by Sir Christopher Wren, likely because Viner himself was Lord Mayor in 1674 and Sheriff of London in 1666 during the fire.

It would be premature to get into the minutia of their actions and reactions at this early stage. But, all in all, Robert Viner[10] and Edward Backwell are the best-known personifications of the goldsmith-bankers who were (eventually) ruined by *the Stop of the Exchequer*. They were deeply involved in all aspects of finance and quite visible on the social scene.

By the year 1672, over 60% of (what today we might call) the state debt was owed to the two of them and both suffered the consequences. As you might suspect by now, Viner was ruined by the national default, but was only declared bankrupt in 1684. While he managed to stay afloat for 12 years, there is no doubt the fatal wound was the "stop" itself.

Backwell and Viner were not, in the end, the only financiers and creditors who were caught up in the storm. The other 40% of the debt—the details of which I'll get to very precisely in Chap. 6—was owed to lesser-known goldsmith-bankers with names like John Colvill(e), Joseph Horneby, John Portman, Thomas Rowe, George Snell and Bernard Turner. Although we know less about them, and they don't have five-page entries in the *Oxford Dictionary of National Biography*, their names are listed in the *Little London Directory* (compiled in 1677) and by F. G. H. Price (in 1876) in the *Handbook of London Bankers*. Sometimes the entry is just one or two lines, but they are all noted as having money deposited at the Exchequer in January 1672. So, although financial historians don't know as much

---

[9] Pepys claims he kept a mummified (child) servant in a box!
[10] The source for the material in this section is G. E. Aylmer (2014), "Viner, Sir. Robert, baronet (1631–1688)," *Oxford Dictionary of National Biography*, Oxford University Press.

about them—and their banking records didn't survive—it's worth noting that we do know many of them not only failed financially, but also ended up languishing in debtors' prison. Similar to Backwell and Viner, their collapse wasn't immediate, but unlike Backwell and Viner, bankruptcy wasn't as dignified and civil. Of course, not every goldsmith-banker in London held the royal debt that imploded. And of those who did have the misfortune to own a bit of the "toxic stuff" in their portfolio, some managed to muddle through the crisis and avoid bankruptcy, presumably if the sums involved were relatively small.

Interestingly, one banker who was caught up in the musical chairs—and in fact had substantial royal debt holdings in January 1672—managed to get his securities fully paid. In a gutsy move I'll describe in Chap. 6, he decided to double up on his bets and the roulette wheel landed in his favor. His name is John Banks and for now I'll provide a brief overview to this nemesis of Backwell and Viner.

John Banks

"The Financier That Got Away (and Paid)"

Born in August 1627 in the county of Kent and died in October 1699. The son of a successful woolen draper, John Banks attended Emanuel College at Cambridge in 1644 and then eventually moved to London to capitalize on his father's connections in the business world. John Banks wasn't a goldsmith-banker or jeweler by profession. Rather, he evolved from a merchant—providing supplies to the Navy and being an associate of Samuel Pepys—to a financier, lender and *investment* banker. But he wasn't a *retail* banker in the modern sense of the word (Fig. 3.3).

It appears that Banks didn't have any strong political leanings—either for or against the monarchy—although he did serve as an MP during the final years of the Commonwealth. During the Restoration, he aligned himself with a so-called moderate royalist faction and was subsequently made a baronet in 1662 for his royal services.

Like Robert Viner and Edward Backwell, he provided loans to the King, both directly via the *Exchequer* and indirectly by discounting (or buying) treasury orders—a process I'll describe in more detail in Chap. 5. Banks was known for embracing a no-nonsense approach to commerce, for fair dealing with his associates and for having a high regard for family.

Fig. 3.3 Banks, Painted by Sir Peter Lely (public domain), via Wikimedia Commons. https://en.wikipedia.org/wiki/File:Sir_John_Banks,_1st_Baronet.jpg

In addition to his involvement in the fixed-income market (aka trading in bonds), he also became a major shareholder in the East India Company (EIC) as well as in the Levant Company, both of which were essentially the equivalent of large-cap blue-chip stocks in the mid-seventeenth century. In fact, according to his biography,[11] he not only diversified between debt and equity, but also held land, property and cash in proportions that are remarkably similar to modern asset allocation models. Some of his surviving financial records indicate that just a few months after *the Stop of the Exchequer*, he held 4% in cash, 9% in stock, 39% in bonds and 48% in land. Although this (1672) portfolio isn't the earliest example of diversification across asset classes—it appears that Dutch households were doing this in the late fifteenth century—the proportions aren't that far off from what a

---

[11] Source: D. C. Coleman, *Sir John Banks: Baronet and Businessman*, cited as Coleman (1963). See also the entry in the *Oxford Dictionary of National Biography*, also edited by D. C. Coleman.

twenty-first-century baby boomer might allocate when one accounts for the present value of pensions and personal real estate holdings.

Sir John Banks' stature in the business community continued to grow as he became a director of the EIC and then eventually (the) governor of the company in March 1672. This was soon after the government's default, the timing of which is not coincidental. As I mentioned previously, although Banks had a substantial exposure at the time of the default, he was shrewdly able to offload the "toxic securities" and get himself paid in full within a few months, while his fellow bankers had to wait years and (their creditors) only received a fraction of the face value. I'll explain how exactly he managed this coup when the proper time comes in Chap. 5, although I should mention upfront that he wasn't a banker per se and thus didn't have depositors to satisfy or didn't need to worry about a mismatch of assets and liabilities on his books. In this, his predicament differed from Backwell and Viner, which might help explain and provide some context around his success in navigating the crisis.

Note that in addition to being a successful and very clever merchant, he was also a fellow of the Royal Society and served on their governing council, all of which was quite rare for a businessman. He was also a close friend and confidant of Samuel Pepys.[12] Needless to say at this point, Sir John Banks didn't declare bankruptcy, get hounded by creditors or flee to the Continent like some of the other goldsmith-bankers caught up in the financial mess of 1672 did. In fact, when he died in the very last year of the seventeenth century, he was one of the wealthiest private citizens in England. One other final anecdote worth noting is yet another connection to the renowned philosopher John Locke. If you recall from Shaftesbury's brief biography, Locke lived in Shaftesbury's household during the late 1660s and early 1670s. Well, after that, Locke moved on to become a tutor to John Banks' son. It's unclear exactly in which subject the greatest known English philosopher was tutoring the child—but at some level, does it really matter?

Sir John Banks "got away," but he wasn't the only banker to get lucky. Another name you will read about later is Sir Stephen Fox—also noted in a number of places in Pepys' diary. He too managed (somehow) to not be on the list of creditors that was published (by Danby) a few years after *The Stop*. But he was in the minority. Why some bankers and financiers

---

[12] Banks actually helped rescue Pepys from jail when he was accused of "popery" during the hysteria surrounding Catholic plotters and the religious plots of the late 1670s.

were caught up and brought down by the default and others were not is something I'll return to in Chap. 6.

Banking and Interest: Was It Legal?

One of the undercurrents that runs throughout this book—which is perhaps appropriate to contemplate[13] at this juncture—is the matter of *usury* or the charging of interest on debts. Recall that our story takes place in England during the mid-seventeenth century, a period when the most important book or text to Protestants, Puritans or Presbyterians alike was the Bible. And scripture takes a very dim view of usury and usurers. Although prohibitions are codified and referenced in a number of places within the Five Books of Moses, here is just one example from the book of Deuteronomy (Chap. 23, Verse 19): "You shall not charge interest to your countrymen: interest on money, food, or anything that may be loaned at interest." Similar injunctions appear in the books of Exodus and Leviticus. Note that there is no mention of a fair or suitable or reasonable[14] rate. Interest is banned, period.

This obviously wasn't only a Hebrew or Jewish obsession. In the New Testament, Luke (Chap. 6, Verse 35) reads: "Lend freely, hoping nothing in return." Moreover, the taint of usury extended well beyond religious dogma. The Greek philosopher Aristotle (in *Politics*) wrote, "Very much disliked also is the practice of charging interest," and Plato echoed similar anxieties with the practice of moneylending. The distaste was universal.

Interestingly, India, in the fourth century BCE, had similar prohibitions in place, although more refined and tied to the use of the funds. In other words, there was a distinction between borrowing money used for commerce (mildly acceptable) and lending money for consumption (unacceptable), since the former was associated with business activity (good), while the latter was associated with taking advantage of the needy (bad).

The influential philosopher and theologian Saint Thomas Aquinas (b. 1225, d. 1274), who as a Catholic priest would likely be opposed to

---

[13] The sources for this section are the article in the *Journal of Law and Economics* by Glaeser and Scheinkman (1998), the book *Beggar Thy Neighbor* by Geist (2013), Richards (1929) and Jones (1989).

[14] In the Talmud, tractate b.Baba Metzia, there is some discussion of a 20% limit on interest rates, but there is no mention of this in the Bible, which is quite clear about the matter.

usury, left the door open[15] for charging interest when the relationship between the parties was structured as a partnership and the payment was a form of profit-sharing.

Nevertheless the official (Catholic Church) position on interest and usury during medieval times can be summarized by the so-called *Third Lateran Council of 1179*, canon number 25, which basically excommunicated anyone caught charging interest on any loan—end of story.[16] This doesn't mean that moneylenders didn't exist or that they didn't charge interest. Rather, the moneylenders (aka medieval bankers) had to be very careful not to get caught and/or charge interest in clever ways that didn't look like interest—for example, by selling annuities and mortgages in which the interest rate is hidden or obscured.[17]

Of course, the threat of excommunication from the Church didn't really concern or worry the Jews, who lived on the margins of Christian society to begin with—and were more likely to worry about pogroms, massacres and expulsions. This then (partially) explains their prevalence in the moneylending business. Jews filled a needed financial gap by offering their lending services in a market with limited supply. Depending on the place and time, they were either immune from punishment, didn't care about the potential consequences or were completely exempt from the prohibitions.

It's also worth noting that the biblical interest prohibition, such as the one quoted earlier from Deuteronomy, didn't apply to Jews lending money to gentiles. Most interpreters translate the word countrymen—the group to whom interest can't be charged—as the colloquial *landsman* aka fellow Jew. So, they (too) could lend with impunity (to gentiles) without worrying about being excommunicated from their own community. A delicate economic equilibrium ensued.

In this way, over the course of 1000 years, lending took place, interest was charged and money was repaid—all in the shadows, hidden in the dark corners of society. Even if a member of the Church was involved (as a lender), sanctions were not always enforced. In fact, some have argued that the Church itself imposed (or encouraged) usury restrictions—but

---

[15] Writing in his book *On Law Mortality and Politics*, he makes clear that the lender is not transferring ownership of the money to the borrower.

[16] For the record and for comparison purposes, canon number 11 excommunicated those who engaged in sodomy or clerics who had women in their houses.

[17] For more on the English approach and attitude to usury, see Jones (1989), as well as Kerridge (2003).

parenthetically turned the other cheek so they could borrow at lower rates than otherwise would have been the case. They apparently needed the money.

And occasionally, when a powerful prince or cleric or monarch found themselves with excessive debt on their balance sheet—or in over their head—they always had the option of simply expelling the lender from their land—which is exactly what King Edward did in the year 1290 and a situation that Jews found themselves in, quite often. Of course, they were expelled for other reasons too, but a discussion of those would take us far afield.

But after a millennium of the status quo, the undesirable attitude toward charging and receiving interest slackened during the Reformation, beginning in the year 1517 when Martin Luther (b. 1483, d. 1546) published (and nailed) his famous theses. Although he wasn't a fan of the rich and powerful, Martin Luther actually took the position of the creditors— that is, those who were owed money—during the Great Peasants' Revolt of 1525. Other reformers such as the Frenchman John Calvin (b. 1509, d. 1564) went even further when he said: "I do not feel usuries are forbidden." Either way, the floodgates were opened. That was the only excuse necessary for the many pro-commerce territories with a "Protestant work ethic" in Europe to abolish the abolishers of usury. Just to be clear, the Catholic Church didn't back down and continued its war on interest. As late as 1745, Pope Benedict XIV reiterated in an encyclical or papal proclamation that usury was interest and vice versa. This will be important when I get to the motives of the various performers in the saga.

Either way, as the sixteenth century turned into the seventeenth century, although the social stigma remained, instead of banning interest or turning a blind eye to its practice, a period of official government toleration—albeit with regulation and caps—begins. The practice of usury was no longer a spiritual offense that should reside within the jurisdiction of Church courts. The concept of usury became associated with *excessive* interest rates as opposed to *any* interest rate. The supply of money (lending) was increased and the Jews were no longer the only money game in town.

In England, for example, during the reign of the various Tudor kings and queens (1486–1603), there was an official interest rate ceiling or maximum allowed. The key milestone was the Act Against Usury in 1571, which despite its title ("against") actually legitimized the practice so long as rates were at or under 10%. Anything above was illegal, and anyone caught charging more than 10% would be prosecuted. In the book *God and the Moneylenders*, the author N. L. Jones (1989) describes the network of usury informers that cropped up to spy on people who might be charging more than 10%, and these whistleblowers would be entitled to a reward if their prey was successfully caught and convicted. The bookseller stalls in London were filled with volumes of interest rate tables (no different from present value tables in business school textbooks) to help determine whether a loan was usurious. Clever financiers labored to engineer structured loans that could fool the authorities and informers and not appear to be charging more than the maximum allowed.

In the year 1624—the old Elizabethan Act of 1571 was cast aside—the interest rate ceiling was reduced to 8% and lending at interest was recognized as a necessary and very normal part of economic life. By the way, this 2% reduction in interest rates was implemented during the reign of James I, who is our royal protagonist's grandfather. It was reduced further in 1660—by acts of parliament, not the King—to a rate of 6% when Charles II was restored to the throne. I should note that these measures applied to private commercial transactions and didn't apply to the King himself.

But the overall process was really no different from today's Federal Reserve or Bank of England committees. parliament would convene every few years and debate the proper (cap for) interest rates. During the 1650s it was set at 6%, a number you will see many times in the pages and tables to come. Also, later on, I'll return to whether or not the 6% interest rate cap was respected or obeyed by the bankers—spoiler alert: it wasn't—since they employed some of the clever methods I alluded to earlier. In the early 1700s the legal rate was reduced to 5%, then 4% and 3% in the early years of the eighteenth century.[18]

Here is the bottom line. Charging interest became legal and completely acceptable in Protestant countries. It was now within the purview or mandate of man's law and not God's law. This (partially) explains how the goldsmith-bankers could openly conduct their activity in public and with impunity, in a seventeenth-century society that was so sensitive to the scriptures. Rather, the debatable details or Sunday sermons were regarding a *fair rate* of interest (a mathematical definition of usury), as opposed to *the activity of moneylending* itself. Technically the dialogue and discourse

---

[18] See the comprehensive book on the history of financial economics by Poitras (2000), and in particular Chap. 11. See also Chamley (2011) for more on the 4% and 3% annuities that were widely available and the benchmark in the mid-seventeenth century.

shifted from absolute zero to the positive real line. In fact, with the legalization of interest—and the newfound power granted to creditors—a far greater concern was the emergence of debtors' prison. A customer who couldn't pay his or her debts (principal or interest) back to the lender now found himself or herself in a type of excommunication[19] from society, the Fleet Prison or the Marshalsea.

The post-Reformation relaxation in the prohibition against usury can also explain another (puzzling) fact, which is the almost complete absence of Jews in the (very) early banking business in England. Note the religious background of the previously introduced Robert Viner, Edward Backwell, John Banks and John Fox—and most of the other goldsmith-bankers who feature in our story. They were all Anglican, perhaps with an occasional Catholic dissenter among them.

Our financial tragedy includes few, if any, Jews. This is a statistic that might appear at odds with the general association of moneylending, banking and interest with Jews. Recall the central character and premise of the great English playwright William Shakespeare's *The Merchant of Venice*.

In fact, from the long list of creditors published after the King's default (in 1672), only one of the approximately 25 names is Jewish (sounding), and I'll get to his interesting story and name in Chap. 7. The historian R. D. Richards—upon whom I have relied for much of the detail on the goldsmith-bankers in this chapter—summarized the homogenous demographics of the industry as follows: "The wealthiest of the great bankers were Anglicans who worshiped God in the Church of St. Mary Woolnoth and mammon in its immediate vicinity."

So, where was Shylock?[20] Well, the answer is multifaceted—and one mustn't expect all financial fiascos to have Jews at their center—but the main reason for their absence in our drama can be laid at the feet of King Edward I and (head of) Oliver Cromwell. At the risk of getting caught up in yet more unnecessary minutia, as I briefly mentioned earlier, in the year 1290, King Edward expelled all the Jews from England because he owed them a lot of money (with even more interest). There were other factors, but they all had to do with money. Fast-forward 350 years and Oliver Cromwell allowed some of them back—or at least gave them legal status—

---

[19] Daniel Defoe, author of *Robinson Crusoe*, wrote and argued passionately against the existence and use of debtors' prisons.
[20] Yes, I know he was Italian and not English (in the play), but you get the point.

after the persuasive lobbying by the (Portuguese and Dutch) Menasseh ben Israel—another story.

Ergo, given that Jews had only been allowed to (officially) return to England toward the end of the 1650s and early 1660s, it shouldn't be surprising it took them a while to get settled and plugged into the financial system. They established themselves as merchants and businessmen and financiers, but the retail banking business eluded them, at least for a while.

Indeed, had the default taken place a century later, in the year 1772 or perhaps 1872 instead of the year 1672, it wouldn't be unfair to speculate that the list of creditors would have included more Hebrew or Jewish names. In fact, 30 years after the events depicted in this book—in the late 1690s, when the Bank of England was established (good times)—and then 30 years after that, when the South Sea Bubble burst in the early 1720s (bad times), one reads of many more Jewish names, both among the winners and among the losers.

For now, 1672 was a gentile affair …

References

Bagehot, W. (1999). *Lombard Street: A Description of the Money Market (1873)*. New York: John Wiley and Sons.

Chamley, C. (2011). Interest Reductions in the Politico-Financial Nexus of Eighteenth-Century England. *The Journal of Economic History, 71*, 555–570.

Clark, D. (1938). Edward Backwell as a Royal Agent. *The Economic History Review, 9*(1), 45–55.

Coleman, D. C. (1963). *Sir John Banks Baronet and Businessman: A Study of Business, Politics and Society in Later Stuart England*. Oxford: Clarendon Press.

Geist, C. R. (2013). *Beggar Thy Neighbour*. Philadelphia: University of Pennsylvania Press.

Glaeser, E. L., & Scheinkman, J. (1998). Neither a Borrower Nor a Lender Be: An Economic Analysis of Interest Restrictions and Usury Laws. *Journal of Law and Economics, 61*, 100–120.

Horsefield, J. K. (1949). The Cash Ratio in English Banks Before 1800. *Journal of Political Economy, 57*(1), 70–74.

Jha, S. (2015). Financial Asset Holdings and Political Attitudes. *Quarterly Journal of Economics*, 1485–1545.

Jones, N. L. (1989). *God and the Moneylenders: Usury and Law in Early Modern England*. Oxford: Oxford University Press.

Kerridge, E. (2003). *Usury, Interest and the Reformation*. London: Ashgate.

Melton, F. T. (1986). *Sir Robert Clayton and the Origins of English Deposit Banking 1658–1685*. Cambridge University Press.

Poitras, G. (2000). *The Early History of Financial Economics: 1478–1776*. Cheltenham: Edward Elgar Publishing.
Quinn, S. (1997). Goldsmith-Banking: Mutual Acceptance and Interbank Clearing in Restoration London. *Explorations in Economic History, 34*, 411–432.
Richards, R. D. (1929). *The Early History of Banking in England*. London: P.S. King & Sons, Ltd.
Selgin, G. (2012). Those Dishonest Goldsmiths. *Financial History Review, 19*(3), 269–288.
Shaw, W. (1904). *Introduction to the Calendar of Treasury Books*. London: His Majesty's Stationary Office.
Steinmetz, G. (2015). *The Richest Man Who Ever Lived: The Life and Times of Jacob Fugger*. New York: Simon & Schuster.
Temin, P., & Voth, H.-J. (2013). *Prometheus Shackled: Goldsmith Banks and England's Financial Revolution After 1700*. New York: Oxford University Press.

CHAPTER 4

Personal Finances of a King

King Charles II—like his father Charles I and grandfather James I—was also not a wealthy monarch.[1] His financial state paled in comparison with his glamorous and affluent French cousin King Louis XIV, or even the current monarch, Queen Elizabeth II, who, according to *Forbes* magazine, has a private net worth exceeding £300 million.

But the story of *why* Charles II incurred these difficulties—and conceivably had no option but to default by the year 1672—is more complex than a simplistic "lack of funds." Instead, one must start at the inauguration of his reign in the spring of 1660. My plan in this chapter is to carefully review his "personal finances" loosely defined during the crucial 12 years between the start of the Restoration and the default. And although—in his defense—Charles II inherited substantial debts and obligations from his father Charles I, and thus started off his reign on the wrong economic foot, I'm not revealing any unexpected plot twists by telling you that he spent money (that he didn't have) prodigiously once he came to power. Remember though, the English wanted a glamorous king. It was widely accepted that "[t]he king should provide in his person and his court an element of grandeur and magnificence … to be the pride of the nation."

---

[1] See Goodare (2009) for an interesting and related discussion of the Stuarts' financial situation in Scotland and how it changed when they came to England.

So, here's the agenda: I'll begin by carefully scrutinizing his *expenses*, or how the monarchy spent its money. Then I'll move on to describe the King's *income* or revenue sources—think of this like wages and salary from a job. I'll conclude by subtracting one from the other to arrive at his *deficits*, or budget shortfalls, and how these were financed over time. As I alluded to in the first chapter, although the financial analysis presented and discussed here is for an English monarch in the mid-seventeenth century, the financial techniques and metrics employed should be no different than it would be for a modern family in the twenty-first century—maybe even yours. In a nutshell, if your expenses exceed your income for prolonged periods of time, you too might end up like the King of England!

Before I continue, I should note with thanks and credits that most of the data in this chapter derives from a detailed study conducted by C. D. Chandaman, a professor of history who (in the mid-1950s) painstakingly hand-collected individual numbers from archival documents in the Public Records Office (PRO) in London. In particular, the key documents are called the *Declaration Books of the Exchequer*, which contain records of receipts, assignments and issues. C. D. Chandaman published[2] this in a book entitled *The English Public Revenue 1660–1688*.

WHERE DID THE MONEY GO?

Tables 4.1 and 4.2 summarize expenses for the first 12 years (1660–1672) that Charles II was in power. I'll discuss what happened fiscally *after* the default (i.e. from 1672 to 1688) in Chap. 6.

Take a moment to look at the numbers for the first complete fiscal year, which is the period from April 1661 to March 1662 (as the fiscal year commenced and concluded at Easter). Tables 4.1 and 4.2 are (my summary of) the occasionally finicky Exchequer records, which themselves comprise half-year statements that I added together to produce the yearly summary.

Recall from your English history lessons (or perhaps not) that 1661–1662 was a few years before the London plague (which took place from the summer of 1665 to the winter of 1666) and the London fire (which happened in early September 1666), which were infamous, significant and very costly events.

In the year 1661, we are very early on in the Restoration period—which I mentioned in the prior chapter—when the English, Scottish and

---

[2] Source: Chandaman (1975); also see the work by D. A. Shaw (1904).

Table 4.1 Expenses of King Charles II during the Restoration period. Twelve years of English Exchequer issues: April 1660 to March 1672

Fiscal year period	Army, navy and ordnance	+ Household and wardrobe	+ Jewelry and goldsmithing	+ Annuities, gifts and rewards	+ Secret service	+ Interest and loan payment	+ All other categories	= Total expenditure
Apr 1660–Mar 1661	£195,986	£59,835	£10,800	£45,000	£5000	£6050	£55,104	£377,775
Apr 1661–Mar 1662	£603,318	£120,649	£12,399	£67,237	£25,950	£43,051	£128,246	£1,000,850
Apr 1662–Mar 1663	£989,984	£141,843	£24,909	£85,885	£29,725	£61,585	£278,600	£1,612,531
Apr 1663–Mar 1664	£755,086	£180,425	£0	£78,244	£43,831	£4814	£300,265	£1,362,665
Apr 1664–Mar 1665	£685,081	£86,243	£44,236	£87,217	£30,622	£123,775	£211,086	£1,268,260
Apr 1665–Mar 1666[a]	£2,009,094	£227,678	£12,967	£103,195	£30,780	£147,021	£193,340	£2,724,075
Apr 1666–Mar 1667[a]	£1,414,634	£123,039	£4250	£131,613	£26,245	£30,978	£197,166	£1,927,925
Apr 1667–Mar 1668	£790,228	£35,277	£460	£102,390	£28,300	£228,158	£208,741	£1,393,554
Apr 1668–Mar 1669	£1,170,624	£64,705	£1230	£97,722	£29,217	£305,470	£152,880	£1,821,848
Apr 1669–Mar 1670	£675,956	£110,300	£1500	£67,966	£25,445	£277,349	£336,298	£1,494,814
Apr 1670–Mar 1671	£513,939	£161,575	£45,553	£92,624	£41,735	£434,583	£286,181	£1,576,190
Apr 1671–Mar 1672	£758,295	£159,134	£40,524	£87,989	£23,600	£648,228	£374,710	£2,092,480
Total	£10,562,225	£1,470,703	£198,828	£1,047,082	£340,450	£2,311,062	£2,722,617	£18,652,967
Average	£880,185	£122,559	£16,569	£87,257	£28,371	£192,589	£226,885	£1,554,414

Note: Based on data reported in C. D. Chandaman (1975)
[a]Period of the Anglo-Dutch war; London plague, from June 1665 to February 1666; London fire, September 1666

Table 4.2 Expense allocation of King Charles II during the Restoration period. Twelve years of English Exchequer issues: April 1660 to March 1672

Fiscal year period	Army, navy and ordnance	+ Household and wardrobe	+ Jewelry and goldsmithing	+ Annuities, gifts and rewards	+ Secret service	+ Interest and loan payment	+ All other categories	= Total expenditure
Apr 1660–Mar 1661	51.9%	15.8%	2.9%	11.9%	1.3%	1.6%	14.6%	100%
Apr 1661–Mar 1662	60.3%	12.1%	1.2%	6.7%	2.6%	4.3%	12.8%	100%
Apr 1662–Mar 1663	61.4%	8.8%	1.5%	5.3%	1.8%	3.8%	17.3%	100%
Apr 1663–Mar 1664	55.4%	13.2%	0.0%	5.7%	3.2%	0.4%	22.0%	100%
Apr 1664–Mar 1665	54.0%	6.8%	3.5%	6.9%	2.4%	9.8%	16.6%	100%
Apr 1665–Mar 1666[a]	73.8%	8.4%	0.5%	3.8%	1.1%	5.4%	7.1%	100%
Apr 1666–Mar 1667[a]	73.4%	6.4%	0.2%	6.8%	1.4%	1.6%	10.2%	100%
Apr 1667–Mar 1668	56.7%	2.5%	0.0%	7.3%	2.0%	16.4%	15.0%	100%
Apr 1668–Mar 1669	64.3%	3.6%	0.1%	5.4%	1.6%	16.8%	8.4%	100%
Apr 1669–Mar 1670	45.2%	7.4%	0.1%	4.5%	1.7%	18.6%	22.5%	100%
Apr 1670–Mar 1671	32.6%	10.3%	2.9%	5.9%	2.6%	27.6%	18.2%	100%
Apr 1671–Mar 1672	36.2%	7.6%	1.9%	4.2%	1.1%	31.0%	17.9%	100%
Average	55.4%	8.6%	1.2%	6.2%	1.9%	11.4%	15.2%	100.0%

Note: Based on data reported in C. D. Chandaman (1975)
[a] Period of the Anglo-Dutch war; London plague, from June 1665 to February 1666; London fire, September 1666

Irish monarchies were all restored under King Charles II. They were three countries under one crown. At this point in the story, the hero returns to London after more than a decade in European exile. In April 1661 the ceremonial coronation of King Charles II took place—an event which required a year of planning and preparation. (You think planning a wedding is hard!) Actually, it took that long to recreate the royal crown, scepter and mace that Oliver Cromwell and his republican cronies had demolished both tangibly and politically. The goldsmiths (before they became bankers) worked very hard on this event.

The background and context here are very important, because in the first few years of the Restoration, England was nostalgic—and thus willing to overlook any (financial) faults in the new king. The full scale of his plight during a decade of exile (for example his escape from Worcester in 1651) was just becoming known. What was a few extra pounds of spending?

Let's get back to the numbers. As you can see from Table 4.1, the King's Exchequer disbursed a total of £1,000,850 during the year starting in Easter 1661. I have listed the various components that add up to the million pounds.

At this point you might rightfully be wondering: was a million pounds a *lot* or a *little* in the year 1661? It's hard to tell, really. As usual, the answer is: *compared to what?* But if you want to approximately convert these units into twenty-first-century estimates, here is a simple rule that puts the numbers in proper context. It's a (crude) rule I'll abide by over the next few chapters, and here it is: **add two zeros to any number to project them 350 years into the future.** In other words, £1 in the 1660s would have the same purchasing power of at least £100 today—if not more[3]—by properly accounting for the time value of money.

To give this rule one justifiable anchor in reality, Samuel Pepys' salary as a clerk at the Navy Board (he was eventually Secretary of the Navy Board) was recorded in his diary as £350 per year. Nowadays, a similar position (clerk, not Secretary) might reasonably pay £35,000 per year (and not including bribes and before personal income taxes, which didn't exist in the 1660s). I'll return to the value every so often, but for now let's continue with the "double-zero rule" to make things easier. Bottom line: consider Charles II as having spent £100 million (in today's values)

---

[3] I believe that number is a lower bound, since the Bank of England website has a calculator that estimates the number might be as high as £200 if one uses a general measure of price inflation.

during the course of his first full year as king. Now, that isn't a trivial sum. For comparison, Queen Elizabeth II's household spent close to £43 million in fiscal 2013—and I'll get back to her majesty (and where that money comes from) later.

Charles II's spending records—which, as I acknowledged earlier, were tabulated by C. D. Chandaman—contain approximately 40 different subcategories, which I have (rather arbitrarily) combined and merged into the seven categories listed in Table 4.1. As you can see, the biggest expenditure, by far, was the charge for maintaining the English Navy, Army and Ordnance, which in 1661–1662 amounted to £603,000 (or 60% of his spending). At the Restoration, England's Navy consisted of 109 ships and between 60,000 and 75,000 soldiers and seamen, all of whom had to be paid by Charles II himself. In total, he owed £445,000 to soldiers, £300,000 to seamen and £378,000 to the Navy—just on day 1, and most of those numbers are not included in the table, which is focused on actual payments made via the Exchequer.

Oddly and most surprisingly to those who aren't familiar with seventeenth-century royal finances, it was the King's personal responsibility to maintain (aka "victual," or provide with food and other supplies) England's entire armed forces. These servicemen, many stationed in far-flung locations scattered around the British Isles, were all on the King's personal payroll—which was a touchy point of extreme consternation in royal circles. As you can imagine, in times of war, the number was higher and the military complex would consume almost 75% of the King's budget. All things considered, 1661–1662 was a relatively cheap year.

I don't mean to flog a dead king's horse, but if indeed one concludes that Charles II ran into trouble because he was spending too much, perhaps it was partially a result of the fact that he was being asked to shoulder so much. Now, to be clear, the claim that Charles II was involuntarily forced to satisfy unrealistic financial demands is controversial among current experts on the finances of the Stuart monarchy during the mid-seventeenth century. But it's a premise I'll return to repeatedly, even if it might be somewhat premature to answer the question: *whose fault was it that Charles II ran into financial difficulties?* C. D. Chandaman writes (on p. 270): "Wasteful extravagance at court and the squandering of money on the King's mistresses was the important factor ... in the dissipation of the crown's resources." But then again, how much could he cut if he actually wanted to? I'll get back to this in Chap. 6, when George Downing enters the scene.

Well, enough politics for the moment. Let's move on to the other 40% of the cash outflows. The second-largest item on the list in the same (1661–1662) year is the category of household and wardrobe, which is rather self-explanatory and accounted for £120,600 (or 12%) of his total expenditures. As the simple description implies, this line item included all the provisions and resources necessary to keep his castles and palaces and many apartments in Whitehall in fine and working order. Using the double-zero rule, this would be 12 million in today's pounds.

In fact, if you translate this 12% fraction into modern household budgetary terms, I suspect that most families in the twenty-first century spend more than 12% of their total budget or expenditures to cover shelter, clothing, utilities and food—let alone the cellular and Wi-Fi bills, which weren't an issue in the seventeenth century. I should note here that "household" expenses to a king of England in the 1660s also included most of what today would be called expenditures for the civil service. This would include salaries of judges (but not the bribes) as well as salaries of customs officials and other items that in the twenty-first century would most certainly not be the financial responsibility of the reigning monarch.

To be honest, there are many other (very minor) items that I didn't explicitly list in Tables 4.1 and 4.2 (remember that Exchequer records list a total of 40) such as the "privy purse" or "master of the horse" or "liveries and messengers," which I included in the "all other categories" entry. My point isn't to drown the readers in budgetary minutia, but rather to provide a broad picture of where the money went and emphasize that it wasn't all spent on good times for Charles and his cronies.

Moving on, the next formally listed item in (my summary) Table 4.1 is the category for "jewelry and goldsmithing," which, as the name implies, was the money spent (out of the Exchequer) on purchasing all forms of jewelry, gems, silverware and other precious metals. In the fiscal year 1661–1662, this amounted to £12,400 or a mere 1.2% of Charles II's expenses. If you browse down the table, this category is rather erratic over the years. Note that in 1663–1664 there were no expenditures at all in this category, and then in the year 1671–1672—which was just prior to the default and the raison d'être of this book—Charles II spent over £40,000 on gold and jewelry—a factoid worth remembering for later. Note also that the jewel category also covered items like gifts for ambassadors and badges for the King's watermen.

The next item in Tables 4.1 and 4.2 is "annuities, gifts and rewards," listed at £67,000 for 1661–1662. The King had the ability to grant lifetime pensions to anyone who pleased him (very broadly and literally speaking) and these life annuities were yet another way in which devoted courtiers and royalists were rewarded for their service. I'll return to these life annuities when we pick through the financial rubble of 1672 in Chap. 6. The next column and category is the mysterious-sounding "secret service," which, unlike the twenty-first century, has nothing to do with a group of ex-military specialists protecting the King. Instead, this was a very large slush fund from which the King could pay anyone he wanted, for various services, without it being publicly disclosed or revealed to the public in Exchequer records. If you are wondering about the difference between Charles II paying someone (e.g. a favored mistress) from the "gifts and annuities" or "privy purse" category and perhaps from the "secret service" category, well the latter was much more discreet than either of the former.

I am almost at the end of expenditures. The second-to-last category (or column) in Table 4.1 is labeled "interest and loan payments," which in 1661–1662 amounted to £43,051. This number which, as the years went on, grew substantially and rapidly is probably the most important figure for the purposes of understanding the default. Let me pause to let this sink in. Although I haven't yet discussed the King's revenues—that comes in Table 4.3 and the attending story—*they obviously weren't enough to cover all his expenses.* As a result, Charles II (via his Exchequer) borrowed money to cover the gap, and slowly paid it back with interest. In the year 1661–1662, the debt repayments amounted to only 4.3% of his total expenditures (see Table 4.2)—a proportion that is relatively small and inconsequential. Over a decade later (by the year 1671–1672), the numbers had mushroomed to an equivalent of over 31% of his expenditures. The very last number listed before the ominous 1672 is approximately £648,000 in loan and interest payments (Table 4.1: this is a 15-fold increase in a mere 12 years. That, put simply, is the core of the problem, although much remains to be explained regarding the reasons for the increase as well as where the debt repayments went, exactly. Nevertheless, it is clear that by the year 1671–1672, Charles II was spending as much on debt repayment and interest as on the Army and Navy. How exactly the loans worked—and the mechanics of the interest payments themselves—is a messy tale of medieval tallies, which is best told in its own chapter (Chap. 5). Let's leave a mental Post-it note here and move on.

Finally, to close the books for 1661–1662 proper, the remaining £128,246 in the penultimate column of Table 4.1 for 1661–1662 is a catch-all category, which brings total expenditures for the year to £1,000,000.

This £128,246 in the "All Other Categories" column consisted of items such as payment for royal messengers, a stipend for the Queen mother (Henrietta Maria, Charles II's mother, who died in 1669), a stipend for Charles II's brother James, the Duke of York, as well as expenses for the Royal Mint, the lieutenant of the Tower of London, salaries for ambassadors (who, like Temple, probably had a tough time getting paid), salaries for the justices of the assizes (traveling criminal courts) and a collection of minor categories that only a king would have to worry about, such as the occasional robe.

All in all, this romp through the royal checkbook should give you a good picture of a typical year's worth of expenditures. Upon first inspection—and we really are only starting the journey—one would be forgiven for concluding that there wasn't anything to be alarmed about in the personal finances of King Charles II, at least in the year 1661–1662.

THE COST OF PLAGUES AND FIRES

Few people—and even fewer children—know that the famous English nursery rhyme *Ring-a-Ring o' Roses*[4] is thought to be a folkloric reference to the plague in the year 1665. Let's start with the symptoms. Approximately 3–7 days after you are exposed, the first signs of bubonic plague would appear—an ominous circle of *rose-tinted* or reddish-colored spots on your skin. The *herbal posy* mentioned in the next sentence of the rhyme was purported to ward off the disease, but if you started sneezing repeatedly, the inevitable end was nigh. Nowadays, when schoolchildren perform the rhyme holding hands and running in a circle, the very last word in the last line—we all fall down *dead*—is conveniently omitted (or has been censored).

The first signs of the outbreak in "noisy, crowded and smelly" London[5] emerged in May 1665, which, recall, was five years after the Restoration. Of course, 1665 wasn't the first case of the plague in English history, as there were known outbreaks in 1348 and then again in 1592. During the fourteenth century, the plague wiped out 20–50% of the population of Europe, with a death toll in the 50 million lives. So, 1665 wasn't the worst case in history—but it was one of the best documented.

---

[4] *Ring-a-ring o' roses, A pockets full of posies, A-tishoo! A-tishoo! We all fall down!*
[5] See Picard (1997) for a description of everyday life in London during the 1660s, as well as the recent book by Larman (2016).

Soon after the outbreak was confirmed, the King left town with the court and royal family and didn't return (from Oxford) to his residence in Whitehall until February 1666. In his absence, he left a minimal staff, which included the enduring George Downing to manage financial affairs. And during the ten months the King was away, the plague killed an official 68,596 Londoners[6] according to reports provided by Lord Arlington. This was an estimated 15%–20% of the population of London and an extraordinarily high mortality rate compared with modern times. Some researchers[7] assert the true number of deaths might have been as high as 100,000. This is important for the actuaries who might use these numbers to estimate mortality rates during the period—but also for any discussion of tax revenues that would have been impacted.

When signs of the plague appeared in a family member, the entire household would be quarantined as a safety measure that (ironically) guaranteed that everyone inside would eventually get "the ring of roses" and then "fall down dead." Every night, city officials would go from house to house—or at least the ones that had been marked with a red cross as having the plague—and collect and count the bodies.

Officials in the city would then publish the so-called *Bills of Mortality*, indicating the number of people who had perished in the various parishes, as well as their cause of death. Historically, the worst week on record was in mid-September 1665, when over 7165 people died in just seven days. Do the math. Approximately, 1000 bodies were collected each night from the streets of London and then buried in large anonymous pits. These macabre weekly statistics, which were carefully monitored and reproduced in the newspapers such as the *London Gazette*, were the precursor to modern mortality tables used by actuaries to price life insurance and annuities.

By the spring and summer of 1666, the numbers in the Bills of Mortality were dwindling to double digits, down from triple and quadruple digits, and city life resumed some semblance of normalcy. But alas, just one or two months later—like a nightmare conjured from the biblical book of Exodus—London was hit with another calamity, the Great Fire.

Early on a Sunday morning, September 2, 1666, a small blaze broke out in a bakery on Pudding Lane in the southwest corner of the city.

---

[6] Source: *National Archives* website (www.nationalarchives.gov.uk), accessed January 19, 2017.

[7] See "The Great Plague of London, 1665," Contagion, Historical Views of Diseases & Epidemics, Harvard University.

The infamous owner of the bakery was Thomas Farriner, a name that is the answer to many a *Jeopardy* question. In fact, the story has been told innumerable times over the centuries. The Great Fire has spawned many TV series, movies, stories and, most vividly (to me), the book by A. Tinniswood (2004), called *By Permission of Heaven: The True Story of the Great Fire of London*. In fact, the 350-year anniversary of the fire was commemorated in September 2016, which generated a renewed interest and awareness of the episode.

To make a long but important story short—and focus on the elements pertinent to budgets and expenses of the King—over the course of five days, approximately 85% of the City of London was burned to the ground. A total of 13,500 housing structures, 87 churches and other buildings, including The Royal Exchange and the Customs House, were completely destroyed. The extent of the damage was astounding, even in an era that was accustomed to natural perils and other man-made hazards. Contemporary estimates put the financial damage at £10 million, which using the double-zero rule would imply a modern-day equivalent of £1000 million pounds. In fact, during the commemoration of the 350th anniversary, the Association of British Insurers (ABI) released a report claiming that the modern-day damage from such a fire would be closer to £32 billion.

Samuel Pepys' entries for early September 1666 are some of the most moving passages in his diary, and much of what we know about the event is linked to his experiences trying to hide his money in the backyard, or ferry his wife and possessions away from the city. There are contemporary accounts of goldsmith-bankers—who had offices inside the city—shipping their money (estimated in the millions) and precious metals on carts to the Tower of London, where they hoped it would be safe. This is all rather ironic given their history. Recall that their business was built and fortified by another calamity, one that took place within the Tower of London, when King Charles I seized money from the merchants.

On a positive note, although nobody should have the temerity to claim that the Great Fire was a blessing in disguise, a few good things did emerge from the ashes. First, although it took many years, the city was rebuilt and remodeled with the help and direction of renowned architect Sir Christopher Wren. Today's London was shaped and molded by designs he made in the aftermath of the fire. His landmark handiwork is St. Paul's Cathedral, which is likely the city's best-known landmark to this day.

Second, oddly enough, after the city was rebuilt, London never again suffered from the bubonic plague that devastated its inhabitants in 1666. At first, it might seem like a coincidence, but a number of scholars claim that, in addition to destroying all the houses, the fire also destroyed the scurrilous rats and vermin that carried the (fleas that carried the) disease. The rebuilding of new houses in the aftermath of 1666 with bricks versus wood also made a difference—for the rats as well as the fires. And although anyone who has been to London knows they still do have rats scurrying about, apparently the infected carriers were torched in September 1666.

Another byproduct of the fire was the creation of property and casualty insurance companies to help individuals cope with (and insure against) these disasters. It might not be an exaggeration to say that one very calamitous fire sparked the creation of an entire industry—one that is built around pooling and sharing all risks and hazards, including fires. Well, at least that was the argument made by the ABI looking for something noteworthy in the smoldering ashes of the city.

In sum, the plague in the year 1665 "cost" almost 20% of the population of London. Within a year, the fire in 1666 led to little (official) loss of life, but the financial "cost" was in the tens of millions of pounds. These costs were borne by individual Londoners and their families as opposed to government, which is why these events aren't immediately obvious in the revenue and expense numbers I have displayed earlier. The years 1665 and 1666 deserve a bold asterisk in our financial statements. Of course, the impact of these two disasters would have been felt or experienced secondhand with a natural delay in government tax payments.

So now let me consider the King's revenues.

A Royal Allowance with Strings

At the Restoration in 1660 King Charles II was promised by the newly elected Cavalier[8] parliament a "salary"—or more precisely a settlement—of £1.2 million per year in financial support, aka *ordinary revenue*. The funds were meant to come from a variety and hodgepodge of sources, but mostly from customs, taxes and rents from royal property, all of which I'll describe in a moment. *These were revenue estimates and not guarantees.* So although they were granted to him and his royal heirs in perpetuity, there was no guaranteed amount per se. Also, there were some strings

---

[8] Source: Harris (2006).

attached to the £1.2 million, such as the King agreeing to surrender feudal rights and not raising taxes without parliament's permission, both of which had cost his father his head. In short, Charles II was told to behave like a "mensch," and in return, he could count on £1.2 million per year. The problem with this Restoration settlement is that (1) Charles II never really received the £1.2 million per year in *ordinary revenue* that was estimated, and (2) truth be told, even if he had received the £1.2 million, that sum wasn't really enough to cover his voracious need and appetite for cash. Remember, he had to support almost 75,000 members of the armed forces (and slightly fewer mistresses and illegitimate children).

Here is a closer look at the revenue side of his ledger: whereas Charles II had approximately 40 or so expenditure categories in his household budget, the income or revenue side had double the entries at approximately 80. Now, usually having 80 different sources of income is relatively good news—most families have two or maybe three sources of income—but in the case of Charles II, most of these 80 sources were actually quite small.

Once again (as in the case of expenses), it's tedious to list every single category (most of which aren't really relevant to the main story). Table 4.3 provides a high-flying bird's eye view of the three broad revenue categories to show where the money came from to finance the various expenditures listed in Table 4.1.

The first category—which is the *ordinary revenue* category mentioned earlier—covers the main (hereditary) branches of tax revenue such as customs, excise and hearth money promised to Charles II at the Restoration. Let's look at each of these individually, since they are quite important.

Customs, Excise and Hearth

Customs, as the word suggests, were taxes imposed on merchants importing (or even exporting) goods from abroad. They included duties on imports (to England) of items such as wines, spirits, linens, silk and tobacco—with particularly high rates if they were imported from France. Alas, not unlike the twenty-first century, certain countries had "favorable nation" status with regard to imports—and in the mid-seventeenth century, France wasn't on England's list. In fact, at some points in English history, all imports from France were completely prohibited—which, much to the chagrin of the King, greatly reduced the yield from his customs. Perhaps this was an early lesson on the consequences of the extreme-right edge of the famous Laffer curve, If the government completely prohibits an activity—no imports from France—they will receive zero tax revenue. I mention France in particular because that country, and King Louis XIV, will reappear in our story as we get closer to 1672. But to sum up the state of customs taxes in Restoration England, every time a bushel of imported wheat—or any other commodity or good—passed through an English port, the Exchequer of King Charles II would (eventually) receive a shilling or two, adding to hundreds of thousands of pounds in annual revenue for the Exchequer. Foreign goods were always taxed once they arrived in England. You can think of this as a type of border tax, if you may, using the current (voguish) discussion of these matters.

In contrast to customs, the excise was a much more recent tax (started in the 1640s) and imposed on domestic or native English manufacturing. (Again, to be clear, customs taxes are border taxes; excise taxes are inland taxes.) It was less popular than customs taxes—assuming taxes are ever popular—and parliament had serious reservations (i.e. debates) over whether to allow this sort of tax at all. As a result of the excise tax, every barrel of ale, cider, beer, vinegar and even chocolate manufactured anywhere in England generated an excise duty of a few pence or a shilling. Many viewed the privacy-invading nature of this tax as degrading and even un-English. (Did I just see you brewing some ale? A shilling please.) Nevertheless, the excise was an important component of the ordinary revenue, also generating hundreds of thousands of pounds per year for the Crown.

The third and final hearth (rhymes with Garth) tax was a type of property tax based on the number of chimneys in your house. This tax, not to be confused with the window[9] tax implemented during the reign of King William III in the year 1696, was even less popular than the excise. The idea for the hearth tax is often credited to the (famous) economist Sir William Petty, but was actually introduced into parliament (circa 1660) by Sir Courtney Poole, which later earned him the unpleasant nickname "Sir Chimney Poole." There was very little debate about the merits of this particular tax before it was introduced. Practically speaking, the Sheriff or Constable would go door to door—enter the house and start counting—and every single chimney would generate a payment of two shillings per year (note 20 shillings per pound), with exemptions limited to hospitals, almshouses and "the poor," provided they had a note from their

---

[9] See the article by Oates and Schwab (2015) on the history and distorting impact of the window tax, as well as an interesting discussion of the definition of windows.

CUSTOMS, EXCISE AND HEARTH 87

Table 4.3 Revenue of King Charles II after the Restoration. Twelve years of English Exchequer receipts and loans: April 1660 to March 1672

Fiscal year period	Ordinary	+ Parliamentary	+ Casual	= Total	Additional loans	Loans as a percentage of receipts
Apr 1660–Mar 1661	£318,768	£55,181	£0	£373,949	–£4999	1.3%
Apr 1661–Mar 1662	£636,030	£243,423	£29,489	£908,942	–£93,533	10.3%
Apr 1662–Mar 1663	£663,659	£671,431	£132,118	£1,467,208	–£148,608	10.1%
Apr 1663–Mar 1664	£795,861	£322,233	£198,436	£1,316,530	–£50,000	3.8%
Apr 1664–Mar 1665	£1,033,884	£112,510	£0	£1,146,394	–£120,000	10.5%
Apr 1665–Mar 1666[a]	£650,045	£1,824,348	£36,616	£2,511,009	–£219,314	8.7%
Apr 1666–Mar 1667[a]	£632,060	£1,098,746	£26,875	£1,757,681	–£189,390	10.8%
Apr 1667–Mar 1668	£359,504	£836,110	£4244	£1,199,858	–£199,184	16.6%
Apr 1668–Mar 1669	£502,409	£1,047,920	£620	£1,550,949	–£312,348	20.1%
Apr 1669–Mar 1670	£751,198	£460,507	£4025	£1,215,730	–£258,253	21.2%
Apr 1670–Mar 1671	£843,116	£159,705	£5726	£1,008,547	–£592,383	58.7%
Apr 1671–Mar 1672	£1,268,836	£378,179	£5650	£1,652,665	–£442,697	26.8%
Total	£8,455,370	£7,210,293	£443,799	£16,109,462	–£2,630,709	
Average	£704,614	£600,858	£36,983	£1,342,455	–£219,226	16.6%

Note: Based on data reported in C. D. Chandaman (1975)
[a]Period of the Anglo-Dutch war; London plague, from June 1665 to February 1666; London fire, September 1666

minister or churchwarden. There are (comical? gallows humor?) stories of Londoners having to petition for a temporary exemption from the hearth tax after the fire of 1666, since they no longer had hearths, chimneys—or a house for that matter. The collection process was extremely invasive, which created additional security problems for tax collectors and is why the hearth tax was replaced in 1696 with the (less invasive, but equally problematic) window tax.

Anyway, these three together, the customs, excise and hearth tax—aka the major branches of ordinary revenue—produced 70% of the *ordinary income* for the Crown during the first few years of the Restoration. All told, that is precisely where most of the money came from to support King Charles II's household. Again, the word *ordinary* was used because it was part of the expected, regular revenue. Think of this as a life annuity in royal perpetuity, but one in which the sums involved fluctuated over time based on economic activity (and kitchen chimney styles).

In addition to the three main sources of ordinary revenue (customs, excise and hearth taxes), there were close to 80 (smaller) items that together added up to the King's *ordinary revenue*. These include items such as rents from his lands, wine licenses, fees from the society of music, fees from the society of tobacco pipe makers and (yes, my favorite) "fees from the custody of idiots." But these were small (potatoes) and rightfully labeled "small branches and casual receipts" in the Exchequer records. Altogether, they amounted to a mere few thousand pounds per year,[10] contributing to less than 10% of his ordinary revenues. Bottom line: in the year 1661–1662, the *ordinary revenues* of Charles II were £636,000, which is half of what was promised (ok, estimated) by parliament at the Restoration. But that was not his only source of revenue. He had some *nonordinary revenue* too.

There were two other very different but important categories (listed in Table 4.3) added to the *ordinary revenue*—one quite big and one small. The big and important category was called the *parliamentary revenue*—under the control and at the discretion of parliament—and the final small category (in Table 4.3) is *casual revenue*, not to be confused with the 80 or so casual receipts from his ordinary revenue. In order to obtain this parliamentary revenue, the King required parliament to meet and pass legislation. Operationally, parliament (or the House of Commons, to be precise) would pass a new (temporary) law to raise taxes directly on the

---

[10] I guess there weren't that many idiots in the seventeenth century; today, however …

King's subjects, as opposed to on goods or activities. In the words of C. D. Chandaman, "Indirect taxation was regarded as the appropriate means of furnishing the settled revenue and direct taxation as the particular instrument of extraordinary supply." These were ad hoc wealth taxes, plain and simple.

To translate this into twenty-first-century terms, it's like the difference between being granted an allowance from your parents—paid via a systematic withdrawal plan at the bank—and asking them for additional (ad hoc) funds to cover any additional expenses you might incur. That is, you need your parents (alive) for the latter, but not the former. If Charles II dismissed parliament, which he could do at any time, that second parliamentary source of income would dry up, as it did much later in the year 1681 when Charles II got fed up with the politicians and fired them all. (I'm getting way ahead of the story here.)

I don't intend to get lost in the minutia of fiscal policy in the mid-seventeenth century, so here's the long and the short of it: look carefully at the year 1661–1662 in Table 4.3. The total revenue from all categories and sources is £908,000. Recall from Tables 4.1 and 4.2 that total outflows were £1,000,000. The result? A deficit, or outflow minus inflow, of approximately £93,000 in that year, as you can see in the "additional loans" column in Table 4.3.

Now, recall that the money to pay the unfunded expenses couldn't be printed or minted. Instead, it had to be borrowed via the machinery of the Treasury (and through the offices of the Exchequer) in the name of the King directly and hence recorded in the table as loan amounts. Take a look at Table 4.3 again and note how the numbers in the "additional loans" column increase over the years, from £93,000 in 1661–1662 to over £592,000 in 1670–1671. Here, we have reached another critical juncture in the story, but one that shouldn't be very surprising: every year Charles II borrowed more.

King's Debts Kept Growing

Here's what we can see when adding the results from Tables 4.1, 4.2, and 4.3 together: the King and the Exchequer would pay interest and principal on the one hand (the sixth column in Table 4.1) and then turn around and borrow even more (recorded in the fifth column in Table 4.3) from the same sources. This is the seventeenth-century equivalent of making a cash withdrawal from one credit card (at usurious rates) only to make minimum payments on another credit card, and so on and so forth.

Let's do some simple math. If we simply add up the difference between the total amount borrowed and the total amount paid off during the 12 years under review, we arrive at a total (owing) of £319,647 on the eve of 1672. That number should be very easy to compute and verify: add the total amount of new loans (in the first column of Table 4.4) and subtract the total amount of repaid loans (in the second column of Table 4.4).

The £319,647 number we have computed assumes the Exchequer didn't have to pay any interest during those 12 years of borrowing. This is most obviously and clearly not the case, as one can see from Table 4.4.

Now, it's nearly impossible to determine or fix the summary interest rate that the King's Exchequer had to pay on the loans, and that is part of the story told in the next chapter. But *assuming* the interest rate was a fixed and constant 10% per year, the balance owing at the end of the 12 years—just prior to the momentous events of 1672—was £1,091,684. This number, which is displayed at the very bottom of the fourth column in Table 4.4, is computed by accumulating the annual deficits at 10% per year. This is basic spreadsheet math. And if we use a 12% interest rate, the balance owing on his debts amounts to £1,316,065 by early 1672. I'm not saying it was 10% or 12%, and you will see reference to 6% in the next chapter, but at the same time, there are sources that mention 20% and 30%. Whatever it was in actuality, the compound interest took its toll.

It's worth noting that although the methodology I have used to arrive at this range of £1.0–£1.3 million is quite crude and makes a number of assumptions (and omissions), it's nonetheless well within the official number reported for the notional amount of the default, once the dust had settled and all claims were filed. In twenty-first-century values—adding the rough and jagged double zeros—it's over £100 million of debt. If that number doesn't impress, then think in terms of the total tax revenues during the year—or the budget. The outstanding debt was more than a year's budget.

Regardless of the actual numbers, the problem is obvious. By the beginning of the year 1672, the King owed a total of £1.0–£3 million (depending on the interest rate assumed[11]) for the 1660s, and onward. The number didn't include prior debts. More critically, these loans had to be *continuously renegotiated every year.*

[11] See R. D. Richards (1929), p. 66.

Table 4.4 Total (net) banking debts of King Charles II by early 1672: at various interest rates

Fiscal year period	New loans during year	Total repaid during year	Net owing at 0% interest	Loan balance at: 10%	Loan balance at: 12%
Apr 1660–Mar 1661	–£4999	£6050	£1051	£1051	£1051
Apr 1661–Mar 1662	–£93,533	£43,051	–£49,431	–£58,679	–£60,528
Apr 1662–Mar 1663	–£148,608	£61,585	–£136,454	–£166,430	–£172,648
Apr 1663–Mar 1664	–£50,000	£4814	–£181,640	–£233,260	–£244,552
Apr 1664–Mar 1665	–£120,000	£123,775	–£177,865	–£264,811	–£284,523
Apr 1665–Mar 1666	–£219,314	£147,021	–£250,158	–£385,516	–£417,276
Apr 1666–Mar 1667	–£189,390	£30,978	–£408,570	–£601,419	–£648,488
Apr 1667–Mar 1668	–£199,184	£228,158	–£379,596	–£652,505	–£721,235
Apr 1668–Mar 1669	–£312,348	£305,470	–£386,474	–£755,868	–£852,143
Apr 1669–Mar 1670	–£258,253	£277,349	–£367,378	–£838,185	–£966,295
Apr 1670–Mar 1671	–£592,383	£434,583	–£525,178	–£1,139,041	–£1,311,136
Apr 1671–Mar 1672	–£442,697	£648,228	–£319,647	–£1,091,684	–£1,316,065

Note: Based on data reported in C. D. Chandaman (1975)
Interest-rate calculations by author

The debts or obligations were very different from the modern mortgage or long-term bond for which the principal isn't due for many years and the terms of the loan are fixed for decades. Instead, the King and his Exchequer were at the mercy of the lenders who financed his deficits—essentially the investment bankers—to constantly roll over his loans.

Now in theory, this rolling-over process could continue for a long time—in the twenty-first century, governments are awash in trillions of dollars, pounds and euros of debt—as long as the investment bankers continued to lend additional sums and the Exchequer did its part to cover the maturing principal and interest.

And yet for some (not-yet-discussed) reason, this delicate refinancing act in which the Exchequer would pay out the bankers out of one small (left) pocket and replenish the other (right) pocket with additional loans came to a crashing halt in early 1672. Why this happened—and why the King and the Exchequer decided to stop this cycle—is laid out in the next chapters of the story.

But first—and next on the agenda—I must explain the mechanics of how exactly the Exchequer borrowed this money. As I said earlier, these were definitely not long-term (i.e. 30-year) bonds, which is how governments borrow in the twenty-first century. In fact, the best way to describe the borrowing scheme in which the Exchequer was embroiled is like the seventeenth-century equivalent of payday loans, but (once again) I'm getting way ahead of the story.

Budget of a Modern-Day Monarch

Before we return to the misadventures at the Stuart Exchequer, for those readers curious about royal expenditures in the twenty-first century, here is a summary of Queen Elizabeth II's outlays. As it stands, parliament supports the Queen, via something called the Sovereign Grant, to meet official expenses of the royal household, the cost of maintenance of the occupied royal palaces and royal communications and travel. For example, in the fiscal 2013, the Sovereign Grant provided £31 million to support the royal household.[12] Her Majesty Queen Elizabeth II also has additional income from rents on her various properties and holdings, amounting to £11.6 million. Loosely speaking, think of the former (£31 million) as parliamentary and the latter (£11.6 million) as ordinary—although I am

---

[12] Source: "Spending Review and Autumn Statement 2015," HM Treasury.

pushing the definitional envelope here. Add them together for a total revenue cash flow of £42.6 million in the year 2013.

Using the earlier-mentioned money-time-machine double-zero rule, but eliminating two digits instead of adding them (because we are going backward and not forward in time), we get an equivalent of £426,000 in the 1660s for royal expenditures. As it turns out, this is *in the same ballpark* of what King Charles spent, if you adjust for inflation. And remember, Charles was entirely responsible for covering all military expenditures, the civil service, entitlements, pensions and interest payments on the national debt, none of which are the (current) responsibility of Queen Elizabeth II.

So who was *really* spending too much?

And by the way, Queen Elizabeth II's household expenditures (in 2013) were £44.9 million, compared to the (lower) £42.6 million in revenue, for a deficit of £2.3 million. This difference had to be "borrowed" (again, loosely) from a royal reserve fund, a pool of money that is running dangerously low, at least according to a (2015) report from the House of Commons. Perhaps royal overspending is in genes.

References

Chandaman, C. (1975). *The English Public Revenue 1660–1688*. Oxford: Clarendon Press.

Goodare, J. (2009). The Debts of James VI of Scotland. *The Economic History Review*, 62(4), 926–952.

Harris, T. (2006). *Restoration: Charles II and His Kingdoms*. London: Penguin Books.

Larman, A. (2016). *Restoration: The Year of the Great Fire*. London: Head of Zeus.

Oates, W. E., & Schwab, R. M. (2015). The Window Tax: A Case Study in Excess Burden. *Journal of Economic Perspectives*, 29(1), 163–180.

Picard, L. (1997). *Restoration London: Everyday Life in London 1660–1670*. London: Weidenfeld and Nicolson.

Richards, R. D. (1929). *The Early History of Banking in England*. London: P.S. King & Sons, Ltd.

Shaw, W. (1904). *Introduction to the Calendar of Treasury Books*. London: His Majesty's Stationary Office.

Tinniswood, A. (2004). *By Permission of Heaven: The True Story of the Great Fire of London*. New York: Riverhead (Penguin).

CHAPTER 5

Paid Upon Orders from the Treasury

We are now getting to the nuclear core of our tale. If you think of this book as a "whodunit," then Chaps. 2 and 3 introduced the cast of characters, Chap. 4 was about the financial motives—and now Chap. 5 describes the murder weapon. The financial crisis of 2007–2008 had its so-called weapons of mass financial destruction, the *credit derivatives*, *credit swaps* and the exotic-sounding *collateralized debt obligations* (CDOs). Consistent with King Solomon's adage that there is nothing new under the sun, the financial crisis of 1672 had its *treasury order*, a copy of which is displayed in Fig. 5.1. Unlike the complicated derivatives of the early twenty-first century, the certificate displayed was one single page and didn't require legal prospectuses of a thousand pages or an army of lawyers to draft. At the very top of the certificate—and referenced within the text of the treasury order—was a number, in this case #91. That double-digit number was likely the most important item on the entire page. It isn't a reference code or an entry made in an archive years later. I'll get to the importance soon enough, but for those who have heard the term "CUSIP numbers" for modern stocks and bonds—CUSIP is an abbreviation for Committee on Uniform Securities Identification Procedures—the treasury order number was a type of CUSIP number which uniquely identified the investment. The number served a greater purpose than identification.

Take a moment to read and appreciate this 350-year-old certificate. Note the mixture of prefilled and typeset text and handwritten calligraphy. In essence, it's a fillable template for a loan agreement, no different from what a casual lender might use in the twenty-first century. The certificate

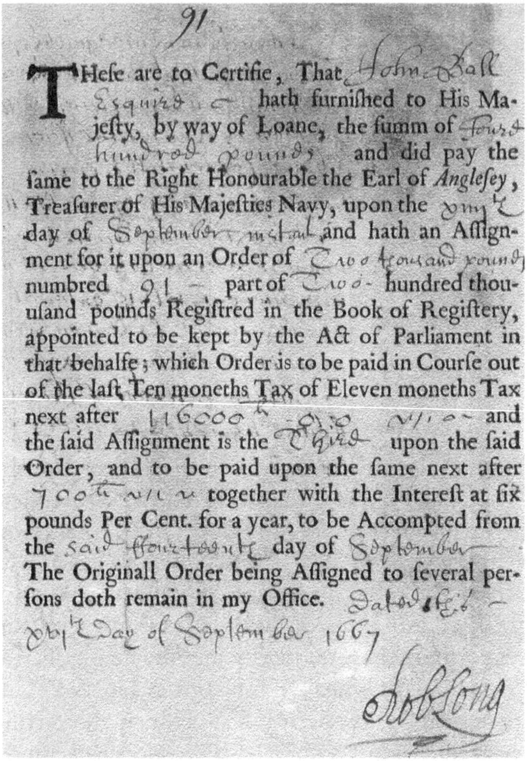

Fig. 5.1 A sample treasury order (Item E407/119). Permission acquired and granted by the National Archives

begins with a reference to John Ball, Esquire, who has "furnished to His Majesty" the sum of £400 as a loan. For the record, John Ball was an official in the Navy office and is actually mentioned by Pepys. More importantly, although the certificate actually says John provided £400 to His Majesty, there is a chance he actually loaned less than this amount. Nonetheless he would be entitled to £400 plus interest at maturity. I'll return to this central (and rather puzzling) fact later.

The phrase "furnished to His Majesty" is a formality, since the cash or coin wasn't handed to King Charles himself. Rather the funds were provided to the Earl of Anglesey, who used it to supply His Majesty's Navy with provisions during the month of September 1667. The borrower (listed as His Majesty) promised to pay 6% interest per year, although you might note some vagueness about when exactly the loan would be repaid to John Ball. That ambiguity, or lack of specified maturity date, was deliberate and an important feature of the *treasury order* system.

Read on. In exchange for the £400 that John Ball was now lending to His Majesty for the use by the Navy, he was given as security "an Assignment upon an Order," with the word "order" appearing no less than four times in the certificate or document. Now, at first this might sound like flowery seventeenth-century jargon but it actually represents a very unique guarantee and financial innovation. What this clause means is that the collateral, or security, backing the loan isn't a house, car or boat that can be seized by the creditor if the debtor doesn't pay. As any heavily indebted home-owning consumer in the twenty-first century knows and fears, if they don't pay the mortgage on time, the bank can seize the house—which is why in some loose sense, they don't really own their home: the bank does. Well, John Ball's collateral for the loan he furnished was a *future stream of expected tax revenues* that His Majesty (or more precisely the Exchequer) was anticipating during the next year. What this means is that if and when the named tax revenue was received at the Exchequer, John Ball would get paid £400 plus 6% interest. This is precisely why no maturity or redemption date was specified. The exact timing was unknown or random. In particular, the tax revenue John Ball would be waiting for—and which would trigger repayment of his loan—was the *Eleven Months Tax*, which was named after the special Act of parliament that had authorized that particular tax. It was not part of the ordinary or the King's hereditary revenue. John Ball had an assignment upon "an order of two thousand pounds numbered 91." Think of it this way: His Majesty's Exchequer was expecting an eventual delivery of £2000—which I will take the liberty of naming tax packet 91—and they used that anticipated packet of pounds as collateral for the loan of £400 made by John Ball. In fact, the tax packet size (i.e. order #91) was expected to be £2000, and presumably, others (like John Ball) had lent money against the remaining £1600 minus a little bit of left-overs for the interest. They too would have a piece, or right, to order #91. These loan certificates weren't secured against a royal castle or a Navy frigate. They were backed by future taxes and a very specific tax, the so-called *Eleven Months Tax*.

Now although John Ball's name was on this particular certificate, he didn't necessarily have to hold on to it until maturity. This certificate, or what I will refer to from here on exclusively as *treasury order*, was assignable. By an Act of parliament[1] (and a small registration fee), the named

---

[1] See the Additional Aid Act 1665.

individual (John Ball) was permitted to transfer, trade or sell it to anyone. Perhaps he might need ready cash, or perhaps he used it as security for his own borrowing. The treasury order could function as collateral for yet another loan. We really don't know the life cycle of this or any particular treasury order, but we do know these orders were liquid. A goldsmith-banker like Robert Viner, Edward Backwell or John Banks—to whom you were introduced in Chap. 3—would be pleased to take them off John Ball's hands, for a small fee of course.

It is quite likely that by the time the relevant tax packet—part of the larger Eleven Months Tax—arrived at the Exchequer and Treasury and order #91 was ready for redemption and payment, the treasury order had passed through many busy hands. Eventually though, somebody would arrive at the Exchequer to get his or her £400 plus 6% interest.

And jumping ahead just a bit in our story, the goldsmith-bankers really liked these treasury orders. As explained in Chap. 1, treasury orders became the assets on their own balance sheets, complementing the liabilities or deposits they held for individual customers. Historians and scholars have documented[2] that, like a mysterious force, by the time of *the Stop of the Exchequer* in 1672, the vast majority of treasury orders were on the books and in the hands of goldsmith-bankers, like gravity pulling on Isaac Newton's falling apple.

Now although it might not seem like much, the innovations embedded within the order system were quite numerous, and most of them are to the credit of George Downing, who implemented these changes. First, the treasury order number (e.g. #91) assured the holder that it would actually get paid *in order*. This wasn't the medieval Exchequer of King Henry VIII or Queen Elizabeth I, where lenders were paid haphazardly—or maybe never—based on court connections, threats or coercion. They had a number and were part of an orderly queue. The actual name *treasury order*, with order capitalized in the certificate, was chosen deliberately and meant to convey an edict of English financial stability. Keep calm and get paid in order.

This was part of a bigger plan involving more than departmental efficiency. One of George Downing's objectives was to open up the treasury market to smaller investors or lenders, accessible to the gentlemen and yeoman, if you like. And by creating an efficient and regulated system he hoped to increase confidence so that perhaps smaller and more risk-averse shopkeepers and merchants would transfer their "retirement savings" into treasury orders. This is no different than (in my corner of the twenty-first century) the Government of Canada offering small investors

[2] Horsefield (1982) and Carruthers (1996).

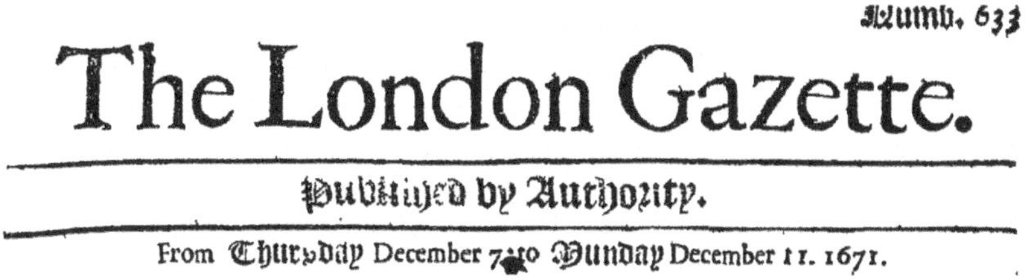
Numb. 633

The London Gazette.

Published by Authority.

From Thursday December 7. to Sunday December 11. 1671.

Fig. 5.2 The masthead of the London Gazette

the opportunity to purchase savings bonds in minor quantities while at the same time borrowing larger sums with many more zeros in the institutional market. It was a different clientele for the same product—loans to the Crown. Since the target audience for these certificates wasn't a handful of bankers and wealthy merchants, you might wonder how the masses scattered around London and beyond were able to find out that a particular tax packet had arrived at the Exchequer and that the order (whether #91 or any other) was ready to be redeemed. They obviously didn't get an email or twitter alert. But they did read the newspaper.

And the best-known and most widely circulated[3] paper was the *London Gazette*. It had been launched in the year 1665 and was managed via the office of the Earl of Arlington (recall, one of the five cabal members introduced in Chap. 2) and the responsibility of his lieutenant, undersecretary Joseph Williamson—a notorious character who appears in many stories (both fictional and true) of the Restoration period. In addition to political news—the newspaper was used as a public relations tool—it contained various financial notices. At the very bottom of the second page, to be exact, was a section in which the Exchequer would announce that a particular order was ready to be redeemed. See Fig. 5.2 for the issue dated Thursday, December 7, 1671, in which it is announced that treasury order #650 was now being paid. See Fig. 5.3. Order #650 was registered or secured against another (separate) source, the hearth tax, which, as I explained in Chap. 3, was one of the King's ordinary sources of revenue. Note again the difference between the two sources of (tax) revenue that could be backing the treasury order; ordinary and parliamentary. Presumably, sometime that afternoon, or as soon as they had seen the notice that appeared in the *London Gazette*, the holder(s) of order #650 hailed a carriage to Whitehall, where the Exchequer was located,

[3] See also *Post Boy*, *Flying Post* and the *Collection for Improvement of Husbandry and Trade*.

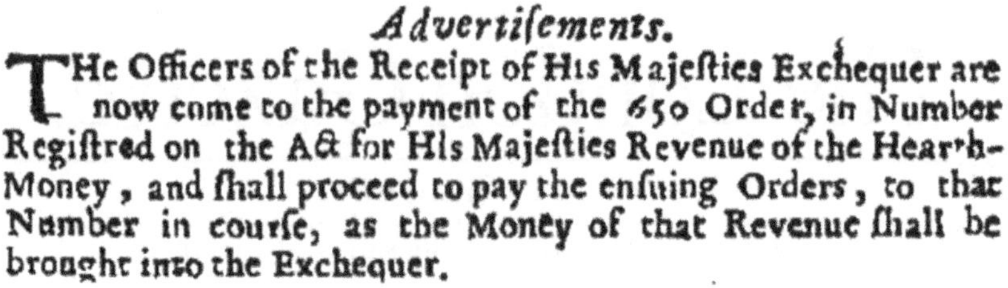

Advertisements.

THe Officers of the Receipt of His Majesties Exchequer are now come to the payment of the 650 Order, in Number Regiftred on the Act for His Majefties Revenue of the Hear᾽h-Money, and fhall proceed to pay the enfuing Orders, to that Number in courfe, as the Money of that Revenue fhall be brought into the Exchequer.

Fig. 5.3 A small corner of the gazette

and received the par value of their treasury order plus 6% interest. Note that the exact amount of cash or coin they received would depend on the time elapsed since the original loan was provided, which is a date listed on the treasury order. Some of these visitors to the Exchequer might have then hurried back to the City of London to spend and enjoy their new-found wealth. Others who didn't need the money—or wanted to reinvest—might have lingered at the Exchequer and used the maturing funds to acquire yet another treasury order, albeit with a higher order number. It's worth pausing for just a bit to recall that all this activity took place 350 years ago, well before any of the financial plumbing we now take for granted. But the concept of a *dividend reinvestment plan* (for savers) or a *systematic withdrawal program* (for retirees) was no different than it might be in the twenty-first century. Money was either consumed or invested.

Another significant innovation involving more than administrative efficiency and media relations was the financial security backing the loan. Recall from the language on the treasury order that the lender (or holder) was assured that as tax revenues arrived at the Exchequer, they were guaranteed to receive their original principal and accumulated interest promptly and without delay. The arrival of tax revenues wasn't only a trigger for payment of the treasury order. The money inside this packet of taxes could be considered the lender's assets. The notice in the *London Gazette* informed the holder of the treasury order that their money had arrived. The security provided by naming and identifying the tax revenues was intended to create more than a psychological—or the more voguish *behavioral finance*—effect. The asset backing had real financial value.

The system of borrowing introduced during the Restoration reduced arbitrariness, reduced risk and—according to George Downing—would eventually reduce the interest (or discount) rate that lenders demanded from the Crown. That was really the long-term goal: a Crown that could borrow at lower interest rates. Apparently, the English treasury commissioners were quite jealous of their cousins and neighbors across the channel, the Dutch, who were (not running perpetual deficits and) paying only 4% interest on their loans. So George Downing and the treasury commissioners were hoping that as the order system matured, they could (perhaps, eventually) lower the 6% rate—and not have to offer bulk discounts to goldsmith-bankers—and thus beat the Dutch at their (much more efficient) money game. In case you are wondering, that dream didn't materialize during George Downing's lifetime or during the seventeenth century. As you might suspect by now, Downing's elegant system blew up in January 1672, but I'm getting ahead of the story.

Many Ways to Skin a Cat

First, I'll start with an admission of sorts. Anyone who attempts to explain the complicated machinations of seventeenth-century finance to an uninformed audience runs the risk of oversimplification to the point of distortion. Alas, the first explanation of any complex phenomenon is most certainly a lie. On the topic of Exchequer borrowings, there were a number of other ways in which the government borrowed money to help finance their operations. These too should be called loans and are certainly part of the Crown's debts. I'll mention and review them now just briefly, but they didn't play a leading part in the events of January 1672. The treasury orders were the lead story in the drama surrounding *the Stop of the Exchequer*, but there were three other methods the Crown used to borrow money during the relevant Restoration period that are worth noting[4]: direct loans, revenue farmers and tallies.

Direct Loans: The Crown borrowed money directly from wealthy individuals, bankers, corporations and even the City of London itself, at least when the City had surplus funds. These loans were negotiated on a case-by-case basis and often involved a bit of political coercion and even some arm-twisting. The common denominator of this category is that these loans were all one-off deals, not tied to any specific tax revenues; nor were they assignable like

---

[4] Source: C. D. Chandaman (1975), *The English Public Revenue: 1660–1688*, p. 296, as well as Nichols (1971), which describes the fact that companies such as the Royal African Company were able to borrow at rates lower than those of the government, in contrast to the modern days, in which the government rate is considered risk free and all other corporate rates are higher.

treasury orders. This is very important. They weren't traded in the secondary market. Instead, they were fixed loans with fixed repayment periods and were not designed to be sold or syndicated. Just as one example, the (famous) East India Company—which received its royal charter from Queen Elizabeth in the year 1600 and ended up controlling most of India for much of the twentieth century—once lent a sizeable sum of money to King Charles II at the (low) rate of 4%. As you might note, this was far under the 6%, for example, being paid on treasury orders. Why would the astute directors and officers of the East India Company agree to this? Well, back in the complicated political climate of the 1650s Commonwealth, they had cozied up to Oliver Cromwell and helped finance his government. A decade later, and as far as King Charles and the royalists were concerned, that was akin to treachery. Indeed, during the Restoration, the company worried they might lose their royal charter—if not their heads—as a result of their prior political sins. So when King Charles II and his ministers came calling for a loan just around the time their Charter was up for renewal, they were more than happy to comply by lending at submarket rates.[5] And yes, the East India Company did obtain a renewal of their royal charter, and the loan was paid back.

Revenue Farmers: Interestingly enough, during medieval times, the King and Crown didn't actually collect income taxes from the masses. Instead of having government agents running around the country amassing the funds, they sold the rights upfront to specialist groups called "revenue farmers." These farmers had absolutely nothing to do with barnyard animals or crops of agriculture. Rather, they were a syndicate of financiers (some of them goldsmith-bankers) who would advance money to the Crown and in exchange would be entitled to collect the tax revenue and keep part of the proceeds—more than the advance, obviously—for themselves. This practice was (mostly) terminated toward the end of 1671, mainly because the King and his council felt they were getting fleeced. Instead, tax revenue collection returned to being managed (and collected by) the government bureaucracy. When farming was used, it was in the form of a loan, and in fact, the suspension[6] of the system in late 1671 was a contributing factor to some of the difficulties experienced by the Exchequer.

Tallies: Without getting too caught up in the minutia, tallies were hazelwood sticks which creditors of the Crown received in lieu of cash

---

[5] See Coleman (1963).

[6] For a careful economic analysis of tax farming in England (as well as in France) during the seventeenth century, see the article by Johnson and Koyama (2014), in which they also reference the suspension of farming in September 1671, which was a few months before the "stop."

and represented a receipt or proof that money was owed to the holder. This system had been in place for centuries. The tally was like a *wishbone* on which the amount owed was etched in the wood and then broken or split right down the middle in two symmetric parts. The Exchequer officials retained one side, while the creditor retained the other. Not to complicate things unnecessarily, but tallies were often attached to treasury orders as "proof of payment," although they also operated as a separate borrowing system. When it came time to repay the loan, the official at the Exchequer would check to ensure the two parts of the tally stick were originally joined together in union and the money was disbursed. This was a clever system to deter fraud, although one that was subject to another hazard, fire. Despite their widespread use, very few of these tallies survive today because of a massive fire (at Westminster) in the late nineteenth century that burned the remaining ones to a crisp.[7] Just to be clear here, the tally recorded a loan, but it wasn't a loan per se.

The bottom line here is that in addition to treasury orders, there were a variety of other ways in which the Crown borrowed money during the Restoration period. And, just as importantly, not all of them melted down (although some burned away) nor did everyone lose money when the King defaulted in 1672. It was mostly the treasury orders that were affected—and not all of them, to be very precise.

Why all the different ways and methods of borrowing money? Well, the government has no choice but to borrow (large) sums of money. To quote G. O. Nichols,[8] writing in the *Journal of British Studies*:

> The government's expenditure was not easily apportioned over the entire year. In most cases large sums were required and consequentially it was necessary for the government to *anticipate* future revenue receipts by *borrowing* in order to meet its current expenditure obligations.

The word anticipation (in the seventeenth century) is another way of saying securitizing (in the twenty-first century). As Nichols points out, the government could have solved this problem by accumulating surplus revenue and using it as a reserve, but during the reign of Charles II, the "demands on revenue" were larger than income.

---

[7] For a broader discussion of debt instruments, tallies and defalcations—which also involved problems with financial fraud—see Desan (2014), Carruthers (1996), Roseveare (1991) and Dickson (1967). The fire (in 1834) was actually caused by burning tallies.

[8] See Nichols (1971), p. 83.

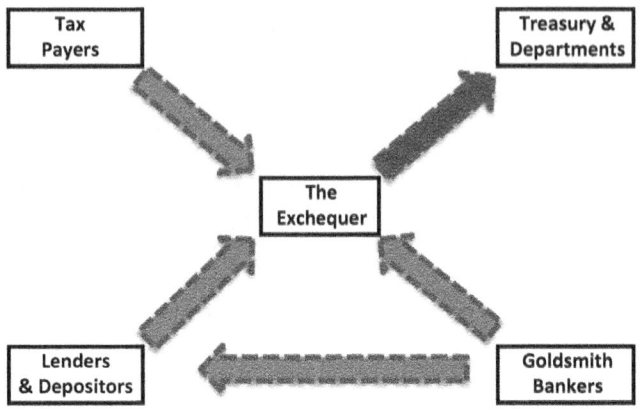

Fig. 5.4 Exchequer and its financial relations

Now that you understand the mechanics of how these treasury orders were issued, circulated and redeemed, and how they differed from other types of borrowing I can move on to a discussion of their valuation and what they were actually worth. Figure 5.4 provides a summary flowchart of the role they played in the financial ecosystem of the Restoration.

Imagine you are John Ball and a few months after lending money to the Crown—but before the Exchequer announces funds are available for redemption—you need ready money and try to sell the certificate to a goldsmith-banker. Recall that John Ball provided His Majesty with £400, which is the "par value" of the bond in modern parlance. In theory the value of this certificate increases over time, as it gets closer to maturity when the interest will be paid. In the secondary market it should be worth more than £400. But it's unlikely the goldsmith-banker offered him the full £400. This is key. After all, the goldsmith-banker was providing a service, offering ready liquidity and taking on some default and credit risk. Also, there is a chance that John didn't actually lend the full £400. It was only a notional value. *What would the treasury orders be worth in a secondary market?*

At this point in the narrative—and with sincere apology to professional historians—I will take the liberty of referring to them as *collateralized treasury orders*, or CTOs for short, to remind you that the certificate and loan was only as good as the tax revenues backing it. Would the projected tax revenues materialize? If not, the guarantee would evaporate. The similarities between the CDOs of the early twenty-first century and the CTOs of the seventeenth were numerous, and much deeper than just two out of three letters in the abbreviation. Let me recap the important assumptions before I move on to modeling. First, 6% is the risk-free rate and everyone would be more than willing to lend at that rate, if they were assured payback. Second, the King issues or sells a whole block of debt at one point in time and the block expires on the date specified by the Act. The next block of debt starts the numbering over again.

VALUING COLLATERALIZED TREASURY ORDERS (CTOs)

In formal (and modern) terms one can think of the financial valuation exercise facing the goldsmith-bankers—or anyone else buying and trading CTOs—in the following way: although CTOs were loans (think savings account) paying 6% interest to the holder upon redemption, they were collateralized or secured against tax revenues. These might be the excise, customs and hearth tax (aka Crown's ordinary revenue) or special Acts of parliament during the Restoration—all of which were collected in packets and arrived at random times to the Exchequer.

The redemption date of a specific CTO number (which I compared to modern CUSIP numbers) linked to a particular tax revenue source was random as well. It could be a matter of weeks before it was redeemed, a few months or even a year, depending on the order number and the implied seniority of the claim. That said, the holder of the CTO earned 6% interest (per year) during the entire waiting period and was assured—by the efficiency of George Downing's system—that a certificate with a higher number would not be paid or redeemed prematurely or out of turn. Recall that the holder of the CTO would monitor the weekly *London Gazette* newspaper announcements. Just as soon as the certificate number appeared in the notices section, the holder would rush to the Exchequer and receive the original principal back plus 6% interest properly calculated and measured to cover the waiting period.

Table 5.1 offers a more detailed analysis of the arrival process from the records listed in the *London Gazette*. In particular, it displays the three different taxes that were used as security for the *treasury orders* during the period 1667 to 1672. They are (1) the £1.25 million tax, (2) the Eleven Month tax and (3) the hearth tax. The table displays the arrival time (in weeks) of orders numbered 50, 100, 150 and so on.

For example, order #700 that was backed by the so-called Eleven-Month tax was announced in the *London Gazette* 57 weeks after payments began. In contrast, order number 700 backed by the £1.25 million tax was announced (and arrived) 45 weeks after payments began. Finally, order #700 backed by the hearth money never arrived. Now, it could be

5 PAID UPON ORDERS FROM THE TREASURY

Table 5.1 How long did it take to get paid? Week in which CTO was first advertised for payment

Order #	(A) £1.25 M act	(B) Eleven Month tax	(C) Hearth tax
1	N.A.	0.0	0.0
50	N.A.	11.0	63.0
100	0.0	18.0	64.0
150	1.0	29.0	67.0
200	4.0	31.0	71.0
250	5.0	52.0	74.0
300	11.0	53.0	75.0
350	21.0	53.0	77.0
400	26.0	53.5	78.0
450	27.0	54.0	97.0
500	31.0	54.5	99.0
550	40.0	54.5	102.0
600	40.0	55.0	105.0
650	41.0	56.0	107.0
700	45.0	57.0	–
750	47.0	61.0	–
800	50.0	62.0	–
850	50.0	63.0	–
900	51.0	64.0	–
950	52.0	65.0	–
1000	75.0	66.0	–
1050	75.0	67.0	–
1100	92.0	68.0	–
1150	123.0	69.0	–
1200	–	70.0	–
1250	–	71.0	–
1300	–	74.0	–
1350	–	87.0	–
1400	–	92.0	–
1450	–	122.0	–

Data source: Hand collected (with thanks to Daniel Tut) from the *London Gazette, 1665–1680*

that such an order number was never issued, or that no tax revenues ever arrived to pay order #700. (It is more likely to be the latter and not the former.)

For a change of view or pace, you can also think of Table 5.1 as arrival times for three different bus routes on a random day. The left-most column ("order #") can be imagined as actual bus numbers, and the listed weeks in the three other columns are minute numbers. For example, the

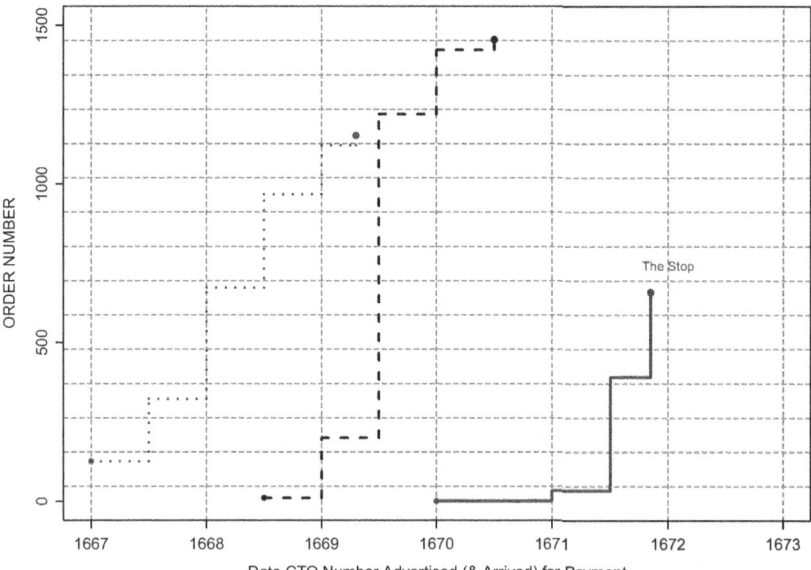

Fig. 5.5 The Tax Revenue Arrival Process

table is reporting that bus #150 on route (A) arrived one minute after bus #100 on the same route (A). Then, three minutes later, or at minute 4, bus #200 arrived. Then, one minute after that, at minute 5, bus #250 arrived. It took another six minutes for bus #300 to arrive at minute 11 and so on. The last bus of the morning commute, #1150, arrived at minute 123, or approximately two hours after the first bus entered service. This (fictional bus stop) perspective will help set the stage for the mathematical (Poisson) model that I will develop later to help value the CTOs. I get to this soon in this chapter.

In Chap. 6, I'll return to the week numbers and link them with actual calendar dates, but you can get a glimpse of the timelines in Fig. 5.5. The figure provides a graphical illustration of the same information in Table 5.1, with lower granularity and the actual arrival dates. Instead of single weeks, it aggregates them to the level of 26 weeks. In other words, in the figure, every jump point indicates an arrival in six-month increments.

Either way, here is the bottom line. Whether you personally held order #10, which was likely to be paid very soon, or John Ball's #91, which might take a while, you (or the goldsmith-banker) knew you would receive the proper time value of money upon redemption. From a financial point of view the risk or concern to the owner was not about being compensated for the waiting time, *assuming your CTO number was announced and you actually got paid*.

Rather, the greater risk to the goldsmith-banker or holder of the CTO was that the total projected tax revenues would not materialize prior to the expiration of the special Act of parliament (or legislated timeline) upon which the loan was secured. This is a concern I didn't highlight or emphasize before, but clearly would have been a consideration. Once the period specified in the Act of parliament had expired, if your particular order number had not been paid, it could expire worthless.[9]

This risk also included the possibility that tax revenues—the security or collateral for the loan—would be redirected by the King to more pressing needs. Either way, if the realized tax revenue packets were not deemed sufficient to pay back all prior orders, and reach your particular order number, you would not be paid either interest or your principal. You can think of this as a type of default, but of the underlying tax revenue. I prefer to use the phrase *revenue shortfall* instead of an outright default, a term which suggests malicious and deliberate actions (which was yet another concern).

To use the language of modern contingent claim pricing—and with apologies if this sounds like Greek to an English speaker—the goldsmith-bankers who purchased the CTOs held a *binary American call option*.[10] The option paid the par value plus interest as soon the tax revenues (aka the underlying stochastic or random process) reached a predetermined level, but prior to expiration of the Act of parliament.

Continuing with the analogy to derivative securities, let's pause and think of this in modern terms. The much-maligned *collateralized debt obligation* is a financial instrument in which many home mortgages, some high quality and some of dubious origin and paternity, were pooled and packaged together into one big (special-purpose) vehicle and then fragmented into smaller shares called "tranches" and sold to investors. Some tranches were (much) riskier than others. Over time, as the underlying homeowners made their monthly mortgage payments, which then flowed into this vehicle, the income is shared and distributed to the investors

---

[9] Although this was never stated explicitly, it is implicit. See, for example, Horsefield (1982) and his comment on top of p. 514.

[10] See the classic textbook by Hull (2014) for the valuation of derivative securities, and in particular fixed-income bonds with embedded options. See also Milevsky (2017) for a more formal and technical analysis of this material.

depending on their seniority, that is, the variety of tranche they purchased. I believe that George Downing would have recognized this idea as his own—perhaps demanded patent payments—and been proud.

Some authors have described the mechanics of CDOs as a "cascading waterfall." The closer you (the investor) are to the top of the waterfall of mortgage payments, the more likely you are to get paid. Conversely, at the bottom of the waterfall is the toxic stuff which if you're stuck there, you may never get paid. If and when homeowners defaulted on their loans, the expected payments (i.e. the water) to the *special-purpose vehicle* (i.e. waterfall) would dry up.

Back to dry land and the mid-seventeenth century. Sure, the Exchequer might redeem your treasury order—from some other source of funds—even if the specific tax revenues set out in the order as backing the CTO didn't materialize, but that was extremely unlikely, since the Exchequer was constantly short of cash. Indeed, the language in the order itself—which you saw in Fig. 5.1—was quite clear: the holder was providing an advance against a specific source of tax revenue. No tax revenue = No payment. In fact, that is exactly what happened during *the Stop of the Exchequer*, although for completely different reasons. King Charles II decided to temporarily, that is for one year, *redirect the tax revenues*. The underlying tax packets were no longer available to redeem the treasury orders, and once the year was over, the security and collateral had evaporated.

POISSON MODEL FOR THE ARRIVAL OF TAXES

Here is an example with some realistic numbers, which will form the basis of the valuation model that follows. Imagine the Act of parliament specified a provision for £1,000,000 in expected tax revenue to be collected over a period of two years—expected revenue which could then be used by the Exchequer as security for borrowing money, that is, for issuing CTOs. Now, some of that million had to be set aside or budgeted for interest payments and other fees, so assume that (the Exchequer would determine) £936,000 could be used to back the principal or par value of the treasury orders.[11]

Let's now say for simplicity that the Exchequer issued 104 of these orders, numbered from 1 to 104, and that each one of these orders was in

---

[11] Very roughly speaking, the £936,000 plus 6% interest (plus a fudge factor) is approximately equal to the £1,000,000. My objective here is to keep the numbers round and simple.

the amount of £9000 and paying 6% interest when (eventually) redeemed. Note 104 × £9000 = £936,000.

Yes, in practice, the order sizes had different par values and a particular order number might be backing a few certificates, like John Ball's order #91, but let's keep things simple for now. Continue to suspend your disbelief and assume that order #1 paid £9000 plus interest when it was redeemed, after the relevant tax revenue packets arrived at the Exchequer. Then order #2 paid £9000 plus interest, but only after order #1 had been paid, which corresponds to a total of £18,000 tax revenues received and so on. Pretty basic arithmetic, thus far.

Lacking any information about the rate at which tax revenue packets were randomly arriving at the Exchequer—they were probably quite seasonal and lumpy—I will assume the tax collections upon which these orders were secured arrived at a frequency of approximately £9000 per week. In other words, a packet of cash and coin containing £9000 arrived randomly at the Exchequer from the assorted tax collectors every week on average, and was then used to pay creditors. Some weeks the Exchequer might receive more than £9000 in collected revenues—and then redeem more than one order—and other weeks it might receive less than £9000, which was not enough to redeem even one new order. In that case, no notice would appear that week in the *London Gazette*.

Think about the process of waiting for a bus that is expected to come every five minutes. Sometimes you wait ten minutes. Sometimes you wait one minute, and occasionally, three arrive around the same time. That's randomness. However, this randomness can still be modeled. In probability theory and statistics, the *Poisson distribution*, named after French mathematician Siméon Denis Poisson (b. 1781, d. 1840), is a discrete probability distribution that expresses the probability of a given number of events occurring in a fixed interval of time (and/or space, but we are looking at time in this example) if these events occur with a *known average rate* and *independently of the time since the last event*. For the purposes of our initial investigation, we will adopt the Poisson distribution to model the arrival of tax revenues.

In the language of stochastic processes, whose basic models I will soon co-opt, I'll denote the order arrival rate by the Greek letter lambda, or $\lambda = 1$, which plays an important role in the valuation of CTOs. Note that if the Exchequer had decided to issue 208 CTOs numbered from 1 to 208 (instead of the 104), then each CTO would have a smaller notional value of only £4500. The arrival rate for orders to be redeemed at the

Exchequer would then be doubled to $\lambda=2$ per week, but the tax revenues would still be arriving at £9000 per week.

My point here isn't to unnecessarily to complicate matters—and what follows doesn't really require advanced calculus—but rather to remind you that the arrival rate λ corresponds to orders, not currency or tax revenues. Another, perhaps simpler, way to think about the arrival rate λ is by computing the total number of CTOs issued against the given Act (call it *M*) divided by the total number of weeks covered by the Act (called it *W*) and then ignoring tax revenue amounts all together. Either way, I hope it's clear. The arrival rate $\lambda = M/W$ is a key variable in the valuation discussion that follows. In fact, it's the only variable.

For those still slogging through the technicalities, my objective in all of this is to get a *mark-to-market* value for the CTO, or a measure of the fair value of accounts that can change over time, such as assets and liabilities. *What is such a security really worth?* How much would you pay for such an instrument in the secondary market? If you were discounting the treasury orders, or buying them from John Ball, would you pay the full notional face value of £9000 per order knowing that you will receive your principal back with 6% interest only if the tax revenue materializes?

The answer depends on a variety of subjective and hard-to-quantify factors, but at the very least they depend on *the seniority of the order number*. Higher-numbered CTOs were worth *less* than their notional value and goldsmith-bankers were perfectly justified in discounting them due to the risk that the tax revenues would not materialize. If John Ball wanted to sell his treasury order to a goldsmith-banker (or any other financier), I doubt he would have received the full £400. In the language of traders, he would have undergone a "haircut." This process of discounting—only offering 90% or 85% of the par value—of course, gave the appearance that the goldsmith-bankers were charging more than the 6% interest to lend to the King and his Exchequer. But in fact, using the language of twenty-first-century finance, it was (1) a liquidity premium and, more importantly, (2) a *risk premium*. Although the liquidity premium is harder to quantify, I'll nevertheless provide an estimate of the justifiable risk premium in a moment.[12]

To get a better sense of the risk of a particular CTO number, let's examine a few of the hypothetically numbered orders in more detail and

---

[12] For the more mathematically inclined reader, a brief mathematical model is available in the technical document listed in the references as Milevsky (2017).

walk through their typical life cycle. For instance, CTO #1, from the 104 issued in my example, was absolutely certain to get paid because it had a claim on the first £9000 of tax revenue. The probability of nonpayment, or shortfall, was near zero. In that specific case, there is absolutely no justification for charging a risk premium and earning anything more than 6% interest on the order. So, CTO #1 should not have been discounted by the goldsmith-bankers, at least as far as credit risk is concerned. The goldsmith-bankers did provide a liquidity service and might have charged for that—but that is a separate (unaddressed) matter.

The same idea applies to CTO (Downing's) #10. It would only be redeemed after the Exchequer received 10 × £9000 = £90,000 of tax revenues. Again, given that they were expecting close to a million pounds of tax revenue, the risk of revenue shortfall was minimal. The revenue *yield* or harvest would surely exceed this threshold. The buyer of CTO #10 had no right to charge a risk premium. Yes, he or she might have to wait a few more weeks or months (than order #1) to get paid, but the CTO paid 6% interest.

Back to the language of modern credit markets: you can think of the CTOs in the range of #1 to perhaps #65 or #70 as being in the highest and safest possible tranche. If the rating agencies Moody's and Standard & Poor's had been around in the seventeenth century, they would have rated them AAA or the equivalent. These CTOs were designed for widows and orphans.

But the situation was quite different and much trickier for higher order numbers, especially as they got close to the maximum 104. The holders

Table 5.2 Valuation of a collateralized treasury order (CTO)

Downing order	Tax revenue threshold	Shortfall probability = threshold not met	Risk-adjusted interest rate
#10	£90,000	0.00%	6.00%
#70	£630,000	0.02%	6.02%
#80	£720,000	0.64%	6.64%
#85	£765,000	2.50%	8.56%
#90	£810,000	7.49%	14.10%
#95	£855,000	17.63%	27.40%
#100	£900,000	33.43%	56.22%

A total of 104 orders issued for £9000 each. Secured against (net) £936,000 tax revenue
Orders pay 6% interest when redeemed. Act of parliament expires in two years
£9000 received per week

of those CTOs took on real credit (shortfall or revenue) risk. Let's focus on CTO #90, for example, the results of which are displayed in Table 5.2.

Note that for CTO #90 to get paid by the Exchequer, the prior 89 orders would have to have been redeemed plus an additional of £9000 of tax revenue received, for a total tax yield of £810,000. And given that total anticipated (expected) tax revenue was £1,000,000 (not accounting for interest and fees that had to be deducted), there was a nontrivial chance that the money would not materialize (i.e. arrive at the Exchequer). *Bottom line: treasury order #90 might never get paid.*

How does one compute the probability that this will occur? Well, if you assume that the tax revenue packets backing the orders (1) arrive randomly at the Exchequer at the rate of (on average) one per week, and that (2) these arrivals are independent of each other, then one can show (mathematically) that the probability that order #90 will not get paid during the two years governed by the Act is *7.49%*. There is only a 92.51% chance of getting paid. It might seem like seventeenth-century witchcraft, to be able to present an explicit number like this, but the arrival rate of $\lambda = 1$ at the number 104 (weeks) is all that is needed to see the CTOs fate.[13]

That number represents the probability that the tax revenues will not be sufficient to pay order #90. It could be that revenues were only £700,000 or £600,000 or £500,000. Either way, there wasn't enough to cover order #90. Ergo, the holder of the CTO doesn't get paid. The CTO defaults. Now, just to be clear, this default I am referring to here is due to the (natural) shortfall in tax revenues and not because of any malicious or deliberate attempt by the Crown to (illegally) redirect the tax revenues from the holders of the treasury orders to other uses.

The Day the King Defaulted is another (structural) matter entirely ...

Here is yet another way to think about this—for those readers who are more quantitatively inclined. The expected number of tax revenue packet "arrivals" after 104 weeks is precisely 104. The standard deviation in the number of arrivals is (the square root of 104 and) approximately 10.2 packet arrivals. By a rough *Gaussian approximation*, the probability that less than 90 arrivals (i.e. 89 or 88 or 87, etc.) materialize can be computed by the z-score of $(89 - 104)/10 = -1.5$, which is close enough to the true value (7.49%) displayed in Table 5.2. Of course, the point isn't the number but what we do with it.

---

[13] This is the CDF (cumulative distribution function) of the corresponding Poisson distribution.

With an actual revenue shortfall probability, we can move to the valuation question, which is: how much would you pay for a security today? The contingent claim pays £1 plus interest at some random redemption time, with a probability of 92.5%. There is a corresponding 7.5% probability of zero payment. The expected payout from this (hypothetical) instrument is £0.925 plus 6% interest, so its present value is simply £0.925 per £1 of par value. The result? You certainly wouldn't pay £1 for this knowing that you might only get £0.925 on average. At an absolute most (assuming you are neutral or ambivalent to any risk), you would pay £0.925 per £1 of par value. If and when you received your £1 (in present value terms), the extra interest rate you earned would be $1/(0.925) - 1 = 8.1\%$. Add this risk premium to the embedded 6% credited interest and *voilà*—you arrive at 14.10% as the (minimum) proper risk-adjusted interest rate that the holder of order #90 should charge the Exchequer.

Now remember that from an intuitional perspective, you couldn't charge the Exchequer more than 6%. That was actually the legal rate of interest at the time and the rate linked to the certificate. So, the goldsmith-bankers and others would discount the treasury order by at least 92.5% of the face value—or by a minimum discount rate of 7.5%—to properly compensate for the revenue shortfall risk on order #90. Well, that is the theory, at least.

In twenty-first-century finance, this is all rather standard. The shortfall probability is obtained using a statistical argument and the risk-adjusted interest rate is the reciprocal of the nonshortfall probability (minus one) added to the 6% interest rate. For order #95, the fair economic interest rate would be 27.40% at a minimum, which is computed via $1/0.8237 - 1 = 21.4\%$ risk premium plus 6% interest, equaling a 27.4% risk-adjusted interest rate.

I repeat that this is only a lower bound—that is, risk-neutral valuation in the modern financial lingo—and a more risk-averse investor would likely demand higher (discount) rates on their CTOs. This number is a solid floor. If I were Robert Viner, Edward Backwell, John Banks or any of the goldsmith-bankers of the Restoration, *I wouldn't pay a penny more if you tried to sell treasury order #90 to me*. I believe that the historical literature discussing the mechanics of treasury orders and the events surrounding *the Stop of the Exchequer* haven't emphasized the order number and the impact on their valuation vis-à-vis a fair discount rate. Perhaps this is my small contribution to the scholarly literature.

To my knowledge there isn't any evidence, one way or the other, whether CTOs trading (i.e. being discounted) in the secondary market were valued differently depending on their order number. It is also unclear whether the (very) high treasury order numbers experienced a termination or cessation of payment due to the late (or nonexistent) arrival of the tax packets at the Exchequer. I do believe this would be a fruitful avenue of potential research.

Treat a Model Like a Gentleman

Unfortunately, there also is a limit as to how far I can "sell" this sort of mathematical model—or analogy to modern CDOs—in the absence of secondary-market pricing data. Much of this is conjecture. Likewise, the assumption that all treasury orders were of the same size or magnitude is simply not true. The tax revenue packet arrival times at the Exchequer were most certainly not independent (exponential) and identically distributed, a critical assumption for invoking the Poisson model as the data-generating process. But I also doubt that any of these realistic additions would change the main conclusion that treasury orders, and especially higher order numbers, deserved to be compensated for the risk of revenue shortfall. These were risky tranches of a CDO, and thus the yield should exceed the risk-free rate. Whenever there is a risk that collateral might evaporate, the owner of the (loan) security incurs risk and should demand a premium. Just because the King and the Exchequer officers claimed it was safe in the mid-seventeenth century, didn't make them risk-free. This is no different from what led up to the financial crisis of 2007–2008. *Instruments were perceived as being safe when in fact the underlying cash flows were unreliable.*

Of course, I am using a microscope invented in the twentieth century to claim that the bacteria (risk) should have been detected by the bankers in the seventeenth century.

Fair Compensation for Financial Risk?

Interestingly enough, Lord Shaftesbury (aka Shaftesbury) wrote a letter in 1674 to none other than John Locke, the well-known seventeenth-century English philosopher and father of Liberalism, addressing this very issue. Recall from Chap. 2, which introduced the *dramatis personae*, that Lord Shaftesbury was one of the five members of the King's so-called cabal—and was present in the room when the critical decisions were made—and was initially vehemently opposed to the idea of defaulting in mid-December 1671. I'll get to specifics very soon in Chap. 6, but Lord Shaftesbury was quite (and rightfully) concerned about the impact a default or even a delay in payment would have on business, commerce and general financial markets.

But two years after the default itself, he had second thoughts about the matter and changed his position—which was quite common for him. In the letter[14] he wrote to Locke, he asserted that the goldsmith-bankers had been "destructive to the nation" by charging an exorbitant rate of interest. He suggested that they were "not content with 12% interest" and "demanded 20% to 30% profit" when lending to the King.

In Lord Shaftesbury's view, 12% was a justifiable interest rate (using our modern language that is a 6% risk premium over the 6% interest rate), but 20% or 30% was too much. Had the goldsmith-bankers been happy with 12%, everything would have been fine. One can only wonder what pricing framework Lord Shaftesbury was using in 1674, and how exactly he came to the conclusion that 12% interest was acceptable but somehow 20% or 30% was "too high."

On a side note, for those readers who recognized my usage of the central limit theorem (CLT) in some of the approximations around the valuation of CTOs, now might be a good time to make a passing reference to Abraham de Moivre. He was the author of the book *The Doctrine of Chances* and (to most historians of mathematics) the intellectual godfather of the "normal distribution." In addition to being an amateur mathematician and teacher, he also toiled as a consultant of sorts to gamblers and financiers. He set himself up in the coffee shops of London and made himself available (from 9 to 5, with 95% certainty) to answer tough probability questions in the late seventeenth century and early eighteenth century.

Although he was a contemporary of Isaac Newton and Edmond Halley, Abraham de Moivre was a mere five-year-old at the time of *the Stop of the Exchequer* in 1672. He emigrated to London in the 1680s after he and his coreligionists were kicked out of France[15] by King Louis XIV. The goldsmith-bankers, and certainly Lord Shaftesbury, couldn't have been using a model developed by Abraham de Moivre to properly value CTOs.

---

[14] Quoted on p. 295 of the Shaftesbury biography by Haley (1968).

[15] Louis XIV revoked the Edict of Nantes in 1685 and many Huguenots (including de Moivre) sought refuge in England.

Position in the Queue Matters

As I wrap up this somewhat technical discussion, at the very least, I hope you have acquired a better understanding of how the CTOs worked in practice. That is the most important takeaway. The mathematical model I developed is really about offering a deeper level of understanding as opposed to pinning specific CTOs down with a definite value. In fact, it isn't absolutely necessary to "get it" to appreciate the story and what happened next.

Although I must admit I do wonder wistfully about traveling back through time (Diana Gabaldon, where art thou?) and returning to the Restoration period, where I start a hedge fund to trade CTOs in the run-up to 1672. Of course, I would short them. No, this isn't sheer fantasy. As I will describe in the next chapter, there actually was quite a bit of (insider) trading taking place just prior to the default. The previously mentioned Lord Shaftesbury conveniently sold his financial holdings in December 1671—just as this measure was being debated among the King's counselors—and used the money to purchase real estate instead—more shenanigans to come.

I'll reiterate one final time that the valuation framework I presented in this chapter is an ex ante model based solely on the likelihood of a shortfall in tax revenues alone. This threat was certainly within the realm of possibility during the entire Restoration period and must have been known to the goldsmith-bankers. The higher the order number, the riskier was the CTO.

In fact, just as important here are the perils and factors I have not included in the mathematical calculations/model. For example, the model doesn't include the threat of the King redirecting tax revenues to other entities (such as his mistresses), nor does it anticipate the prospect of a plague that kills a quarter of the population of London (in 1665), a great fire that displaces over three-quarters of the inhabitants of the City of London (in 1666) or that the English declare war on the Dutch (in 1665 and then again 1672). All of these *unknown unknowns* were yet another reason to discount treasury orders (even) more deeply and charge higher interest rates on loans to the Crown. The war on interest inadvertently became a war on credit risk premiums.

Even in the absence of all those extraneous (exogenous, unforeseen) hazards, the holder of a fixed-income security secured against random revenue streams should be entitled to much more than the (risk-free) rate of

6%. And when you include the risk of being thrown into the Marshalsea, Clink or Fleet prison for debtors—and where many of the goldsmith-bankers ended up—it's doubtful any credit spread can compensate for that sort of punishment.

A Hint of What Went Wrong

Regardless of whether or not you agree with my mathematical valuation model—or whether you personally would have ever trusted the Exchequer to pay back your order number on time—let's now look at things from the issuer's perspective. Imagine yourself for a moment in the role of treasury official, or even His Majesty King Charles II himself, on the off chance he took the time to wander into the Exchequer on his daily walks around St. James' Park. *What do you see going on in the Exchequer?*

Well-to-do people were entering the Exchequer every day and voluntarily handing over large or small sums of cash and coin. They were not coerced. These weren't tax payments they were making. In exchange for the loan, they received a piece of paper (perhaps with a wooden tally) whose three most important features were (1) an *order* number, (2) the name of the tax backing the *order* and (3) the assignability of the *order*, that is, the important ability to transfer ownership. The Exchequer welcomed all the money the officials could get their hands on. As you saw from the tight personal finances of His Majesty in Chap. 4, the number of treasury orders the officials were issuing—investors depositing their money, so to speak—was nowhere near enough to cover the Crown's expenses. Just as soon as the money was deposited at the Exchequer, the officials handed the actual money over to the arms of the government (e.g. His Majesty's Navy or the Master of the Horse or the Lieutenant of the Tower) to pay the outstanding and long-delayed bills.

The same observers might have noticed that soon after the deposit, the John Balls of the world were transferring and trading certificates among themselves and other goldsmith-bankers, using them just like currency. It was a piece of paper with a promise and the merchants and bankers were treating it as if it was as good as cash and coin. But it was only a piece of paper that derived its value from a promise. And so, with the unfailing human ingenuity that brought us fire, gunpowder and nuclear weapons over the millennia, at some point in the late 1660s the light bulb (ok, candle) "turned on" in the mind of the Exchequer officials and the penny dropped, so to speak. No different than the goldsmiths who discovered fractional reserve banking.

You see, if everyone on the street was treating these treasury orders like currency, why shouldn't the Exchequer, the Crown and the government itself do the exact same thing? The officials at the Exchequer could simply print new treasury orders—with increasing numbers, preserving the Downing system—even *without receiving any cash at all.* They could then give those (new) treasury orders to the departmental treasurers and treat them as if they were cash. And when queried by the various departmental officials—"Hey, what's this? We need real money!"—presumably, the Exchequer officials answered them: "This is as good as cash. Go sell them in the secondary market"—which they could. Any goldsmith-banker would purchase them for cold hard cash and coin, albeit at a discount.

Now these treasury orders weren't quite like the ones I discussed so far because the Exchequer had never received any physical coin deposit. There was no John Ball to name on the certificate. But nobody really cared as long as there was an order number. Let me make this very clear. The paper was not backed by specific tax revenue but was still assignable to others. These CTOs were based on a fictitious transaction—and to separate them from their legitimate siblings, I'll use the abbreviation fi-CTO for the fictitious treasury order.[16]

Was this fraud? Was it illegal? No, not at all. According to many historians,[17] what these Exchequer officials did—with the blessing of King Charles, no doubt—is that *in addition to creating new credit, they invented paper money!*

As long as there was a proper deposit to the Exchequer, the treasury order was a reflection of existing cash in circulation. The monetary base of the economy wasn't expanded by the transaction. Real money came in today and would be returned tomorrow. Those were the regular treasury orders. But the fi-CTOs were a different story. They created new money where none had existed. They didn't reflect or encourage credit; they created it.

Alas, the temptation was too great. Like a teenager who is given a blank checkbook with only a vague sense of how much money is in

---

[16] These are known to historians as fiduciary orders; see Chandaman (1975). I can use the abbreviation *fi-CTO*.

[17] Source: See Shaw (1904) or R. D. Richards (1927). Note that English historians are more likely to make this claim. The Dutch, French and Spanish historians scoff. And there is some evidence that the Chinese got there before anyone else in the sixth century. That paper was made of lovely silk too!

the underlying bank account, the Exchequer officials—egged on by the financially pressed departmental treasurers—wrote postdated checks backed by a source of tax revenue that was eventually watered down. And like the experience of most teenagers new to credit management, these seventeenth-century checks eventually bounced in early January 1672, to the tune of a few million pounds.

So, with the twitter version of the story behind us, in the next Chap. 6, I will present in chronological sequence the financial, economic and political events leading up to and including *the Stop of the Exchequer in 1672*, as well as its aftermath.

References

Carruthers, B. G. (1996). *City of Capital: Politics and Markets in the English Financial Revolution*. Princeton: Princeton University Press.

Chandaman, C. (1975). *The English Public Revenue 1660–1688*. Oxford: Clarendon Press.

Coleman, D. C. (1963). *Sir John Banks Baronet and Businessman: A Study of Business, Politics and Society in Later Stuart England*. Oxford: Clarendon Press.

Desan, C. (2014). *Making Money: Coin, Currency and the Coming of Capitalism*. Oxford: Oxford University Press.

Dickson, P. G. (1967). *The Financial Revolution in England*. London: Macmillan.

Haley, K. (1968). *The First Earl of Shaftesbury*. Oxford: Clarendon Press.

Horsefield, J. K. (1982). The Stop of the Exchequer Revisited. *The Economic History Review, 35*(4), 511–528.

Hull, J. C. (2014). *Options, Futures and Other Derivatives* (9th ed.). New York: Pearson/FT.

Johnson, N. D., & Koyama, M. (2014). Tax Farming and the Origin of State Capacity in England and France. *Explorations in Economic History, 51*, 1–20.

Milevsky, M. A. (2017). Valuing the Debt that Stopped the Exchequer in 1672. *Social Science Research Network (SSRN)*, 1–20.

Nichols, G. O. (1971). English Government Borrowing: 1660–1688. *Journal of British Studies, 10*(2), 83–104.

Roseveare, H. (1991). *The Financial Revolution 1660–1760*. London and New York: Longman.

Richards, R. D. (1927). The Evolution of Paper Money in England. *The Quarterly Journal of Economics, 41*(3), 361–404.

Shaw, W. (1904). *Introduction to the Calendar of Treasury Books*. London: His Majesty's Stationary Office.

CHAPTER 6

Diary of a Default

1667: Downing Gives Orders

In the words of W. Lowndes and D. M. Gill, writing in the *English Historical Review*,[1] the year 1667 marks "the beginning of the treasury system as distinct from the exchequer and of the treasury's independence from the privy council and its committees." So, if the tale of the financial default requires a formal beginning, then Thursday, April 4, 1667 is as good a place as any at which to start. That was exactly seven years to the day after King Charles II issued the Declaration of Breda (April 4, 1660), in which he promised a pardon to his enemies and to pay arrears to all soldiers. Back in the year 1660, the anticipation and excitement for the Restoration of the monarchy and the return of the King from exile was widespread. But then seven years later, in 1667—the year after the ominous setting of John Dryden's poem *Annus Mirabilis*—the enthusiasm had all but vanished and some were longing for the good old Puritan days. In fact, John Milton was back in town and *Paradise Lost* was available for sale by local booksellers.

On this particular day (April 4) Samuel Pepys wrote in his diary (yet again) about the "sad condition of the King's purse," which in and of itself wasn't newsworthy, although he also went on to comment about how hard it must be for the King to have to "pass by his officers daily," knowing that they

---

[1] See Lowndes and Gill (1931).

haven't been paid their wages for over four years. By April 4, it would have been seven months[2] since the fire destroyed most of the City of London—and England was (again) at war with the Dutch. The financial situation was as grim as ever. It is therefore worth noting and quite apropos that the *London Gazette*, for the first time ever, published on April 4, 1667 a small advertisement at the very end of the two-page broadsheet which stated as follows:

> It is hereby advertised that all persons that will lend or advance any sums of money for his majesties services, according to the Act of parliament for the Eleven Months tax … shall have tallies of loan and *orders* here upon for the due payment of their principle and interest according to the rules and directions prescribed by the Act.

As I carefully explained in the prior chapter, investors (i.e. lenders) would learn that their collateralized treasury order (CTO) was ready for payment when their unique number appeared and was published in the *London Gazette*. But the same newspaper was also used for advertising or soliciting loans and April 4 was the first date such a notice appeared. The English with money to invest—clearly not those who hadn't been paid in years from the Exchequer for their work—were invited to contribute or lend money to the same Exchequer.

Arguably, a more significant and serious event in the chronology occurred a few weeks later when, in mid-May, the same newspaper announced that the (fourth) Earl of Southampton had died. This particular Earl had been the Lord Treasurer from the very beginning of the Restoration. Southampton was a staunch and loyal monarchist—fidelity of course being more important than financial acumen—who had presided over all the Treasury's financial affairs single handedly. Upon his death in May 1667, the King didn't replace him with (or name) a new Lord Treasurer—much to the chagrin of dignitaries like Shaftsbury and Arlington, who had coveted the job—and instead put the Treasury's management and operations into commission. This meant that a small committee (aka Treasury Board) of counselors managed the day-to-day financial affairs of the entire country. Note that a committee replacing a single bureaucrat wasn't unprecedented and was actually the norm during the 1650s, under Oliver Cromwell. But this change of administrative procedure—from one to many—had direct and immediate bearings on our story.

---

[2] And ten weeks after the infamous John Wilmot (Earl of Rochester) had eloped with Elizabeth Malet and got married at a chapel in Knightsbridge.

The members of the new commission, announced in late May 1667, consisted of Clifford and Shaftesbury—who have already appeared in our story—as well as other notables such as William Conventry, John Duncombe and the Duke of Albermarle (aka General Monk). These were all highly respected names—whom I haven't mentioned yet—but would ring familiar to aficionados of Samuel Pepys and the Restoration. A few of the new commission's members had some prior experience with commerce and finance—such as Lord Shaftesbury—and others were appointed solely for the purpose of establishing prestige. In particular, the Duke of Albermarle was a military war hero and English celebrity. He served as the head of the commission and added stability, gravitas and heft to the proceedings. The commission certainly had a tough job to do and could use all the credibility they could muster.

The mandate of the Treasury commission was threefold. The first task on the agenda was to cut the King's expenditures. This was easier said than done. The second task was to increase the yield or revenue from the King's ordinary sources of revenue, which were the various taxes I described in Chap. 4. The third task (eventually) was to convince parliament to approve additional taxes to cover the gap between tasks 1 and 2. None of these would prove to be stress free. The Navy, Army, ambassadors, judicial system, civil service as well as the King and his court were being told to make do with (much) less.

One member of the commission, Thomas Clifford, wrote to the manager of the King's household and told him to cut back expenses and—as a benchmark for proper spending—to use the reign of the King's late father, Charles I, as a yardstick for proper spending. In particular and for some unknown reason Clifford selected the year 1634—the sixth year of Charles I's reign—as the appropriate year to emulate.

But it wasn't only about cutting back on expenditures. Exchequer officials, from the lowest clerk to the highest commissioners themselves, were warned to improve their output efficiency and work longer hours in the office. Apparently the era of long (gin) lunches was over!

The first meeting of the new commission took place on May 27, 1667—an event that was noted with much interest in Pepys' diary as well.[3] Just as important as the existence of the commission itself was the

---

[3] Another notable (but unrelated) event, which took place around the same time, was the attendance of the first woman, Margaret Cavendish—poet, writer, scientist and philosopher—at a meeting of the Royal Society (founded in 1662).

person responsible for documenting the meetings, or the main administrative officer of the (new) Treasury. His name was Sir George Downing, the secretary of the commission. And although he wasn't a formal voting member, his influence on the Treasury department was far-reaching, and as I pointed out in the prior chapter, he was the architect of the new order system of borrowing. In a manner of speaking, his fingerprints were on every document. It really is difficult to overestimate or exaggerate the impact Downing had on the administrative and bureaucratic affairs of His Majesty's Treasury. He introduced Dutch methods of funding—techniques he had likely acquired from his time as an ambassador in The Hague—into the fabric of national credit.

In the words of his fawning biographer,[4] "Downing erected a scaffolding of order out of the confused mass of business handled haphazardly by the (previous) Lord Treasurer Southampton." There was a new sheriff in town—there to clean up the financial paperwork—and his name was Downing. The sheriff corralled his commissioners and they scheduled to meet regularly, usually three times every week (Tuesday at 3pm and then 8am on Wednesdays and Fridays), and Downing ensured that everything they did, said or requested was documented in minute books, which have been preserved to this day (350 years later) in the National Archives.[5]

All requests for payments and appropriations were required to abide by new procedures, most importantly proper documentation. The *Calendar of Treasury Books* (*CTB*) documents most of this activity and contains (much of) the seventeenth-century records of the activity of the commission and is a testament to Downing's skill.

Now, it is worth pausing for a moment and noting here that there is a difference between a calendar and the original records or manuscript (of the Treasury) itself. Occasionally—in the heat of writing—I might play a bit loose and fail to differentiate between a "calendar" and a "record," but in the case of the Treasury, Shaw's work compiling the minute books is relatively complete.

Whether we focus on calendars or the original records, Downing's biographer asserts that he created the first (modern) governmental bureaucracy

---

[4] See Beresford (1925), p. 217.

[5] In fact, you can read digitized versions of the minutes online at http://www.british-history.ac.uk. The full State Papers are available (by subscription) at http://gale.cengage.co.uk/state-papers-online-15091714.aspx and provide access to both the calendar and the manuscripts. Both locations are a virtual goldmine of information for English history buffs.

and proclaims that he invented "red tape." The above-mentioned *CTB* contains many instances of notices sent to delinquent revenue collectors to question their sums and ask them to justify their numbers. This would be the modern-day equivalent of getting a notice from the federal tax authorities probing the numbers you reported on your tax returns.

One example of many such communications is a letter (July 1667) to tax collectors in Northamptonshire who had remitted a total of £200 in hearth money (aka chimney tax) when it was clear to the commission that there were a total of over 8000 chimneys in the county. Recall that each chimney should generate two shillings in tax, which is a tenth of a pound. So the 8000 chimneys should result in £800 or four times the revenue "yield" recorded. The commission asked: where did the rest of the money go? Of course the English (in the seventeenth century) hated paying taxes, and the hearth tax in particular was the most odious of them all. But Downing and the commission were going to (root out the corruption and) get to the bottom of the matter.

It wasn't only wayward tax collectors who fell into Downing's bureaucratic dragnet. Arlington, a member of the cabal who was responsible for the intelligence and security operations, including the mysterious secret service, had his departmental budget slashed and was told to subsist on an allocation of £4000 per year. In mid-July, the Earl of Sandwich, who was the English ambassador to Spain, submitted his expense claims and requested payment or reimbursement from the Exchequer for £5000, which he had incurred out of his own pocket. Well, that particular claim was sent back to him—presumably all the way to Spain—with a request for additional documentation and expenditure specificity. One can only imagine the frustration. (I certainly know what it feels like with much smaller sums.) But the new directives were clear. No payments were to be made from the Exchequer unless they were preapproved by the commission.

But this bureaucratic and rigid adherence to documentation—as annoying as it might have appeared to the recipient of Downing's queries—had the positive effect of generating confidence among investors and bankers that *lenders would be paid on time*. The ambassadors might have to beg for their money—and the seamen could starve—but the bankers would get their principal and 6% interest while standing in a proper English queue.

The order system which I explained in Chap. 5 was Downing's handiwork and fully consistent with his philosophy for efficiency. Holders of the CTOs were confident that the full tax revenues would eventually be received and the "bonds" would be redeemed at the *Exchequer* in due time. In the goldsmith-bankers' minds perhaps, the fickle King might play fast and loose, but Downing would ensure their money was secure.

Now, lest we posthumously award him sainthood or the Nobel Prize for Peace and Economics, it is also worth noting that as a clerk of the Exchequer, Sir George Downing was entitled to a fee or commission every time a penny, shilling or pound passed through its doors. In other words, a shilling belonging to His Majesty's Treasury that was lost to corruption or inefficiency anywhere in England was a personal matter for him. It affected his pocketbook. Alas, like most other government employees who got "kickbacks" for lack of a better word, Downing enriched himself while in office. In fact, he was a wealthy man before he became secretary to the commission and continued to enrich himself while documenting[6] that "My Lords represent to the King the impossibility of finding money to disband the army and to take care of paying the seamen."

To historians who are notoriously stingy with credit, Downing's reputation has been tainted by his conflicts of interest. But to his credit, he certainly was instrumental in expanding credit.

As far as the timeline is concerned, the spring and summer of 1667 served as the first time the Exchequer issued the (fictitious) treasury orders (fi-CTOs) that I described in Chap. 6. The fi-CTOs were those loans or debts that were not backed by specific tax revenue sources. The idea of course was to expand the number of CTOs issued to the public—and raise more money—so that the government could reduce its reliance on goldsmith-bankers, who were the major lenders.

Reducing the reliance on bankers was Downing's stated objective and in return the goldsmith-bankers (apparently) loathed him. Although considering the fact that he ensured they got paid on time, the relationship between them must have taken on more of a love-and-hate dynamic. For example, Pepys wrote that Downing wanted to "put the bankers out of business" and that he hoped eventually "money would pour" into the Exchequer so the "king could dispense" with the bankers. Although, interestingly, Pepys also quoted Sir John Banks (whom I introduced earlier) as saying that the Exchequer could never really compete with the bankers because of its distance from the bankers. The bankers were based in and around the famous Lombard Street in the heart of the City of London, whereas the Exchequer was based at Whitehall—two miles away from the

---

[6] See Lee (1965), p. 130, for example.

bankers. It might not seem like much of a walk (30 minutes perhaps), but in the seventeenth century, it mattered.

In sum, by the early summer months of 1667, the new Exchequer machinery was rumbling into action, and despite the unpaid wages, budgetary austerity and probing tax audits, the financial outlook appeared to be improving. Things were starting to look up (from the very bottom).

But the month of June brought another tragedy and even greater embarrassment to the English.

June at Chatham

Recall that at this point in time the English had been at war with the Dutch for over two years, and despite an early advantage, the balance and momentum were moving against the English. Then, in early June, the Dutch fleet, led by the great sailor and admiral Michiel de Ruyter, daringly led 50 ships (on June 8) and sailed across the English Channel, up the Thames river and then unto the Medway river in the heart of the county of Kent. They broke into the lightly guarded Chatham dockyards about 35 miles east of London and burned down most of the ships that were based at port. To add insult to injury they then towed England's most illustrious ship—the HMS *Royal Charles*—out of the Chatham port and down the river. They gleefully passed under the nose of King Charles and the stunned English public, taking the captured ship all the way back to their port in Holland.

To this day—350 years later—the Dutch have the stern piece of the Royal Charles displayed in the Rijksmuseum in Amsterdam and the Raid on the Medway has gone down as the British Navy's worst defeat in history.

Needless to say, the recriminations were furious. Where were the guards? Where were the seamen? Why had the watchmen not been alerted? The King and his council wanted heads to roll. But in the ensuing inquiries, the answer to all these questions sounded the same. They abandoned their post—or perhaps had not been there to begin with—because they hadn't been paid (in years, as noted by Pepys). There was no money. Of course, it wasn't only about money and the strategic mistakes went beyond payroll—unpaid seaman and officers aren't very motivated.

The embarrassment following the raid and assigning blame was the least of the King's problems. The financial environment got even worse. The goldsmith-bankers suffered a so-called run on the bank when depositors—panicking about the Dutch boats menacing them in the Thames river—rushed to the bankers in the City of London and demanded their deposited money back, immediately. England feared it was facing another armada invasion, except this wasn't the Catholic Spanish in 1588, with a Protestant Queen Elizabeth I to protect them. This time it was the Protestant Dutch attacking and a (possibly Catholic) King to defend them.

Pepys wrote (on June 12): "[H]undreds are coming to them for money and they will soon all be broke." This continued for a few days, and Pepys commented (on June 15), "It is feared this will undo the bankers," and then again (on June 17), "[B]ankers are broke as to ready money." Many depositors learned (the hard way) the difference between a demand deposit—that can be withdrawn at any time but didn't pay any interest—and a time deposit that paid some interest, but a 20-day notice was required before being withdrawn.

To make matters worse, the most illustrious member of the new Treasury commission, the Duke of Albermarle[7] (aka General Monck), also withdrew his savings from the goldsmith-bankers, cashing in £12,000 in one day, a sum which today would be worth 100 times that amount. This would be the equivalent of, say—in early September 2008, just before Lehman Brothers collapsed—the noted US General Colin Powell (who happened to be a member of the Federal Reserve's Board of Governors) withdrawing all his money from his local Savings & Loan or bank. That would certainly not instill confidence in the financial system! The diarist John Evelyn mentioned to his good friend Samuel Pepys that "wise men move their money abroad." Perhaps even a box buried in the backyard wasn't safe.

And yet, somehow the Exchequer's treasury order system survived. According to the notices in the *London Gazette*, orders #319–#321 were ready for payment on June 13. These orders were backed by and paid under the Act of £1.25 Million. Two weeks later, orders #322 and #323 were ready for payment on July 4, 1667. Then, on July 18 the entire series to #358 was redeemed. The CTO market was operating normally. Although there are a handful of inconsistencies in the records of the *London Gazette*, when (for example) #336 appeared to be listed two weeks

---

[7] Some early American history aficionados might recognize his name from Albermarle County in North Carolina, which is actually named after the Duke. He was one of the original eight Lords Proprietors of the Province of Carolina, which just goes to prove that he did have a diversified investment portfolio. See Isenberg (2016) for more on him, along with the philosopher John Locke, and their role in Colonial America. The county eventually dissolved and merged with others in the vicinity.

after #346, overall the queue evolved properly. Occasionally, there would be a reminder in the *Gazette* that a prior order number—that had been ready for collection a few weeks earlier—was still waiting for redemption at the Exchequer. Perhaps the owner was hoping that interest would continue to accumulate on the money even though the tax packet had arrived, or perhaps it was the general confusion of the times. Either way, the order system survived and thrived.

What calmed the market? Well, the financial panic of mid-June 1667 eventually subsided when King Charles I announced—in a vital statement that was being quoted and debated five years later—that "he will make good their assignments for money." The King stood beyond the CTOs. It's unclear whether Downing and the commissioners crafted the statement of support or merely encouraged him to be proactive. But what is clear is that the King declared that no matter what the Exchequer would honor and pay all that is owed to the bankers (although perhaps not the seamen or any of the other officers who hadn't been paid in years).

In the language of financial accounting, by guaranteeing that the *assets* the goldsmith-bankers held on the left-hand side of their balance sheet were secure and properly valued, the depositors whose *liabilities* were on the right-hand side could be assured they would (eventually) be paid. In other words, the crisis was one of liquidity and not solvency. The CTOs were as good as gold—and being redeemed in order—at least for the time being.

By the end of the summer the English were ready to end the unpopular and embarrassing war with the Dutch and ready to move on with their lives and commercial ventures. On August 23, King Charles II laid the foundation stone for the new Royal Exchange and the next day (St. Bartholomew's Day) peace was proclaimed with the United Provinces.

In fact, soon after the earlier mini financial panic, even Pepys himself felt comfortable enough to lend money to the government—that is, purchase some treasury orders—as an alternative to investing the money in a box in his backyard, which fans of his diary know was his preferred mode of safety.

Pepys reports having invested or purchased £300 worth of treasury orders after Downing twisted his arm by claiming that William Penn had purchased £500 worth. Recall that Penn (senior) was a next-door neighbor of Pepys and this is perhaps one of the earliest community bond appeals. Downing strong-armed other civil servants to lend (even small) sums upon The Act and get in queue for a CTO. He claimed that even the lowest clerk would be investing £100, which of course was wildly optimistic.

In an interesting side note, Pepys (August 30) commented that he had a choice between lending to the Exchequer for a short period of time at 6% per annum, or for longer in exchange for 10% interest annualized. This is an (very early) example of an upward-sloping term structure of interest rates, or term premium. For the record, Pepys selected the 6% and kept his duration short. He half-joked that with the war over and the Exchequer paying 6% (or perhaps even 10%) on loans, even the Dutch themselves would soon be sending their money to invest—since the Dutch treasury only offered 4% interest.

The English nation's (and parliament's) attention shifted to locating scapegoats for the failed war. In their crosshairs was the King's chief advisor and Chancellor, Lord Clarendon (Edward Hyde), who after decades of service was tossed to the parliamentary lions and was (eventually) forced into exile in France—where he wrote a wonderful (and biased) history of the fascinating period he lived through.

With Clarendon gone and stripped of his chancellorship, it was now time for a younger group of advisors to take root and gain influence. Enter the full power and influence of the cabal—whose cast of characters were introduced in Chap. 2. There were Clifford, Arlington and Buckingham—who had been released from the Tower of London in July and reconciled with the King in September—as well as Shaftesbury and Lauderdale, the fourth and fifth members.

Recall that Clifford and Shaftesbury were already members of the Treasury commission by this point in time and a new era of administrative competence was dawning. The City of London (six months after the fire) was in the process of being rebuilt, the plague had been dormant the entire summer and the hostilities with the Dutch were in the past.

Like clockwork, in late December, the *London Gazette* advertised that order #673, which was secured against the so-called Act of £1.25 Million, was ready for payment. The notices continued appearing with regularity every few weeks and the CTO owners—mostly goldsmith-bankers who had discounted the notes and purchased them in the secondary market—were getting paid without delay.

So, although the court held minimal Christmas celebrations in 1667—perhaps to honor the austerity that Downing and his commission were directing—it did appear that the financial situation was improving, even after the Medway affair.

Members of parliament (MPs) were exceedingly impressed with the new efficiency of the Treasury commission and attributed the positive turn to the fact that a committee was always better than one individual (i.e. Lord Treasurer) at managing financial affairs. In fact, some in parliament worried that if this continued—and Downing's whip continued to crack—the King wouldn't need them (i.e. parliament) anymore. After all, the only reason a king called his parliament in the seventeenth century was to approve and grant supply (aka new taxes). Well, that particular fear was completely unfounded, and four years later (in 1672) they would all realize, in hindsight, the comical nature of such anxieties.

ALLIANCES, DUELS AND A LIQUOR TAX

The year 1668 began—or according to the Julian calendar, the year 1667 continued—with *all members* of the Treasury commission continuing to scavenge for new sources of revenue while *some members* of the King's privy council were working on a Triple Alliance. That was a peace treaty between England, Sweden and the United Provinces signed in late January, with the objective to slow down the expansion plans of the imperial King Louis XIV of France. Soon after the Triple Alliance was cemented, France reached its own peace agreement with Spain, which in turn reached its own harmony with Portugal, and for a while, the wars abated[8]—but only for a while. In the spirit of tolerance and reasonable dialogue, the year 1668 saw the philosopher John Locke inducted as a member of the Royal Society, together with John Banks—a banker who will soon make an appearance. Perhaps as symbolic foil to Locke, the year 1668 also saw the (revised) publication in Latin of Thomas Hobbes' monumental book *Leviathan*, a treatise that was no sooner banned by the Anglican bishops.[9]

I should emphasize that in early 1668, while "some members" of the King's privy council were busy promoting universal peace and reconciliation, not all were focused on nonviolent matters of state or prudent finance. In particular, the Duke of Buckingham (aka George Villiers), who was one of the cabal members, was busy preparing for (what became) an

---

[8] See Hutton (1989), p. 299, or Lee (1965), pp. 128–150, or Beresford (1925), Chap. 12, as well as *the Calendar of Treasury Books* (1668), for most of the references in this section.

[9] See the comment by Pepys, who purchased a copy of *Leviathan* in September 1668 and comments about the increasing price of the book in the secondary market once the bishop's ban restricted supply.

infamous[10] duel with the Earl of Shrewsbury. Now, technically speaking, in the late seventeenth century, duels were already outlawed in England, but were still practiced and were very serious business. Recall that over a century later (in 1804), the first American secretary of the Treasury, Alexander Hamilton, lost his life in a tragic duel with Aaron Burr, who was then the vice president of the United States. The Duke of Buckingham's duel, which took place on January 16, 1668, was over less weighty matters—namely over the wife of the Earl of Shrewsbury—as opposed to political disagreements. It wouldn't merit a mention were it not for the fact that the Earl (eventually) died of his sword (not gun) wounds and the entire affair became the social scandal of 1668. Now, given the illegality of duels, some crafty MPs—during the long debates over taxes and the need for new sources of revenue—suggested that the duelist's (namely Buckingham) estates should be confiscated, sold and the funds used to pay off debts. That particular suggestion went nowhere, although it took a personal pardon by the King to get (his boyhood buddy) the Duke of Buckingham out of the hot seat.

Conflicts and wars were expensive hobbies and the second Anglo-Dutch war, which had ended in the summer of 1667, was still generating invoices—and recriminations. Before they were willing to approve or vote for any new taxes or supply, as it was then called, MPs wanted a detailed accounting or report of the (disastrous) war expenses incurred from 1665 to 1667. Needless to say, the last thing the King wanted was detailed scrutiny of his personal expenses. If the rumors and innuendos were to be trusted, a large fraction of his budget was going to support his lavish lifestyle and many mistresses.

The *CTB*, which (again) summarizes the minutes of the committee meetings, includes many insightful and some amusing entries illustrating the tension between a free-spending king and austerity-minded commissioners. On January 17, 1668, the King's Jewel Office under the auspices of Gilbert Talbot is warned to stop further deliveries, presumably of jewels and precious stones. The same Gilbert Talbot is warned a few days later that "new and useless" deliveries in the Jewel Office must be stopped. On February 3, 1668, there is an entry in the *CTB* in which the King—who apparently prized his tennis courts—is informed that the "sail cloths and new nets" that he wanted installed were too expensive. There were multiple requests for pensions to be granted to people who had helped the

---

[10] See Pepys (1997), p. 648.

King escape from Worcester, an event which took place 15 years ago. On February 28, 1668, there is an entry regarding the King's primary mistress, Lady Castlemaine (aka Barbara Palmer, aka Duchess of Cleveland), who asked that her two sons (presumably with the King) be granted some land, which would generate an annuity of £500 per annum for each child.

Remember that this was all taking place during a period in which the Navy, Army and other officers hadn't been paid in years. The commissioners had to scrutinize these requests on a case-by-case basis and decide who would receive a warrant for payment and who would have to wait. Some appeals were immediately deferred or denied and others, such as the request for payment of Colonel Thomas Fairfax's pension, were promptly approved with little hassle.

Even respectable members of the nobility had to grovel for their (back) pay. I have already noted the many ambassadors who had their expenses scrutinized by the commission. Even Lauderdale, who was a member of the cabal, made a personal appearance in front of the commissioners to complain that he hadn't been paid a pension for work he had done almost five years ago as a Groom of the Bedchamber.

The *CTB* is replete with references to the two main goldsmith-bankers Robert Viner and Edward Blackwell, who, it seemed, often visited the Treasury commissioners on a daily basis, settling their accounts, providing additional documentation and offering additional loans. Everything was for sale and the goldsmith-bankers were best positioned to handle the finances of the transactions. In March 1668 the King "sold" the City of Bombay (today called Mumbai)—which he had received as part of the Portuguese dowry upon his marriage to Queen Catherine of Braganza— to the East India Company (EIC). The company in return agreed to supply the King with 10 pounds of gold per year, which (today) would be equivalent to an annuity of 160 ounces of gold. The King claimed the city was too much of a nuisance to rule and he (obviously) would rather have the ready cash.

Throughout the year 1668 Downing continued his relentless push for accountability and proper recordkeeping, such as when he sent a letter admonishing the Commissioner of Sewers, Street and Highways for not having sent their accounts for over five years. Where was the paperwork? He demanded to know.

In early April 1668 the King (again) appeared in person before MPs and gave a passionate speech in which he asked for new taxes. The Treasury commission was doing everything it could on the expense side, but it needed more revenue. The response the King received was lukewarm at best and hostile at worst. In addition to very detailed and personal expense reports, they wanted the King to produce—akin to what Downing was demanding from others—they also asked for his personal commitment to stop "conventicles, assemblies of papists and non-conformist." These were gatherings and prayer houses that were outside the established norms of the Church of England. Basically, the King would get more money in exchange for less religious freedom (for the country).

To put this in perspective, at the time, there was a growing awareness that the King's brother, the Duke of York, who was next in line to the throne, was a practicing Catholic. He openly took Holy Communion in a Roman Catholic Church and MPs were (again) seeing ghosts of the Gunpowder Plot and Bloody Mary's rein. They wanted spiritual assurances. So, the King nominally agreed to their terms and made some half-hearted declarations or statements restricting religious freedom to nonconformists and was eventually rewarded the new tax. Of course, the irony here is that a year or so later he borrowed the idea of "selling his religion" on a much grander scheme, but let's not get ahead of the story yet.

After much pleading and praying, in early May 1668, parliament finally approved a new tax in the amount of £310,000 to support and pay for the Navy. This tax would be levied on imported wine and liquor, with specific reference in the Act to the French and Spanish varieties, although any wine imported from abroad during a two-year period (June 1668–June 1670) would be subjected to new levies. In particular, wines imported from France would be charged a third of a shilling (4 pence [d]) per quart, whereas wines from Spain would be charged half a shilling (6d) per quart. Finally, spirits (other than wine) such as brandy or "strong water" would be charged a full shilling (12d) per quart. The Act specified that commissioners had the power to grant warrants to search cellars and warehouses and if necessary "in the case of resistance, to break open doors," to search for wines or liquors that might be concealed—and to then seize the offending cargo.

In addition to favoring domestic production, the fact that the number £310,000 appeared in the Act meant that somebody had estimated that between 6.2 million and 18 million quarts of liquor would be imported during the two-year period, which is of course is a very wide estimate. There was no guarantee that the new tax would generate this sum of money—and this gets to the heart of the risk when these sources of revenue were used as security for loans. Moreover even if it would materialize, the £310,000 sum of money paled in comparison with the £2 million to possibly £3 million in total that the King owed by this point. If (to make things look better) one focuses on the cumulative deficit from 1660 onward—not including any debts inherited from his father or prior to the Restoration—then by mid-1668 the total stood at between £700,000 and £800,000 depending on the assumed interest rate on debt and borrowing.

But every pound was helpful and it was a step in the right direction. The commission got to work implementing the Act. With some money having finally been approved, parliament was then prorogued or dismissed until October of the following year. But in an interesting follow-up to the new Act, the Treasury commissioners launched a lively discussion over how to monetize the tax. The income from "wines, spirits and strong waters" would trickle in over two years, but the cash was needed immediately.

The *CTB* reveals an interesting discussion (mid-May) in which the Treasury Board sought legal advice on whether the £310,000 allotted was a strict limit (upper bound) or only an estimate. They optimistically wondered, what if the levy on imported wine yielded more than £310,000 during the two-year period covered by the Act? Would the King be entitled to the shillings per quart regardless of how much liquor was imported? They also debated the extent to which they could farm out or borrow against this (new) tax, and whether the £310,000 accounted for the 6% interest that the Treasury or Exchequer would have to pay on any borrowing.

On May 20, one enterprising merchant came to the meeting of the Treasury commissioners and offered to immediately lend £50,000 against the security of the supply and to be repaid in order once a total of £70,000 had been received. It's unclear whether this implied he would receive an additional £20,000 for his trouble, or whether the £70,000 was the trigger (arrival) that would generate a repayment of £50,000 plus interest. Meanwhile, representatives of the Vintner's Company came with a proposal to collect the levy or tax themselves—far more cheaply than any advance or loan—since they have the "ancient power" to search cellars and root out any malfeasance.

For the record, when the dust eventually settled on the liquor tax (and the Act expired in 1670), approximately £50,000 less than the estimated £310,000 had been generated. Like most other sources of the King's ordinary revenue, the original *expected* yield fell far short of the *realized* yield and no doubt there was another £50,000 hole in the budget.

And so, toward the end of the year 1668, the King's attention was focused on yet another way to improve his financial situation, and that was via a union of England with Scotland, which, recall, was the land of his grandfather King James, and much of the Stuart clan. And, although the motivation was political, the financial angle was never far behind. The King sent his primary minister responsible for Scotland and oldest member of the cabal, the Earl of Lauderdale, to Edinburgh to handle the negotiations. But the months progressed with little to show and the diplomatic efforts to unify both under one flag withered under the watch of commissioners who couldn't see eye to eye. Indeed, it wasn't until 30 years later during the reign of Queen Anne in 1706 that the Act of Union was finalized and the two countries were finally brought together, with one parliament of Great Britain located in the Palace of Westminster.

So, as 1668 Christmas celebrations were taking place at court—and perhaps the courtiers were enjoying Isaac Newton's recently discovered reflecting telescope—King Charles II's gaze shifted to another country to help with his financial challenges, namely his cousin Louis XIV's France.

Selling Your Religion at Dover

The period from 1669 to 1671 was unique in the history of the seventeenth century because it was the only three years in which there were no wars being fought in Europe. The other 97 years had some conflict taking place somewhere.[11] Perhaps the rare calm starting in 1669 allowed King Charles II to grasp that his monetary problems would never be resolved by a suddenly generous English parliament or the brilliant efficiency (i.e. budget cuts and austerity) overseen by George Downing. The many commissions and official reports tabled in parliament since the second Anglo-Dutch war had ended in the summer of 1667 all concluded the same thing. The King's regular revenue yield (of approximately £900,000) was simply not enough to pay off the budgeted expenditures (of approximately £1,200,000). Parliament in turn believed that the King was simply mismanaging his resources and the budget gap was his fault. The £9 "in" versus £12 "out" numbers didn't even include the growing tally of interest and debt payments that had accumulated since the beginning of the Restoration, which I discussed at length in Chap. 4. The King's financial situation was dire and the outlook was hopeless.

Alas, sometime in the winter or early spring of 1669, the King came to the solemn realization that the only possible solution to his problems would

---

[11] My source for this claim is Grayling (2016).

be to *sell* something vast and cherished. He would have to locate something far more valuable than the City of Bombay or the few pounds of gold it had generated. And what he decided to sell this time around ended up changing the course of English and European history. King Charles II made the decisions to sell his personal religious beliefs and convictions to the highest bidder. And the man with the deepest pockets for such an unconventional purchase was his first cousin, the Catholic King of France, Louis XIV.

So, King Charles II offered to change (or sell) his religion and publicly profess to be a Catholic and attend mass at a Catholic Church—all for the right price of course.

Now, this was an absolutely preposterous undertaking, considering that he was the official head of the Church of England and king of a Protestant country. England was an 85% Protestant nation that was still reeling from the trauma created by the civil war's religious turmoil and persecutions. Recall that King Charles I had lost his head to Oliver Cromwell and his band of Puritans in 1649. Catholics were widely (and erroneously) blamed for setting the Great Fire of London in September 1665 and loud cries of "no popery" could still be heard in the streets whenever the masses were frustrated. The national holiday on November 5 was still memorialized and celebrated every year, which is when the (Catholic) Guy Fawkes tried to blow up the House of Lords during the reign of King James I, grandfather of King Charles II. Effigies of the Pope were paraded every year through the streets and cities all across England. Nobody had ever forgotten that the Catholic Pope had excommunicated their beloved Queen Elizabeth I, ostensibly for being a Protestant heretic.

But despite all this emotional and national baggage, King Charles II decided sometime in early 1669 that he would offer King Louis XIV the most astonishing business deal of the century. One can only imagine the shock the French king must have experienced when the top-secret letter arrived at his Palace of Versailles.

In this letter Charles offered to *eventually* profess the Catholic faith—and denounce the official Anglican or Protestant state religion—in exchange for an *immediate* payment of £200,000 in cold hard cash. Moreover, in addition to offering to "switch sides" on the religious front, Charles also proposed to join forces with the French in a (future, to be named) war against the Protestant Dutch Republic. Recall that this was while England was openly and officially part of the so-called Triple Alliance with (Protestant) Sweden and the Dutch. The duplicity of it all was simply breathtaking. Charles knew that Louis wanted to (eventually) fight the

Dutch and would also welcome an expansion of the Catholic faith. He also knew that Louis had the budget for both.

But the £200,000 wasn't all he requested. The promised war—against the Dutch—would cost King Louis XIV an additional £1,000,000 before the war, plus £600,000 per year until the war ended plus ships, guns, armaments and a few port cities in Europe. The £200,000 cash payment—for the religious conversion—would be due immediately and Charles promised or assured Louis that he would publicly announce his conversion "when the time was right."

Now, the value of religion isn't absolute or determined by God and King Louis pushed back on the price tag. He attempted to bargain down the numbers and terms with carefully measured counterproposals. This went back and forth (in highly secret communications) between England and France for almost a year until the deal was actually consummated. In the end, Charles agreed to a price of £160,000 (which today would be equivalent to £16 million) to profess his Catholicism and also committed to supply 60 warships and 4000 infantry to join the French against the Dutch. The timeline for all this activity was rather loose, but the money would flow to Charles just as soon as the agreement was signed. In fact, the person who was served as the go-between was Charles' younger sister Minette (aka Madame), who was living in France at the time and married to King Louis XIV's younger brother.

Now, whether or not King Charles II had any intention of proclaiming himself a Catholic has been debated for centuries. Some historians claim that he actually did convert on his deathbed, but 15 years later, in 1685. Others claim this was all part of his pragmatic and cynical attempts to raise new money and align himself with the most powerful monarch in Europe, King Louis XIV. Regardless of his motives and true beliefs, he most certainly did not announce publicly that he was no longer Protestant anytime within the decade of the 1670s. He did uphold the other part of the deal though, which was to (again) declare war on the Dutch, and I'll get to that critical episode in a moment.

Charles' brother James, who apparently knew about the secret deal and was himself an exceedingly open Catholic, wrote in his memoirs that Charles was indeed sincere about the religious epiphany as early as January 1669. James wrote of a moving story in which sometime before the secret negotiations with France began, Charles called his trusted (Catholic) advisors Clifford and Arlington together. With them, he professed his devotion to the true Catholic faith (teary eyed, according to James).

Either way, King Charles II was playing the lead in a Shakespearean play—no different from his actress mistress at the time, Nell Gwyn—and deserving of a modern-day Tony or Oscar award. Even if Charles was not sincere, the fact remains that he was taking an enormous risk if anyone (Catholic or Protestant) ever found out about this sale. This is why the King and his few trusted cronies took extreme cautions to ensure that nobody learned the details of the deal, and this was achieved by creating a parallel (fake or simulated) agreement with France that said nothing of religion or wars.

Charles announced the existence of the secret agreement with Louis to his close and trusted advisors (Clifford and Arlington, but not Buckingham, Shaftesbury or Lauderdale) in December 1669. The agreement was then taken to France in March 1670 and was finally signed by representatives of both sides on May 22, 1670 in the port city of Dover. It is therefore known to history as the Secret Treaty of Dover.[12]

As soon as this agreement was signed and the English king's sister returned to France from Dover with the paperwork, King Charles began the official cover-up. He sent the (unknowing) Duke of Buckingham to France to formally negotiate a treaty with King Louis XIV. This particular agreement talked about cooperation and alignments and was signed by all five members of the cabal—quite publicly and with much fanfare—on December 21, 1670. That treaty was really a sham and Buckingham himself commented on how easy it was to negotiate with the French. Of course, everything had already been predetermined months ago.

The Treaty of Dover had two levels—like a painting with hidden layers—the public one and the private one. In the hidden or secret agreement France committed itself to support and underwrite Charles' deficit and (partially) solve his money problems once and for all. The only condition was that he would *eventually* profess the true faith—when the time was right.

It took over a century before the historian John Dalrymple discovered (in 1771) details of this strange and treacherous pact in the French archives. Needless to say, this finding caused quite a stir in the late eighteenth century and one can only imagine the political implications—for

---

[12] The source for most of the material in this section comes from Hutton (1986). Some say that the English were forced to make a treaty with the French, before the Dutch beat them to it.

the Stuarts as well as for the reputation of the monarchy—if this pact had been uncovered in the late seventeenth century.

Arguably, it is at this (Dover) inflection point that Charles' attitude and relationship to parliament, the Treasury commission and especially the bankers changed in a fundamental and irreversible way. Basically and quite frankly, in his mind he no longer needed them.

The key here is that when we try to understand why the King took the actions he did in late 1671 and early 1672—the decision to default and alienate the bankers on whom he had been so dependent for a decade—one can argue that the financial deal he struck with Louis XIV was the single most important political and financial factor.

Of course, the devil was in the details and not everything worked out exactly as King Charles II had planned. The 30 or so months between his initial outreach to France in the spring of 1669, the preparations for war with the Dutch and the formal decision to default on his debts in the late fall of 1671 included many tragedies and setbacks along the way. It was a not smooth path or a direct line to redemption. Ironically, the King's proper (ordinary) sources of revenue were actually starting to improve, although not anywhere nearly enough to cover his expenses.

As for the exact timeline, in early September 1669—for the record, three months after Samuel Pepys stopped writing his diary due to his deteriorating eyesight—the Queen Mother, Henrietta Marie, who had been residing in France ever since she fled London to escape the plague (and bronchitis) in 1665, died at the age of 59. That marked the end of an era.

The Catholic Queen Henrietta Marie, after whom the US State of Maryland is actually named, didn't have the best relationship with her eldest son Charles, but her death must have been a blow, nevertheless. The entire English court was put into official state mourning. The death left Charles (and the immediate Stuart family) with a younger brother James—Duke of York, who would eventually become King James II in 1685—and a dear sister Henrietta Anne, whom he lovingly called Minette. It was this same Minette who served as the (dangerous) liaison between her brother Charles and her brother-in-law Louis. To cement and finalize matters, in June 1670, she traveled to the English port city of Dover to meet her brother—for the first time since the Restoration—and to oversee the signing of the appropriately named Treaty of Dover. Charles' trip to Dover in May 1670 was to officially meet his sister, whom he had not seen in almost a decade, but unofficially, it was to sign the treaty. This is exactly how he managed to pull it off. It was an innocent family reunion.

Alas, when she returned to France from Dover in mid-June 1670, she suffered some sort of stomach ailment—some say she was actually poisoned by her jealous, unbalanced and sadistic husband—and then died a few days afterward. When the news reached her brother in England, soon after he had returned from Dover, the King was simply inconsolable. He shut himself up for days and refused to be comforted. He had lost his sister—the single person with whom he was the closest—less than a year after losing his mother. King Charles II's many biographers all write that he was never the same after that loss. Dover changed him on many levels.

But he soldiered ahead with the provisions and commitments—perhaps in memory of his beloved sister—and by early 1671 the King was wholly dedicated to fulfilling his obligation under the treaty. He was getting ready to provoke yet another conflict with the Dutch and all he needed was an excuse. The preparations were evident to all—and King Louis XIV expected nothing less. After all, he was paying for it. War was in the air. Needless to say, the (secret) money the French were sending Charles to pay for his "religious conversion" was most certainly *not* being received at the Exchequer or passing through the hands of George Downing and his Treasury commissioners. The money was going directly to King Charles.

Prelude to the De(fault)

How things stood towards the end of December 1671. The King's cumulative deficit from the beginning of the Restoration in 1660 added to between £1.1 million and £1.3 million in debt. That range is based on the revenue and expenditure data I presented and calculated in Chap. 4. The budget deficits were financed by short-term loans, primarily from the city's goldsmith-bankers in the form of CTOs. In fact, the total outstanding debt was likely in the range of £2.0–£2.5 million if financial obligations prior to the Restoration were added to the tally. That number is consistent with estimates quoted by Clifford and Downing at various parliamentary meetings and appears in the detailed analysis by Dr. William Shaw in 1904. Either way, the underlying treasury order system—which I described in Chap. 5—was such that by late 1671 the King was enjoying (i.e. spending) tax revenue that would only be received at the Exchequer in another 12–18 months. In other words, the next year and a half of revenue belonged to someone else, namely the holders of the CTOs. That, in a nutshell, was the financial situation.

On the political side the King had just signed a (secret) treaty with France that obligated him to wage war on the Dutch, yet again. The prior war (known as the second Anglo-Dutch war) had ended in June 1667, soon after the military embarrassment known simply as "Chatham." Four years later England (or at least the King) was ready for a rematch. In addition to his legal commitment to France, the King also hoped that a resounding victory at sea—against the economically powerful, dominant and rich Dutch—would lead to commercial prosperity and greater financial security for England. And although there were no specific timelines imposed by the French King and master puppeteer Louis XIV, naval engagements required advanced preparation. Those wouldn't have been cheap either. Yes, the financial subsidies King Charles II was receiving from the French would cover some of those expenses (eventually), but there was a cash-flow imbalance upfront. In sum, all the actors were in place and the stage was now set for an historic debt crisis. The only items still missing were some matchsticks and someone to light the fire.

Matchsticks Versus Tally Sticks

The first indications that a financial calamity was imminent came in late September or possibly early October 1671. In terms of social context and what else was going on, this was two months after—the very odd and sensationalized story in which—King Charles II had pardoned Colonel Blood for attempting to steal[13] the crown jewels. It was two months before the King's mistress Nell Gwyn gave birth to his illegitimate child.

The exact date of what follows isn't known precisely. What we do know is that the King and his cabal of privy counselors (discretely) approached the main financiers and goldsmith-bankers at Lombard Street. These were notables like Robert Viner and Edward Blackwell, and the King and his cabal officially requested a very large sum of money (i.e. a loan) to help outfit a fleet of 60 ships that were to sail sometime in the spring. Recall from the terms of the Treaty of Dover that King Charles II had signed, he was obligated to contribute these ships and join France in the war against the Dutch. And, again, although King Louis XIV had committed money to King Charles II, it clearly wasn't enough, or perhaps the funds were squandered on other expenditures.

---

[13] See Hutchsinson (2016) for a recent telling of the story.

Either way, what is for certain is that the King approached the bankers for (yet) more money.

Financial historians do not know—and the records do not indicate—the exact sum of money that was requested at that critical meeting (hundreds of thousands? Millions of pounds?), but it must have been sizeable. It's also not clear whether the requested loan would be backed by a particular source of tax revenue and would thus be part of Downing's treasury order system, or whether it would be a new stand-alone debt such as the alternative methods of borrowing described in Chap. 5. The interest rate offered to the bankers is also unknown. Perhaps the contract negotiations never reached that stage. The details are sparse.

What we do know about the encounter—from a single letter that has been preserved in the British Library[14] and written by a Richard Langhorne to Lord Hatton—is that the bankers outright refused to advance any more funds or money to His Majesty, with all due respect of course. The answer was a flat-out no.

Apparently, sometime in October 1671, the English goldsmith-bankers—with millions of pounds of CTOs on their balance sheets—decided that enough was enough. In their professional opinion, committing any more funds to His Majesty was simply too risky. Perhaps they were weary of throwing good money after what they perceived was bad money? Or maybe they prudently examined the King's financial situation, books and financial statements—not knowing about the secret money flowing from King Louis XIV—and determined that his business model was untenable. In the language of modern financial risk management, one would say that they determined that allocating any more capital to that particular trade would breach their internal "risk budget" limits.

Here is the bottom line. We don't know their motives for declining the investment, but we certainly know the aftermath. One can only speculate if these same goldsmith-bankers would have made a different decision at the time, knowing what would unfold six weeks later. Either way, a resounding no was the symbolic matchstick struck in late 1671. The red phosphorous was about to turn white and ignite.

---

[14] Manuscript 29553, folio 358, and reproduced in Browning (1966). Note that the author of the letter, Langhorne, was apparently an important and well-known Catholic, which might have clouded (slightly) his recollection of the matter.

Alternative Facts and Faults

According to Langhorne's letter,[15] the King's counselors—after some internal debate—decided then and there to "stop all payments" from the Exchequer to the bankers. Was this revenge? Payback? Or was it an inevitable by-product? Either way, George Downing's elegant and efficient treasury order system was about to be thrown out the window. The rest, as they say, is history. And although there are many contemporary sources and descriptions of the aftermath of the default, the same Richard Langham wrote that the impact was "greater than in the Chatham business" when the Dutch sailed up the Medway in June 1667 and towed away the HMS *Royal Charles*. But that is just one single account or metaphor of the immediate result. I'll discuss the public reaction from a variety of authors and perspectives later on, but first let's review the mechanics of what a "stop" really meant and how it was implemented in practice.

First, let me be clear that King Charles II didn't physically go to the Exchequer down the street from his palace at Whitehall and seize gold or silver coins from the goldsmith-bankers' account or safety deposit box. That's a medieval view of kings, money and finances. I say this because some erroneous and highly exaggerated accounts have (perhaps deliberately) obfuscated the events surrounding January 1672 with an episode which took place decades earlier. That is what I described in Chap. 3, when the King's father (Charles I) temporarily took control of the mint or vault in the Tower of London. In fact, some writers—dare we call them historians—in the nineteenth century asserted that the "stop" was an outright act of thievery. For example, the famed author Walter Bagehot, writing[16] (in 1873) in his book *Lombard Street*, claimed that this event was a "monstrous robbery" and the "credit of the Stuart government never recovered." That was his opinion two centuries after the episode.

Another description of what took place in early January 1672 was offered in a series of high-profile lectures[17] delivered by the Earl of Iddesleigh in 1865. He claimed and then wrote that the "stop" was effectively an "impounding of a million and a quarter of money from the goldsmiths" which they had placed for safekeeping in the Exchequer. Iddesleigh goes on to say that the funds were immediately used to attack the Dutch fleet.

---

[15] Dated January 6, 1672.
[16] Page 93.
[17] Published in Iddesleigh (1887), p. 252.

It's worth noting that these exaggerated narratives appeared during the Victorian era in the late nineteenth century, a period which perhaps was more hostile to the loose moral standards of the Stuart era. These embellished versions of what happened likely caused the next generation of writers and historians (in the early twentieth century) to "swing the pendulum" in the other direction and downplay the story, or certainly the King's role in all of it.

For example, Dr. William Shaw—who, recall, was the modern-day editor of the *CTB*—wrote the following in 1904, in the introduction to his masterwork: "Misrepresentation arose first at the hand of Whig politicians, followed therein by Whig historians." Recall that Whigs were a political party or faction opposed to the Tories and (absolute) monarchy. As a general rule, a Whig would have welcomed any story or tale that would malign King Charles II's reign. This is why Shaw went on to write: "It has been reserved for modern writers to improve such misrepresentation by the most absurd and unhistorical innuendos." And as you just saw in the description by Iddesleigh and Bagehot, "In its grossest form the modern version of the myth states that the bankers had been in the habit of depositing in the Exchequer cash balances or reserves for safe-keeping and that Charles II simply seized upon these deposits." Dr. Shaw then concludes that "the inference is invariably drawn that Charles profited instantly by the amount of the bankers' assignments which were stopped." Ok, well, here Dr. Shaw might be pushing it. What is the definition of the phrase "profit instantly"?

Redirect the Financial Plumbing

So much for what didn't happen. Let's move on to what actually took place. From here on I'll rely on the descriptions provided by noted historians Keith Horsefield (writing in 1982) and Henry Roseveare (writing in 1991), who can't be accused of sympathy to either seventeenth-century Whigs or Tories. Indeed, the process of stopping the Exchequer was more subtle (and perhaps cleverer) than robbing a bank, although the long-term impact was just as devastating.

By this point the reader should be quite familiar and appreciate how the CTO system worked and how it was tied to anticipated revenues. As these payments were arriving into the Exchequer the cash was *supposed* to be immediately redirected or transferred to the holder of the numbered CTO to which it was linked. The announcements in the *London Gazette* since 1667 attest to the integrity and efficiency of the process. Even the CTOs that were of the "fictitious" design (fi-CTOs) and not linked to a particular revenue source were also designed to be paid in order. Order #101 was paid after #100 and so on. That was Downing's innovation, or at least what he is known for.

What was announced in January 1672—and I'll get to the pomp and circumstance around the text in the next section—is that the incoming revenue was to be *redirected* to other sources and not used to redeem the treasury orders. Instead of paying the current holders of the CTOs, or those to whom they had been assigned, the Exchequer was given strict orders to divert the funds to other departments and pay immediate bills for goods, not bankers.

So, in some sense—and from a cash flow or a monetary point of view—nothing really happened immediately. Perhaps Dr. Shaw (quoted earlier) had a point. One can think of it as rewiring the cables in a house and then waiting a while to turn on the electricity. Or perhaps the proper analogy is the mouth of a tunnel with a very small trickle of traffic that was suddenly uprooted in the middle of the night and reconnected to a completely different highway. Yes, the immediate impact was that a few disoriented drivers (tax packets) found themselves arriving in a completely different city. But as soon as the announcement was made public and everyone knew that the Exchequer's pipes had just been redirected, the financial "inferno" broke loose. From that point onward, once a tax packet came in through the door, instead of announcing the arrival in the *London Gazette*, Downing's number was simply ignored. The treasury orders weren't paid.

On Thursday, December 14, 1671, an announcement appeared in the *London Gazette* that order #660 was now ready to be paid at the Exchequer. Please hurry up and collect your money. Like the many other such announcements that had appeared during the prior six years, this particular treasury order was secured against the hearth tax, which, recall from Chap. 4, was one of the King's ordinary sources of revenue. To be honest, it was just another day for the printers at the *London Gazette*. The prior week, the play *The Rehearsal*, written by the Duke of Buckingham, had been performed at Theatre Royal on Drury Lane and enjoyed by many in the royal entourage. The King's favorite mistress (at the time) Nell Gwyn would give birth a week later to her second son, called James. Those were happy times. But what set this day in December apart—and only became known a few weeks later—is that it was the last day when treasury orders were paid by the Exchequer. That was the finale or last act of the last scene. Sir George Downing's system and the innovation of government finances during the Restoration and the late 1660s came to a crashing end with order #660. *And then ladies and gentlemen, the King defaulted.*[18]

Was Downing Down?

Where was the financial architect Sir George when all his hard-earned work was thrown into turmoil? Well, in early October 1671—just as the rumblings and tremors were starting to be felt—he was effectively removed as secretary of the Treasury commission. Did his boss, the King, and the Treasury commissioners know something that he didn't? He was immediately replaced by Sir Robert Howard, a man whose skill would never match his predecessor. In fact, Dr. William Shaw, the archivist and historian, would bitterly complain over two centuries later that "this created a deplorable break in the treasury records." Much to the dismay of modern financial historians, the eminent Sir George Downing was sent to the United Provinces (the Dutch) to ostensibly "rattle their cage" and set the stage for a war. This was the war which King Charles II would provoke and declare just a few months later, as per the terms of the Secret Treaty of Dover. Sir George Downing left the country and was (effectively) unreachable.

And while speculation might be futile and pointless, it is hard to imagine that the professional (puritanical) and organizational champion Sir George Downing would have stood by quietly—in late December 1671—and watched his meticulous wall of orders come tumbling down. Poignantly, at the time, he probably had no knowledge of these events and decisions, since he was safely tucked away in The Hague.

Perhaps this is one of the great ironies of financial history and a lesson to future defaulters everywhere. Before you shaft your creditors and create deliberate chaos, send your most efficient bookkeepers and accountants on a long vacation to Europe.

---

[18] In fact, there is an argument to be made that the *Day the King Defaulted* was actually on December 18, 1671, although I will discuss the exact timing and calendar dates competing for anniversary mentions, later on.

Whose Idea, Exactly?

According to historians and authors such as K. D. Haley, the idea of "stopping" the Exchequer was considered well before the bankers turned their financial back on the King and refused him any more loans in early October 1671. The "no" might not have been a real match. Shaftesbury wrote in his personal notes—after the event, of course—that the idea was considered repeatedly and many years earlier. According to Shaftesbury, sometime in July or August 1671, Clifford was very close to formally suggesting this to members of the privy council—the "stop" would have taken place six months earlier—but Shaftesbury managed to talk him out of the foolishness. Or at least so he claimed. It does seem from Clifford's personal notes in 1667—well before the Treasury was even put into commission and Downing was made secretary—that Clifford himself had studied precedents from the reigns of King Edward II in the fourteenth century and Queen Elizabeth in the sixteenth century.

Then again, some—like historian Laurence Echard, writing in the 1720s—laid the blame for the (idea of) the "stop" at the feet of Lord Shaftesbury and claimed that he suggested this to Clifford as a solution to the King's financial troubles during an evening of heavy drinking. The moral of the story was, perhaps, that only two drunkards could honestly believe this to be a good idea. Likewise, in his treatise on English history, Bishop Gilbert Burnet, writing in the 1690s, also laid the blame squarely at the feet of Lord Shaftesbury. Burnet wrote unequivocally when describing the events and aftermath: "The Earl of Shaftesbury was the chief man in this advice."

Trading on Early and Inside Information

Now, whether or not the blame for the idea should be assigned to Clifford or Shaftesbury with his extensive financial ties is not really a matter of extreme importance. The jury's verdict leans toward Clifford. But the fact is that the privy council and all members of the cabal accepted the plan and acted on the idea. They claimed that nobody could come up with a better or alternative plan. Rather, the more interesting issue is the following question. Did either of them or any other members of King Charles' inner circle—knowing this was being debated and was in the cards—personally benefit from the "stop"? Well, the answer to that question seems quite unequivocal. Shaftesbury had inside information—that is, knew about the "stop" before it was announced and acted upon it, profitably and decisively.

According to his (mostly sympathetic) biographer,[19] starting in early October 1671 just as the London bankers had said no to any more loans, Shaftesbury began to unload and sell the treasury orders and assignments he personally held. Moreover, he also withdrew cash deposits from various goldsmith-bankers with whom he had business dealings. Think of it as a bank run with one person in the queue, Shaftesbury. Then, he took all this cash and used the capital to purchase land around England, an investment that would likely appreciate if and when financial assets melted down. This took place over a period of two months until early December 1671, discretely and with little apology or explanation. By Christmas time, just a few days before the formal announcement, he had—in the language of modern capital markets—unloaded all his bonds.

Again, his biographer K. D. Haley found no fault in this front running of treasury orders and claimed that the norms of the times allowed it. It was acceptable and perfectly standard to act on this information. In Shaftesbury's mind, this didn't make him culpable—although one can certainly appreciate that when people eventually found out (and eventually they did), he was blamed. When looking for who committed a financial crime, motive, ability and smoking gun were all in Shaftesbury's possession.

To be fair, Shaftesbury wasn't the only person who knew (and probably acted) on the information. John Evelyn noted in his diary[20] that he had confidentially been told about the "stop" a few days—but not months—earlier, by Thomas Clifford. Evelyn also wrote that some have pretended or claimed that the idea for the suspension of payments out of the Exchequer was Shaftesbury's idea, but he personally knew it was Clifford.

In sum, despite a few claims to the contrary, modern historians have in fact concluded that although Shaftesbury—and perhaps even Lauderdale—profited from the "stop," it was Clifford's idea. On a side note, yet another reason why it makes sense to ascribe the move against the bankers to Clifford was his personal religious beliefs. Recall that Clifford was a Roman Catholic—one of the few of them in positions of power—and the Catholic Church still held very negative views on charging and paying interest. I discussed this in Chap. 3.

---

[19] See Haley (1968), p. 294.
[20] Entry for March 12, 1672.

Could Catholic doctrine have been part of the deliberations? I would suggest that the "stop" was more than simply a financial decision or attempt to pacify the country. It had religious and moral undertones as well. For example, in the immediate aftermath of the "stop"—as the public was grappling with the concept of shirking financial obligations and commitments made to bankers—the framing of the crisis took on a moral dimension. Were the bankers charging too much interest? I have already described in Chap. 5 how Lord Shaftesbury—who initially was opposed to the action and then traded on it—eventually came around to the notion that implied interest rates were excessive. The legal rate for private commercial loans was 6%, which was the rate on the treasury orders. But the effective rate for loans to government (after the discounting) was much higher.

Also it appears that when Lord Shaftesbury wrote to John Locke that bankers were profiting at the expense of the King, the King himself was ordering inspections of the bankers' and scriveners' records. For example, the personal letters of Robert Clayton—a prominent London scrivener and banker in the 1660s and 1670s—indicate that in early 1672 a Sergeant Pemberton was looking for evidence of usury and had (for lack of a better word) subpoenaed his banking records. Clayton wrote that no evidence was found of usury in his ledgers (lucky for him), although perhaps the scriveners were adept at hiding the true[21] rate. It's unclear whether the "stop" was part of a concerted war on interest or whether it was used as an excuse afterward, but it was part of the dialogue and narrative.

The bankers weren't bailed out because they had profited at the expense of the country. Indeed, many of the bankers had to request personal pardons from the King for charging usurious interest rates. I'll get to that particular drama once we clear up the financial details. With the possibilities of the *why*, *when* and *how* behind us, in the next section, I'll move on to the official announcements and the immediate aftermath.

Tuesday, January 2, 1672

January 2, 1672 was a Tuesday in England, and although New Year wasn't celebrated according to the Julian calendar, it was the first day of work after a break for the Christmas holiday. For the three days of Tuesday (January2), Wednesday (January3) and Thursday (January 4), the minutes

---

[21] See Melton (1986), pp. 120–222, for more on this.

from the meeting of the Treasury commissioners, which are summarized in the *CTB*, are replete with the usual mundane items. A customs officer at Dover was ordered to send a shipment of private goods that had arrived from France to Whitehall to determine the proper tax rate. Another item involved a request to the King to provide five soldiers to accompany a large sum of money from Liverpool to the excise office in London. Late on Thursday a letter was sent to the Archbishop of York inquiring about "first fruits and tenths," which was a tax clergy had to pay, which in his case was overdue. These were the usual sort of activities and discourse that took place in the meetings and there was no indication of what was to happen during the coming weekend (Figs. 6.1 and 6.2).

The entry in the *CTB* minutes for Friday, January 5, 1672, is quite brief but extremely ominous. It starts with, "All businesses that were to be heard this day to be adjourned till Tuesday morning," and then it states: "His Royal Highness the Duke of York, Prince Rupert, the Lord Keeper, Duke of Monmouth, Duke of Buckingham, Duke of Ormonde, Earl of Lauderdale, Lord Arlington, Lord Shaftesbury, Treasurer of the Household, Secretary Trevor, Sir John Duncombe, Sir R. Long, Sir Robert Viner, Alderman Backwell, Mr. Meynell, Mr. Lyndsy, Mr. Snow, Mr. Portman, and other bankers concerned are to attend at the Treasury on Sunday, 7th of January, at four in the afternoon." Most of these are names you should be able to recognize by this point in the narrative.

And that was the last entry for the day (and the week) in the *CTB*. No other business was conducted, discussed or mentioned. Instead, all the bankers and financiers were told to show up on the Lord's Day at a hastily arranged meeting at the offices of the Treasury. From the records of the *CTB* one would be hard-pressed to appreciate what exactly was unfolding. There certainly was no mention of "stops" or defaults. But in fact, the die had been cast and the *CTB* for Friday, January 5, contains the entry which announces the "stop" itself. It is a four-page document dated Tuesday, January 2. A copy is stored in the British Library and is reproduced in the following pages. I will quote a few of the key passages. The document starts off with a long list of dignitaries—members of the King's privy council and others—who were either in attendance or endorsed the decision. Later on in this chapter, I'll return to the issue of Tuesday, January 2 versus Friday, January 5 and the precise dating of the "day" the King defaulted. The advertisement of the text itself appeared in the *London Gazette* in the issue dated Thursday, January 4 to Monday, January 8. You will soon learn why the precise dating really does matter.

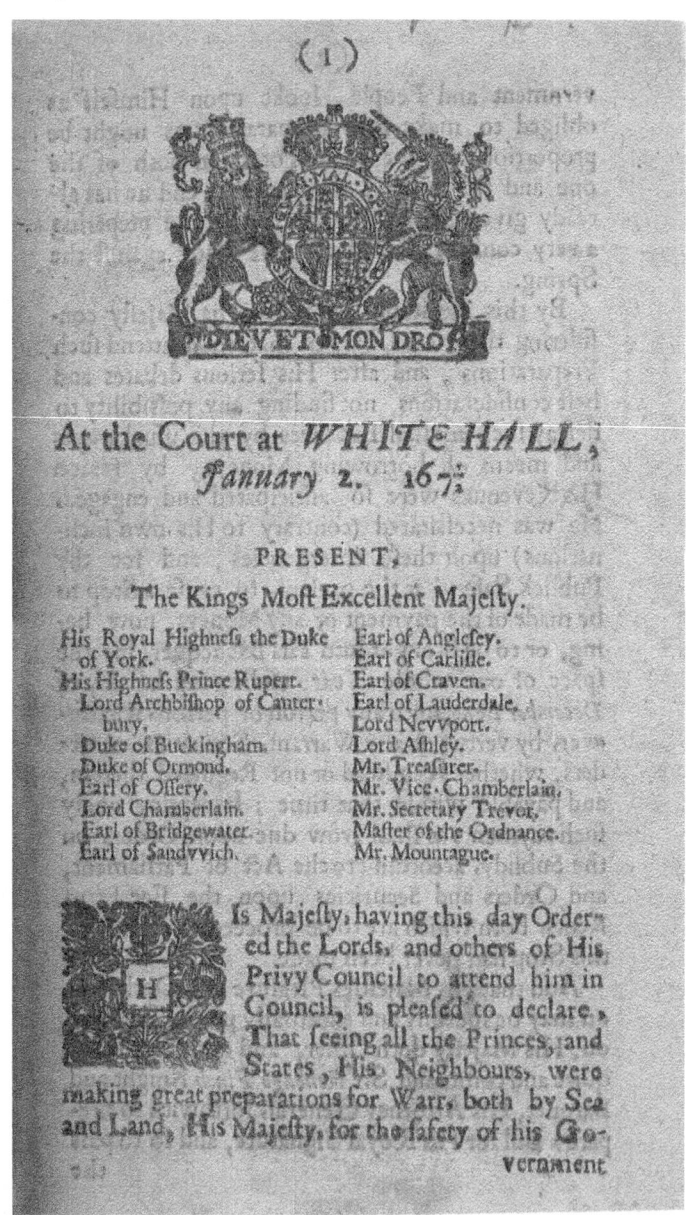

Fig. 6.1 Announcing the Stop of the Exchequer 1/4. Permission granted by the British Library. Item 8132.h2

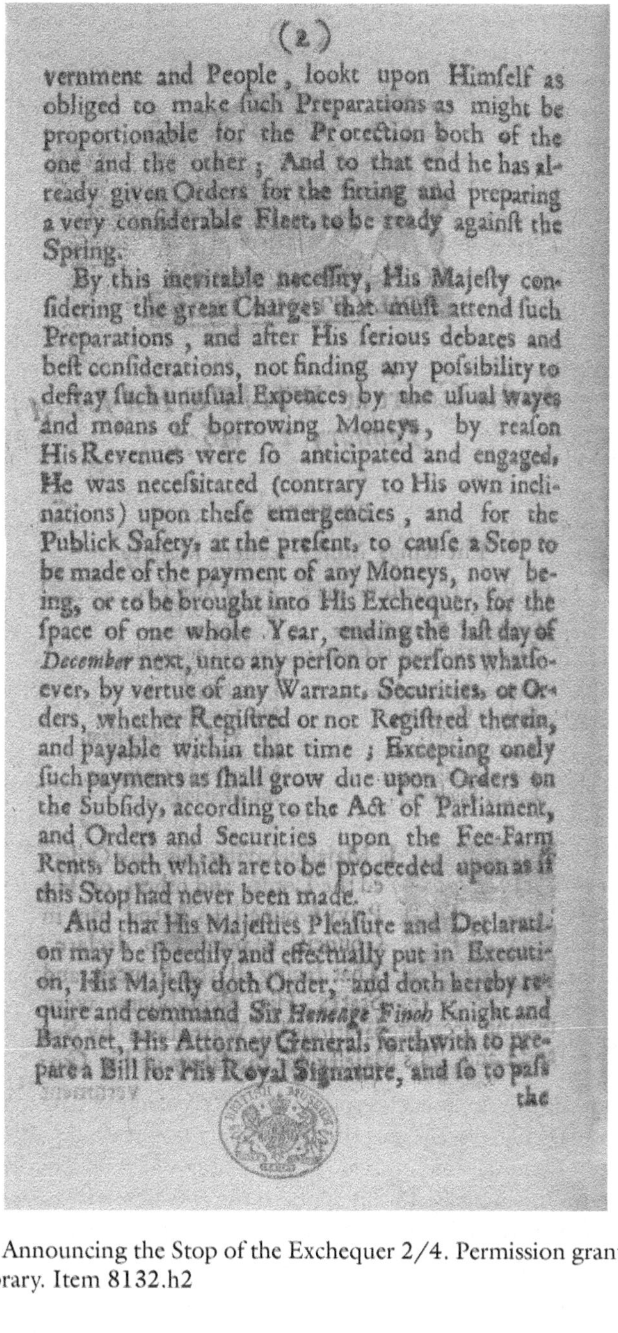

(2)

vernment and People, lookt upon Himself as obliged to make such Preparations as might be proportionable for the Protection both of the one and the other; And to that end he has already given Orders for the fitting and preparing a very considerable Fleet, to be ready against the Spring.

By this inevitable necessity, His Majesty considering the great Charges that must attend such Preparations, and after His serious debates and best considerations, not finding any possibility to defray such unusual Expences by the usual wayes and means of borrowing Moneys, by reason His Revenues were so anticipated and engaged, He was necessitated (contrary to His own inclinations) upon these emergencies, and for the Publick Safety, at the present, to cause a Stop to be made of the payment of any Moneys, now being, or to be brought into His Exchequer, for the space of one whole Year, ending the last day of *December* next, unto any person or persons whatsoever, by vertue of any Warrant, Securities, or Orders, whether Registred or not Registred therein, and payable within that time; Excepting onely such payments as shall grow due upon Orders on the Subsidy, according to the Act of Parliament, and Orders and Securities upon the Fee-Farm Rents, both which are to be proceeded upon as if this Stop had never been made.

And that His Majesties Pleasure and Declaration may be speedily and effectually put in Execution, His Majesty doth Order, and doth hereby require and command Sir *Heneage Finch* Knight and Baronet, His Attorney Generals forthwith to prepare a Bill for His Royal Signature, and so to pass the

Fig. 6.2 Announcing the Stop of the Exchequer 2/4. Permission granted by the British Library. Item 8132.h2

The document opens in the finest of modern PR traditions with a very positive message about how "His Majesty is pleased to declare" that after observing that England's neighbors were making preparations for war on both sea and land, "His Majesty looked upon himself" to make similar preparations for the "protection both of one and the other" and that his people should rest assured that "he has already given orders" for the fitting of a considerable fleet that would be ready in the spring (of 1672). Coincidentally, these plans and the date are consistent with the earlier mentioned story in which the goldsmith-bankers refused to advance a loan to His Majesty to help prepare the fleet.

After the positive and uplifting message of the first paragraph, the notice continues to discuss that after "best considerations" and "serious debates" on how to defray these costs, the King had been unable to borrow the required money because his "revenues were so anticipated and engaged." We, of course, know exactly what this meant. He had mortgaged 12–18 months' worth of tax revenue and that income—which would soon be arriving at the Exchequer—couldn't be used for anything other than paying back the treasury orders. Therefore, the King was "necessitated contrary to his own inclinations upon these emergencies and for the public safety at the present" to—and here it comes—"cause a stop to be made of the payment of any money now being or to be brought into his exchequer for the space of one whole year ending the last day of December next." The released or free funds, which were no longer being used to pay maturing treasury orders, would then be available to pay for the fleet, cover the expenses of war and so on. The announcement did exempt from the "stop" loans that were backed by the subsidy (aka special taxes) from Acts of parliament as well as loans that were backed by fee "farm rents." Both of those were to proceed "as if this stop had never been made" (Fig. 6.3).

At this point it's worth pausing to remind readers that CTOs could be backed by specific sources of revenue—such as customs or excise or hearth taxes—or by special taxes voted from time to time by Acts of parliament. To be clear, the Stop of the Exchequer was limited to the former only. The default was on the *hereditary* revenue of the King, which was explained in Chap. 4, and didn't apply to the other source of revenue that made up the King's personal finances, the so-called *parliamentary* revenue. Also, revenue that had been *farmed*, which was also explained in Chap. 4, was not affected. Of course, the announcement did apply to the fi-CTOs that weren't backed by any pre-specified source of tax revenue, other than a general promise to

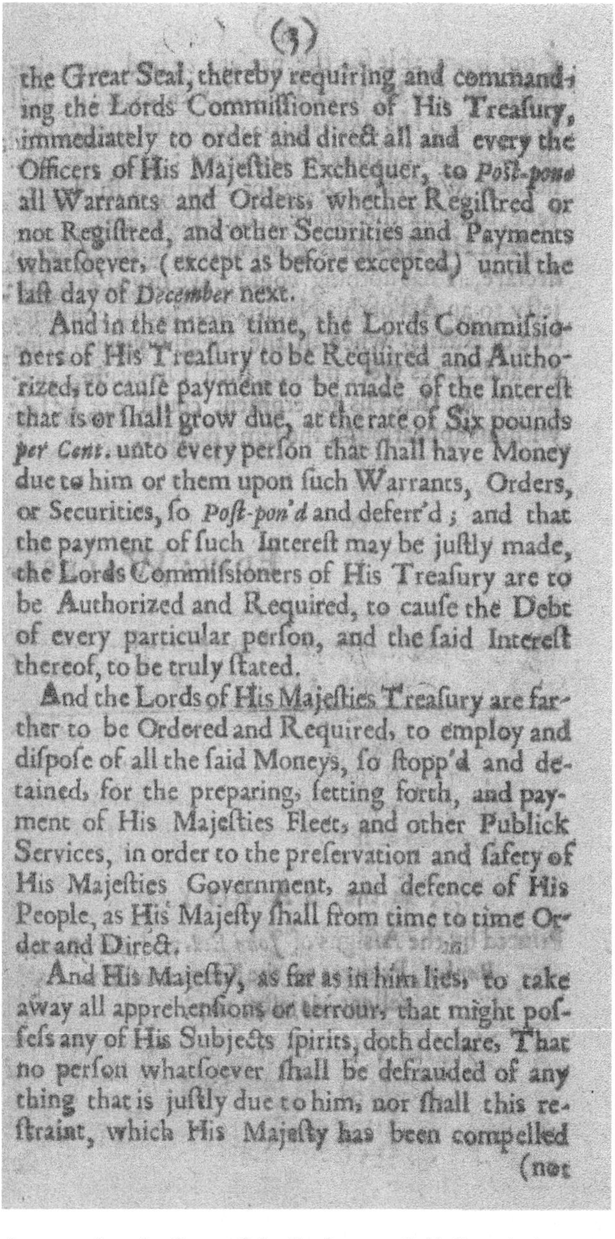

(3)

the Great Seal, thereby requiring and commanding the Lords Commissioners of His Treasury, immediately to order and direct all and every the Officers of His Majesties Exchequer, to *Post-pone* all Warrants and Orders, whether Registred or not Registred, and other Securities and Payments whatsoever, (except as before excepted) until the last day of *December* next.

And in the mean time, the Lords Commissioners of His Treasury to be Required and Authorized, to cause payment to be made of the Interest that is or shall grow due, at the rate of Six pounds *per Cent.* unto every person that shall have Money due to him or them upon such Warrants, Orders, or Securities, so *Post-pon'd* and deferr'd; and that the payment of such Interest may be justly made, the Lords Commissioners of His Treasury are to be Authorized and Required, to cause the Debt of every particular person, and the said Interest thereof, to be truly stated.

And the Lords of His Majesties Treasury are farther to be Ordered and Required, to employ and dispose of all the said Moneys, so stopp'd and detained, for the preparing, setting forth, and payment of His Majesties Fleet, and other Publick Services, in order to the preservation and safety of His Majesties Government, and defence of His People, as His Majesty shall from time to time Order and Direct.

And His Majesty, as far as in him lies, to take away all apprehensions or terrour, that might possess any of His Subjects spirits, doth declare, That no person whatsoever shall be defrauded of any thing that is justly due to him, nor shall this restraint, which His Majesty has been compelled

(not

Fig. 6.3 Announcing the Stop of the Exchequer 3/4. Permission granted by the British Library. Item 8132.h2

pay back when the Exchequer had the money. The goldsmith-bankers mostly held those. They were actually the hardest hit, as we shall see in a moment. This carve-out under which some orders were paid and some were not is important for two reasons. First, anyone examining the Exchequer's payment records for the months of January 1672 onward might be surprised to find ongoing and large cash outflows—repayments for loans—to many goldsmith-bankers. Of course, these were payments for the exempted securities. Unlike a bank that closes operations after an insolvency, the "stop" didn't lead to a total shutdown of the largest government agency, the Treasury. In fact, there is a case to be made that the Exchequer would be busier than ever before, because the anticipated tax revenues that had been released or rescued from servitude to the bankers could now be spent on goods, services, merchants and tradesmen. Indeed, the Treasury commissioners would now be as busy as ever. The best way to think of what happened in modern terms would be to announce that all 20-dollar bills with serial numbers ending in digits 7–9 were no longer legal tender. Those ending in digits 1–6 were still good to go and accepted anywhere. Well, one-third of the population of consumers with 20-dollar bills would be holding useless paper. Chaos would surely reign, but it would be distributed randomly across the population. Well, in 1672, it wasn't random at all. It seems that the goldsmith-bankers held most of the sevens, eights and nines. They also held the other digits, but that wasn't enough to stave off bankruptcy (Fig. 6.4).

The carve-out or exemption is noteworthy for another reason, which might have legal undertones as well. While the King could pretty much do anything he pleased with heredity revenue—such as excise, customs or the hearth tax—expropriating the parliamentary supply was a trickier proposition. It's unclear whether he could do that (legally) and he certainly didn't want to jeopardize any future grants or supplies. The hope had always been that parliament would provide him additional funds to pay for the war and making a "stop" on payments backed by those revenues, even if they had been granted in the past, would risk the future.

Moving on down in the announcement itself, the third and fourth paragraphs discuss various technicalities about "using the great seal" and "royal signatures" to command the Lord Commissioners of the Treasury to order and direct the officers of His Majesty's Exchequer to implement the declaration postponing the payments. But in yet another concession to the holders of affected treasury orders—that is, those with digits 7–9—during the postponement, they would be entitled to 6% interest. In other words, they might not get paid until the end of the year (in December 1672), but they would be fully compensated for the time value

(4)

(not being able for the present to find any other expedient) to lay upon such Monies, as are or shall be paid into His Exchequer, continue longer then the aforesaid last day of *December*: and that then no new Warrants, Orders or Securities shall intervene, to break the course of such Payments.

And His Majesty is graciously pleased farther to declare, That nothing could have urged His Majesty to an Act of this Nature, but such a conjuncture of Affairs, when all the Neighbouring Princes and States were making such Threatning preparations, that His government could not be safe without appearing in the same posture.

E̅D̅W̅: WALKER.

In the SAVOY,
Printed by the Assigns of *John Bill*, and *Christopher Barker*, Printers to the Kings most Excellent Majesty, 1671/2.

Fig. 6.4 Announcing the Stop of the Exchequer 4/4. Permission granted by the British Library. Item 8132.h2

of money, so to speak. In fact, the Lord Commissioners of the Treasury were themselves ordered to carefully tabulate and list the debts of "every particular person" that had been affected by this and that "the interest thereof to be truly stated". In other words, the commissioners were to report on who exactly was owed what. Well, spoiler alert here, that never happened. It took almost five years before a full list of government creditors was prepared, but I'm getting ahead of the story here.

The notice then goes on to direct the Lord Commissioners of the Treasury to "employ and dispose of all said moneys, so stopped and detained" to pay for the fleet, public services and the defense of His Majesty's people. That, quite naturally, was the main point of the entire exercise. Money that would slowly trickle into the Exchequer could be used for other (more important) sources rather than paying back bankers.

Finally, the notice ends with another reference to the "neighboring princes and states that are making threatening preparations" that leave the King no choice. But, in an odd choice of language in the very last paragraph, it says that "to take away all apprehensions or terror that might possess any of his subject's spirits," His Majesty declares that (1) "no person shall be defrauded of anything that is justly due to him," and that the "stop" will (2) "not continue longer than the last day of December."

Well, neither of those statements would prove to be correct, unless one uses a very loose definition of the words *defrauded* and *December*.

So, what happened next? Well, presumably on Sunday, January 7, at 4 pm, all the bankers that were listed in the *CTB* entry attended the meeting at the offices of the Treasury in Whitehall and were informed in person of the details and rationale for the "stop," although there is quite a bit of evidence to suggest that they knew about this by Friday, if not earlier. Recall that the date of the announcement was listed as (or backdated to) Tuesday, January 2, and later documents make reference to the "stop" having been implemented as early Monday, December 19. Recall that the last announcement in the *London Gazette*—for order #660—was announced on Thursday, December 14. Moreover, in a document that is abstracted in the *Calendar of State Papers Domestic* (*CSPD*) for January 17—in which the action was further explained—the date given for the "stop" is December 18. Either way, whether the "stop" is said to have taken place as late as January 5 or two weeks earlier in mid-December, by Sunday, January 7, the goldsmith-bankers knew exactly what they were facing—financial chaos.

One can't help but see parallels to the infamous bankruptcy announcement of Lehman Brothers, when the paperwork and notices were sent to the Federal courthouse very late on Sunday, September 14, 2008, New York time. And, just as soon as the financial world learned of the bankruptcy filing, stock markets in Asia—which would start trading late on Sunday, New York time—immediately started to tumble. Twenty-four hours later, by the end of trading in North America, the Dow Jones Industrial Average would have had tumbled 500 points in one day.

Well, back in 1672, there were no Asian markets that would tumble late on Sunday evening; in fact the biggest market at the time was in Amsterdam and they would not hear of the news for at least another few days—when the mail arrived. And I'll get back to the mail and Amsterdam markets in a moment. But the (smaller) stock market in London and especially the deposit banks, well, I believe they had their personal "Lehman moment" very early on Monday morning, January 8, 1672, London date and time.

You see, the bankers were now facing two intertwined financial problems. They were holding treasury orders with the "wrong digits" so to speak. Pieces of paper that last week would have entitled them to principal and interest payments in the next few months were now worth (much) less than had been just a few days ago. And although the declaration or the King had promised to compound 6% interest on the debt and guaranteed that the "stop" was only for a year, he had broken his earlier word—in June 1667, after the Chatham crisis—that all debts would be paid on time. Regardless of whether or not there was a market for these debt instruments, in the language of financial accounting they would have to "write down" the value of those investments.

But the second and much greater problem all the goldsmith-bankers faced is that individual depositors from London and beyond had placed cash in their respective banks—and bright and early on Monday morning, they all queued up (in fine English fashion, no doubt) and wanted to withdraw those funds, immediately. The commoners, gentry and peers had heard what happened over the weekend and they all wanted their money back. The goldsmith-bankers now faced a classical "run on the bank," and unlike the twenty-first century, there was no deposit insurance to pay depositors, central bank or lender of last resort to "bail them out" or a secondary market in which to liquidate their CTOs—which nobody was going to purchase. Bank runs are much better understood[22] today in the

---

[22] See, for example, the seminal article by Diamond and Dybvig (1983), in which they use a game theoretic model to describe the process of a "run on the bank" and the need for government-based deposit insurance to avoid banks runs.

early twenty-first century—as well as what is needed to avoid them—compared to banking science in the mid-seventeenth century. But even the twenty-first century has had its share of bank runs. A recent one took place at a bank called Northern Rock (in the United Kingdom) in September 2007. That episode[23] was in the early stages of what we now call the financial crisis of 2007–2008 or the Great Recession. The prior bank run (in the United Kingdom) took place at Overend, Gurney & Co., which was a London bank that ran into financial difficulties in the year 1866.

So, in the year 1672 it's unclear that anyone would have called what was happening a bank run and perhaps there weren't the long lineups either, but the impact was exactly the same. Depositors couldn't get access to their cash.

So although it took many years before the famed goldsmith-bankers Robert Viner, Edward Backwell, Gilbert Whitehall, Jeremia Snow, Robert Welsted, Thomas Rowe and John Portman went bankrupt—yes, all of them—their miserable fate was sealed early on that Monday morning when hundreds and possibly thousands of Englishmen lined up in the (cold fog of) the City of London, demanding, asking or pleading for their money back. And these same bankers froze them all out. They refused to pay anyone, even those—and this is key—depositors who had not invested in interest-bearing accounts. It seems that even English men and women who had used the goldsmith-bankers' services for safekeeping only were also locked out of their money. Whether this extreme act was justified or not is debatable. It could be that in times of such financial chaos, the initial instinct is to put a halt to all cash outflows in the safest course of action, but the uproar and implications were widespread. It is quite possible that many of the inaccurate descriptions I mentioned earlier regarding the mechanics of the "stop"—phrases such as the seizing of money or thievery—and might have been tainted by political biases, more accurately described the actions of the goldsmith-bankers. Later on, when I get to the discussion of public opinion and the general lack of sympathy for the bankers, a strong case can be made that their actions on that Monday morning revealed their true priority.

---

[23] See Shin (2009) for a detailed analysis of the Northern Rock bank run within the context of a Diamond and Dybvig (1983) framework. That article also discusses the rather peculiar fact that the queues to pull out money started only after the Bank of England announced (September 13, 2007) that it would provide emergency liquidity support to Northern Rock.

Either way, the King himself had to intervene. The bankers were called in for yet another impromptu meeting and this time were told in no uncertain terms that they must return funds and cash that had been given to them as demand deposits, immediately. The savings accounts which themselves paid 6% to depositors and were locked up (like modern-day certificates of deposit) or those that required 20 days' advanced notice could justifiably remain frozen. But the cash had to be returned—and the bankers promptly complied. They knew they were at the King's mercy, since many of them now faced a slew of legal challenges and problems as well. And in those days, it would require more than high-priced bankruptcy lawyers. One of the bankers' first requests—and quoted as the epigraph to this book—was to obtain an exemption or assistance against arrests. Think about this for a moment: this was a request from the most important banker in the realm, Alderman Edward Backwell. Just a few days earlier he was at the center of every important financial transaction in London. His name appears more than anyone else in the *CTB*—documenting the daily activity of the Exchequer—and his bank depositors included a *who's who* of royalty. The Queen, the Duke of York, Prince Rupert, the Duke of Monmouth and many other nobles, all had accounts at Backwell's bank in the City of London. They trusted him and used his services for all types of financing. Here, he was begging or pleading—together with his banking colleagues—to protect them from being arrested. The response? Well, the Lord Commissioners of the Treasury would "ask the King's pleasure in it."

Desperate Dowry Measures

Edward Backwell's case in particular is quite interesting because he didn't sit back silently as the "stop" massacred the value of his holdings. The Alderman had extensive dealings with the finances of the nation via the Exchequer. And if the King was about to sever an artery in a complex network of cash flows, he could retaliate in other parts of the Kingdom's blood supply. In particular, Backwell was responsible for importing and exchanging Queen Catherine of Braganza's dowry. Recall that this money, which was long overdue to the King, was coming in (very) slowly and being processed by Backwell's own agents in Lisbon. The Portuguese cruzados would be carefully transported to London, weighted and then exchanged into English pounds, all by Edward Backwell. Well, in the finest games of "tit for tat," Backwell apparently decided—at some point on Monday, during the pandemonium—to send orders to his agent in Lisbon to seize the Queen's dowry. Presumably, the plan was to keep it hostage until his CTOs were paid. Well, the King and his cabal were one step ahead of Backwell on this one. On Tuesday, January 9, the *CTB* has an entry in which a letter is sent to a Captain John Holmes informing him that there are 19,000 cruzados aboard a ship in Lisbon, called (quite appropriately) *The Diamond*. The captain is informed that under no circumstances is that money to be handed over to Edward Backwell. To reinforce the order, the Treasury commissioners also asked Arlington to write a letter to the same effect providing that power be given to the government agent in Lisbon to supersede any agents of Backwell. The *CTB* entry contains an extract of the letter sent to the captain of the ship. It says:

> The money belongs to His Majesty. You are not to dispose of any part of the said money upon Alderman Backwell's orders but are to secure the same on board and give notice to my Lords of your arrival, upon which they will give order how the said money's shall be disposed.

The score for day 2 of the financial crisis of 1672 was: King 2, Backwell 0. But that didn't stop Backwell from trying again. Later on, he proposed a scheme in which he would get paid or reimbursed from (new) taxes on wine and vinegar. That scheme also went nowhere. And he wasn't the only one trying to be clever.

Order on the Sabbath

In contrast to the successful attempt by Shaftesbury to capitalize on—and trade on—his inside information about the Stop of the Exchequer *before* it was announced to the London market in early January 1672, the *CTB* includes a rather curious story in which the exact opposite is alleged to have occurred. Namely, it references an enterprising individual who attempted to trade on the information—and quickly sell his devalued treasury orders—*after* the news was released in London, but *before* it actually arrived in Amsterdam.

Recall that (at that time) London and Amsterdam were the two single-largest financial centers in which "capital assets" were bartered and transacted. A handful of corporate securities available in London—for example, those of the EIC—also traded in Amsterdam and vice versa. Technically speaking, the world's first organized stock market was launched in the Netherlands (in Amsterdam) in the year 1611; Germany was next, in the year 1685, and then (in third place) was England, in 1698, all according to economic historians.[24] So, although England wouldn't have a formal or centralized exchange for another 25 years, there certainly were individuals trading English corporate securities in London during the 1670s. Likewise, merchants and bankers were trading or marketing English bonds—for lack of a better term—in the Dutch Republic. Therefore, even if there wasn't quite a flourishing stock exchange until the last decade of the seventeenth century, the CTOs could be disposed of in Amsterdam, for the right price of course.

And so an enterprising London-based investor who heard the announcement about the "stop" immediately tried to get his order routed to Amsterdam before the market or individual traders there learned the news. I'll get to the details in a moment, but one might view this as the seventeenth-century version of high-frequency trading, that is, to get your order placed in queue before everyone else. The previously mentioned Dr. William A. Shaw, writing in 1908 in the introduction to the *CTB* that he edited, had another name for this case. He called it: *The amusing story of a Jew*.

Here are the known facts. On January 9, 1672, which was the Tuesday following the weekend of the crisis, Sir Joseph Williamson, who was a protégé of Lord Arlington (member of the cabal) and responsible for the post office, received a short letter from a Mr. Silas Taylor. Now while my strict practice has been not to introduce any more names or new people than are absolutely necessary, Mr. Taylor was the keeper of the naval stores in the English port city of Harwich. Geographically, Harwich is directly across the water from the Dutch Republic's port city of Hellevoetsluis, or approximately 260 kilometers (160 miles) to the east. The relevance here is that all the mail or post from London to Amsterdam—including news that would be relevant to traders and merchants in both cities—would first traverse from London to the port city of Harwich by horse and carriage. Then the mail package would sail from Harwich to Hellevoetsluis by a so-called packet boat, and finally, it would resume its travel by land to Amsterdam. Information flowed much more slowly than the speed of (e-mail or) light.

In the sixteenth and seventeenth centuries, the entire journey took approximately four days to complete. What this means is that the traders

---

[24] See the book *The World's First Stock Exchange*, by Petram (2014). See also Goetzmann and Jorion (1999).

or merchants in Amsterdam learned what had happened in London four days earlier—or 14 days earlier if you convert from Julian to Gregorian—once the mail courier finally arrived. In fact, during periods of bad weather, traders in Amsterdam often had to wait weeks (instead of days) for important market-moving news from London. To this exact point, a recent study by Professor P. Koudijs[25] demonstrated—among other interesting facts—that trading in markets in Amsterdam was much more active (or volatile) on days when these (mail) sailboats arrived versus days when they were delayed due to poor weather or unfavorable winds. Koudijs referred to the traders in Amsterdam as being "starved for news" when the boats didn't sail. So, although stocks in Amsterdam moved in the absence of mail or packet boats, they didn't trade (or fluctuate) as much.

Either way, getting from London to Amsterdam before the mail arrived—if at all possible—could be quite valuable if you had the right news. And the "stop" of the Exchequer would have been *the* breaking financial news of the 1670s. Speaking personally, Amsterdam would be the first place I would run to if I lived in London (in the 1670s) and had some private information about financial securities. My second choice for dumping toxic debt would be the lovely city of Venice, again in the seventeenth century.

Well, according to said Silas Taylor, on the afternoon of Friday, January 5—the day on which the announcement was formally made (but officially dated January 2) in London—a harried traveler arrived at the port city looking to cross from Harwich to Hellevoetsluis. I use the term "harried" or perhaps haggard because the distance from Harwich to London is 135 kilometers (or 85 miles). In a horse and carriage winding its way along (seventeenth-century) unpaved roads, it would take 12–14 hours, which means that our traveler must have departed London very early on Friday, the 5th, or more realistically late on Thursday, the 4th.

If the story is to be believed, then rumors of the "stop"—to people outside the immediate cabal—must have circulated prior to the meeting of the Treasury commissioners on Friday, the 5th (in the late morning) and well before the fateful assembly of the bankers at the Exchequer on the Lord's Day of January 7. For the record, the issue of the *London Gazette* with the banner date of Thursday, January 4 to Monday, January

---

[25] See Koudijs (2016). His study focuses on a period in the late eighteenth century, but the mail and post system was in place by the late 1660s. See also Koudijs (2015) for related work on insider trading during the same period.

8 included the entire text of the declaration. It's not clear exactly when that issue would have hit the streets of London, but it's not unreasonable to suggest that the local market knew all details about the "stop" by Thursday afternoon. Now, remember that Shaftesbury knew this was happening (and had acted) many months earlier. Either way, by Friday (January 5) afternoon, the above-mentioned traveler was in Harwich and looking for a quick boat. And here is exactly what Mr. Taylor wrote to Joseph Williamson[26] in a letter that arrived back in London the following Tuesday. I'll quote verbatim:

> Last Friday a Jew came post from London, who endeavored to get a boat for Holland, but could get none that day.

Now, in terms of maritime background, normally there were two mail boats that sailed from Harwich every week; one would leave on Wednesday and the other on Saturday.[27] Ordinary travelers who were willing to trek and keep the mail company could also use the packet boats to get across. At other times, such as on a Friday afternoon, travelers could charter or rent a private boat, if available. On this exact Friday afternoon, our Jew missed the last boat. Mr. Taylor goes on to write in his letter:

> But he got one for £18, and went the next afternoon, even though it was his Sabbath and the ordinary packet would have gone at 6 or 7.

I'll carefully unpack that statement since there is a lot going in that sentence. The £18 price the traveler paid for the chartered boat was (much) more than a normal or scheduled fare, which would have been approximately[28] £5 for a one-way trip. He clearly overpaid. Of course he wanted to leave as soon as possible (ideally on Friday), and well before the packet boat left with Saturday's mail at 6 or 7 pm. The extra few hours' head start in the race to beat the news appeared to be worth much more than the £13 markup in price. Remember yet again that these aren't trivial sums and could conceivably feed a family of the "middling sort" for an entire year. Note also the somewhat anti-Semitic or accusatory undertones in reference to the transgression of the Sabbath. This is something I'll return

---

[26] Source: *State Papers Domestic*, Car. II, 302, No. 39.
[27] See W. G. S. Dibden (1965) for more on this.
[28] Thanks to Peter Koudijs at Stanford University for providing this information and related references.

to later. In fact, I'll argue that it might have all been quite kosher with the proper ingredients.

The dispatch or letter to Joseph Williamson in London then goes on to describe the apparent motives of "the Jew," which is where we rejoin our main story:

> He said his business required haste and being about it before the mail was opened, I believe it concerned money, because of his story that the King had shut up his Exchequer and all the bankers and their shops refusing to pay ant bills until all were open.

This final paragraph doesn't require much interpretation. The Jew had to get to the other side and then to Amsterdam before the "mail was opened," at which point traders in Amsterdam learned that the CTOs he (probably) had with him and was (probably) trying to offload were close to worthless. Or, in Danby's famous words, "the orders were not now money."

And that is basically all Mr. Taylor wrote (in his letter). The same dispatch goes on to discuss other topics. It describes tensions over trade in the Indies between the Dutch and English and then rumors of deals with the French, but nothing more about the "stop" or whether the Jew was successful in getting to Amsterdam before the news packet arrived. Mr. Taylor (based in Harwich) couldn't possibly know that—when he sent the letter on Monday—and the *CTB* records and even Dr. Shaw himself (writing in the early twentieth century) are completely silent on that matter.

Who was this crafty and spirited Jew? When did he actually get to Amsterdam? Did he manage to sell his CTOs to some unsuspecting Dutch merchant before the (delayed) market realized their true value?

Well—after a bit of digging—I believe I have the answer to both questions, pieced together from some (albeit) circumstantial evidence. First, I think the Jew's name was Isaac Alvarez, who was also known in the (small, nascent) Jewish community of London as Isaac Israel Nunes. (It was quite common for Jews to have a secular name used for business purposes.)

But Isaac Alvarez wasn't a goldsmith-banker like Edward Backwell or Robert Viner, or even a merchant like John Banks. Rather, he was listed in the records of the Jewish community of London as a court jeweler who provided gems to His Majesty. Although he was a prominent member of the Jewish community, he apparently moved in the same social circles as members of the infamous cabal. In particular, records indicate he was quite friendly with the Duchess of Buckingham, wife of the most rakish and witty member of the cabal, the Duke of Buckingham. Don't hold this against him. Isaac was a court jeweler and must have been acquainted with all the female members of the King's entourage out of necessity. In one remarkable story[29] that circulates about our Isaac, he apparently convinced the (very non-Jewish) Duchess of Buckingham to donate funds to help build the Creechurch Lane Synagogue in London. Was it for the women's section perhaps? Either way, I would venture to guess that Isaac the jeweler was quite the persuasive fellow and one can only imagine what a man with his skills might have achieved in a twenty-first century synagogue, during the High Holiday's Israel Bond campaigns. When Isaac passed away (in 1683) and was buried—in the Jewish cemetery Beth Holim in London—his epitaph included the following, which is a subset of the entire version, which is reprinted in the *Jewish Historical Society of England* (1937), Vol. 3, pp. 94–107:

> Under this marble all that's left behind
> Of Issac Alvarez Nunes Lies Confined
> Of Hebrew Race, by Birth a Portugall
> In London his abode and funeral
> Whose far gained knowledge in mysterious gems
> Sparkled in the European diadems.
> A loving husband, a tender parent, a true friend
> Sincere in his dealing to the end

Note the reference to mysterious gems and (without any trace of irony, on my part) sincerity in dealings. The monument and the text are preserved in the records of (another) Bevis Marks Synagogue in London, dedicated by his wife Sarah and their children Abraham, Daniel, Marianne and Deborah. Also, when he died, he was relatively wealthy and left £2000 to Sarah and another £1000 to each of his children. In debtors' prison he wasn't.

But back to our story, as someone close to the royal court—with "far gained knowledge in mysterious gems"—it is quite natural that he was paid with treasury orders instead of cash. The *CTB* is replete with such notices of payment to suppliers. I'm not speculating here. There are records in the privy council Register of a petition by Isaac Alvarez to King Charles II

---

[29] Reported in the annals of *Transactions of the Jewish Historical Society of England* (1937), Vol. 3, pp. 94–107.

himself, asking His Majesty to pay an overdue account of £4000. Apparently Isaac Alvarez had received "treasury orders backed by the customs" from yet another court jeweler named Isaac Le Gouche. This was in exchange for jewels that he had supplied His Majesty in January 1670. So we have established that Isaac Alvarez indeed owned some treasury orders and might have still had them in January 1672.

But in fact, there is even stronger evidence that he still owned them at the time of the "stop," and I'll get to that in a minute. But it's not inconceivable that he is the Jew who spent that Friday night in Harwich. If he could smooth-talk the Duchess of Buckingham into donating to his synagogue, I'm sure he could convince someone to purchase his defaulted bonds.

But did he make it in time? Alas no, for those readers who were rooting for him, I don't think he made it to Amsterdam before the market opened. Unlike his Anglican compatriot Lord Shaftesbury, Isaac wasn't able to successfully trade on inside information. He was stuck with the CTOs—for a very long time.

How do I know this? Here is the final piece of the puzzle. The names of all the creditors who were owed money as a result of the "stop"—a list that was published in 1677 and will be presented and carefully discussed later in Table 6.1—includes 25 prominent goldsmith-bankers and notable members of the gentry. The list is mostly Anglican (for reasons I explained in Chap. 3) except for one single name at the bottom. The one Jewish name was, yes, you guessed it: Isaac Alvarez.

He was listed as being owed a total of £1580. As a reminder, in today's terms, that would be hundreds of thousands of pounds—and certainly worth more than an overpriced boat ride (£18) from Harwich to Hellevoetslius on a weekend.

Once you have his background, it really should come as no surprise that he was stuck with some of the CTOs in early January 1672, when the music stopped playing and everyone rushed to find their chairs. Now, the £1580 paled in size relative to the much larger sums owed to Robert Viner and Edward Backwell—with more on their story to come—but it was close enough in size to his (Isaac) wife's inheritance and dowry. In other words, it was worth a (quick) trip to Amsterdam and perhaps missing a Sabbath with the family.

Interestingly, yet another court jeweler on the list of creditors was Isaac Le Gouche—who I mentioned earlier as the jeweler having business dealings with Alvarez—and who actually was a Huguenot immigrant from

Table 6.1 Bankers' Debt created by the Stop of the Exchequer

Name of creditor	Sum due £	Interest due £
Sir Robert Viner	416,724.65	25,003.46
Edward Backwell	295,994.82	17,759.68
Joseph Hornby	22,548.27	1352.89
Gilbert Whitehall	248,866.17	14,931.96
George Snell	10,894.72	653.67
Bernard Turner	16,275.48	976.52
Jermiah Snow	59,780.93	3586.85
John Lindsey	85,832.85	5149.86
Robert Welsted	11,307.60	678.45
Thomas Rowe	17,615.88	1056.95
John Portman	76,760.90	4605.65
Isaac Collier	1784.32	107.05
John Thruston	5208.40	312.50
Isaac Legouch	5370.18	322.20
Robert Ryves	16,368.21	982.08
Edmund Turner	4592.58	275.58
Edward Chamberlain	706.09	42.35
George Toriano	129.73	7.76
John Shaw	9355.51	561.32
Francis Millington	1285.36	77.12
Henry Johnson	1388.55	83.28
Robert Wynne	567.35	34.00
Richard Lant	1844.02	110.60
Isaac Alvarez (for S. Bickford)	1580.66	94.80
William Gomeldon	2157.82	129.50
Total	**£1,314,941**	**£78,897**

As of February 1677.
Source: *Calendar of Treasury Books*, III, p. xlviii

Antwerp. Isaac the Huguenot was owed three times as much as his fellow jeweler Isaac the Jew. Either way, think of Isaac Alvarez as the token Jew in the scandal.

Needless to say, the fact that Isaac is listed as a creditor almost five years later implies that he did *not* make in time for the start of trading on Monday morning, January 8 (Julian), in Amsterdam. I'm not sure when he returned to London, or if he met Mr. Taylor in Harwich on his way back, but I suspect he wasn't in a rush anymore. Now, even if they were Isaac's CTOs that were trying to cross from Harwich to Hellevoetsluis, could Isaac have sent someone else in his place? Perhaps. Could it have been a completely different "Jew" who held the CTOs—who learned about this news early on Friday—and was trying to get to cross the Channel before the news (boats) arrived? Maybe. Unfortunately, we will never know the true facts in this story unless someone from the Alvarez family can step forward and provide him with an alibi for that Friday night.

Here is the bottom line: naming Isaac Alvarez—a Jew close to the court and king, which was rare at the time—as Mr. Taylor's "Jew" and the one who spent that Friday night in Harwich fits the timeline. The critical information about the "stop" would have only been disclosed to the London market (by the King's privy council) on Thursday or Friday, and it made sense that a court jeweler would be among the first to learn of the news.

Isaac had the motive and the means. But instead of rushing to the nearest bar or tavern in the City of London to drown his sorrows in a pint of beer, he headed straight to Norwich. This was a clever idea, but not quite fast enough.

In the end, despite being owed a sizeable sum of money from the Exchequer, the "stop" didn't bankrupt him or ruin him or send the Jewish jeweler to prison. Remember, when he died (in 1683), he left sizeable sums and assets to his wife and children. This was very different from the legacy and fate reserved for the goldsmith-bankers, to whom I'll return in just a moment.

Oh yes, as for the final religious transgression bit. Well, it seems that getting on a boat during the Sabbath is perfectly acceptable *if* the person follows a few simple measures before sunset on Friday evening. Namely, the traveler would (1) have to board a boat before the Sabbath, even if it wasn't going anywhere, and then (2) make the appropriate benediction with wine for the Sabbath after sunset and (3) quickly get off the boat and spend the evening in a (presumably nice) hotel, instead of sleeping on the boat. Then, the next day—on Sabbath afternoon, perhaps after a fine meal—he would be permitted to board the boat from Harwich to Hellevoetsluis, according to Jewish law.

This[30] is according to the interpretation of Rabbi Joseph Caro, writing in the canonical text of Jewish law, dictating what is allowed—actually and come to think of it, mostly what is not allowed—published in Venice exactly one century before that fateful weekend in Harwich.

---

[30] I would like to thank Rabbi Jeremy Milevsky, spiritual leader of the B'nei Torah congregation in Toronto, for bringing this technical permit to my attention.

But all in all one can't fault Mr. Silas Taylor—the English keeper of the naval stores in the early 1670s—for not being familiar with the *Rabbinic Responsa* from the late sixteenth-century Italy. The optics namely getting on a boat on the Sabbath looked bad, and perhaps in this case, some secular skepticism was justified.

Clarifications and Limitations

One week after the so-called Lehman moment, on Wednesday, January 17, the King and his privy council were forced to issue a follow-up with additional details and stipulations. In this new bill that was prepared for the King's signature, a number of ambiguous items appearing in the January 2nd notice were clarified and others were strengthened. This particular item is noted (aka calendared) in the *CSPD* and interestingly makes reference to December 18 as day on which the "stop" was implemented. The notice repeats the same motivation and language from the earlier announcement. It references the temporary (one-year) length, the 6% interest that would accumulate during the 12 months and that it did not apply to the orders secured by the Act of parliament granting the King supply for the present war. That was standard. But—and this is key—the second notice also included a long list of departments and specific individuals that should continue to be paid from the Exchequer. In particular, it was to "authorize the Commissioners of the Treasury to cause payment to be made … payable to the Queen, the Duke of York, his children, Prince Rupert, secret service" as well as a long list of court officials, from the President and Court of the Marches of Wales to the Judges at Westminster, Master of Chancery and an assortment of other clerks, officers and persons. The key takeaway here is that the King wanted to ensure that the "stop" wouldn't affect the day-to-day functioning of the government. The King and his privy council were trying to isolate the financial damage into the hands of the bankers.

And with that announcement, further official references to the "stop" and its aftermath begin to dwindle. The affected goldsmith-bankers are left to resolve their own personal and business crisis, but commerce continued and life went on. In late January the EIC established a trading post in China, and many bankers who weren't holding the wrong digits on their treasury orders and didn't have any exposure to the affected bankers stepped in and flourished as their unlucky competitors floundered. Banking establishments such as Hoares, Childs, Heriots and Ballards—many of which survived into the twenty-first century and continue to have a presence in London—continued to finance, lend and take deposits. Life continued. England moved on to the next milestone of the year, which was the actual war with the Dutch—the raison d'être of the "stop"— which began two months later on April 7, 1672, to be precise. English forces attacked the Dutch fleet at Smyrna on March 12, and almost simultaneously, King Charles II issued a so-called Declaration of Indulgence, in which he allowed religious congregations who dissented from the Church of England to worship in their own way so long as they hired licensed preachers. Moreover Catholic recusants were also given freedom from fines and penalties, and allowed to practice their faith with fewer restrictions. Perhaps this was a step in the direction—at least symbolically—of King Charles II himself fulfilling the terms of his deal with King Louis XIV and (eventually) professing his own Catholic faith?

In late April 1672, as the war with Dutch was getting off the ground, King Charles II rewarded his closest advisors, the cabal, for their loyal service and dedication. Presumably, this includes the "stop" as one of the successes of the regime. Lord Shaftesbury became an Earl (of Shaftesbury)—he also became Lord Chancellor (and holder of the Great Seal of the Realm), which was an even greater honor[31]—and Henry Bennet was rewarded with the title of the Earl of Arlington. Thomas Clifford was awarded with a Barony, and the Earl of Lauderdale became a Duke (of Lauderdale).

And what happened to the goldsmith-bankers?

Well, that brings us to the last episode of our story, albeit a chapter that took 34 years to unfold.

Danby Makes Assignments

Throughout the year 1672, the Exchequer continued humming along as busy as ever despite the "stop"—as fresh new cash from the King's ordinary revenue was now freed from the financial bondage of its CTO masters. In contrast to the activity at the Exchequer, the deposit-taking banks owned by the affected goldsmith-bankers were (much) less busy, since the deposit notes or paper slips that prove a deposit that the bankers had issued as part of their own banking activities—which historians view as the origins of paper money—were now practically worthless. These notes were no longer accepted by merchants in and around London or (ironi-

---

[31] The lineage for Lord Chancellor was Clarendon to Bridgeman to Shaftesbury.

cally) even the Exchequer itself. One Treasury official referred to them as "not now money," and it wasn't until the year 1680 that any goldsmith-banker's notes would be recognized for payment again. And, of course, the bankers themselves would soon face another type of bondage, debtors' prison, if they weren't able to satisfy their many creditors. But let us progress through the timeline in proper order.

By mid-June of 1672, the official auditor of the receipts of the Exchequer was able to certify the total amount of the stopped debt. Recall that one of the promises made in the announcement on January 2 is that a full and proper accounting would be made so that all creditors knew where they stood. Well, six months after the "stop," early estimates were made available and they were in the range of £900,000, although no public list was released. In fact, the total outstanding debt was an underestimate relative to the final tally, which was certified a few years later at closer to £1,200,000.

During the summer[32] of 1672, it also became clear exactly *who* among the goldsmith-bankers held the—for lack of a better description—toxic debt and *who* had managed to steer clear or perhaps get their treasury orders paid despite the "stop." As I mentioned in Chap. 3, when I introduced the goldsmith-bankers and the financiers of the era, through some clever machinations, some prominent merchants and financiers did not appear on the list of government creditors even though they were "still standing" when the "musical chairs" stopped playing.

For example, Sir Stephen Fox—a name that appears quite a bit in the extant literature of the Restoration—apparently held over £360,000 in treasury orders by the Christmas holiday of 1671, but somehow managed to get paid and was never listed. We don't know the details of how he managed to pull off the feat, but by June 1672, he wasn't listed as a creditor and presumably wasn't owed any money. Note that he wasn't a goldsmith-banker with depositors, which might help explain.

Another person who got his CTOs paid was Sir John Banks—who around the same time became the governor of the EIC. His case is quite interesting, because instead of cutting his losses, he decided to double down on his bet and he actually won. In the (early, incomplete) list of creditors that was compiled in June 1672, John Banks was recorded as being owed principal and interest in the amount of £60,202 with 6s and

---

[32] Not to distract, but the Dutch were having convulsions of their own, and Prime Minister de Witt (together with his brother) was lynched by a mob, bringing an end to a distinguished career.

8.25d, which incidentally is quite a remarkable level of detail. The debt (or the underlying CTOs) was secured against a mixture of the hearth, customs and excise (tax) revenue, which meant that it was covered by the "stop" or (the CTOs) had the wrong serial number or digits, using the earlier analogy. But what John Banks did was to offer another loan for £51,500—yes, good money after bad—to the Exchequer. This might seem irrational, but in exchange for the additional loan or money, he was promised that *security* for the entire debt would be transferred from the above-mentioned sources of revenue to the so-called fee farm rents. Recall from Chap. 5 that this was yet another form of Exchequer borrowing, which in this case was tied to landownership and payments by tenants. In particular, fee farms were properties confiscated by the Tudors from the Church in the sixteenth century, which then generated payments in perpetuity and now (partially) belonged to the Crown. Now, I don't want to get caught up in the minutia, but these payments had a life-contingent element to them and were dependent on Queen Catherine of Braganza. To be precise, they were *reversionary annuities*, which would only start paying after the death of the Queen. So, John Banks (or his heirs) would not be able to recover some of that money until she died—and for the record, she lived for 34 more years until 1705. Of course, John Banks didn't know that in 1672, but he did perceive the overall package of cash flows was more secure. And he was right! The bad debt itself was being swapped for good debt—in other words, more than a change in the security of the debt—and Lord Treasurer Clifford had to write a special endorsement or instructions to allow this. Basically, Banks used £60,000 in (defaulted) CTOs plus his own cash to purchase another type of bond, linked to fee farms rents.

In addition to the financial aspects of the deal, John Banks also sought and obtained a pardon from the King for charging interest above the legal 6%—think of it as acquiring liability insurance against certain crimes "to be named"—which is something other goldsmith-bankers sought out as well. In fact, staying with John Banks, in September 1672, the EIC itself, of which Banks was the governor, made another loan to the Crown. For that loan of £30,000, the repayments would come from and would be linked to the customs tax, which the EIC had a hand in collecting. It was all rather foggy and incestuous, but the bottom line is that John Banks doubled down on his losses and was quite successful. He died as one of the wealthiest men in England. So, when the Danby published his final list of goldsmith-bankers who were creditors (in 1677), John Banks was definitely not on the list. The details of this rather fascinating transaction or modern-day swap are carefully described by Banks' biographer D. C. Coleman (1963) in a book that is rightfully subtitled *A Study of Business*. As I mentioned earlier, Backwell tried to suggest a similar deal or proposal for himself but wasn't successful.

Returning to the timeline, in November 1672, Shaftesbury was named and promoted to Lord Chancellor—he who first argued against and then wrote John Locke, complaining about usurious interest rates—and in December 1672, the temporary "stop" was extended by another six months to May 1,1673. The announcement appeared in the *London Gazette* and was dated December 11, 1672. The text contained the usual flowery references to "his majesty hath not been wanting" and "contrary to his own inclinations," but that he had no choice and was "compelled at present to continue the same 'stop' of payments of any moneys now being brought into His Exchequer." The announcement goes on to say, "And his majesty is graciously pleased further to declare that he continued the 'stop' of payments to as short a time as May 1st next, to show his intentions of taking the first opportunity … to restore to his good subjects all that is justly due to them,"—which in other words is saying that it could have been worse and the "stop" could have been extended for another year. For the record, the complete stop continued for another two years after that, and I'll get to that in just a bit. The December 11 notice concludes with a statement that the King wanted to "render them under his government both safe and happy." Of course, the war with the Dutch was still raging in late December 1672, which wasn't rendering most of the King's subjects happy or safe.

Continuing on the war footing—against bankers and the Dutch—in January 1673, Lord Shaftesbury gave a memorable speech (*Delenda est Carthago*) to parliament in the name of the King—they were still on good terms, but within 12 months, he too would be turfed—in which he asked for support for the ongoing war with the Dutch and also asked for further supply (aka taxes) to support the war. Parliament (upset at Charles for his Declaration of Indulgence the prior year and) in turn responded by passing something called the Tests Act in March 1673. This Act—which places us at the risk of taking us far from financial defaults to religious fault lines—forced anyone who wanted to hold public office or vote or preach or teach in England to take a particular oath. The language of the oath stated: "I do declare that I do believe that there is not any transubstantiation in the sacrament of the Lord's supper or in the elements of the bread and wine." If you wanted public office, you had to accept those terms. And quite frankly, although the reader might not be certain about the exact meaning of this oath, a Catholic (at least in the seventeenth century) would be—and would never swear to it. Now, some government office holders like Arlington (remember, "he leaned toward Rome") took the oath. Ever the diplomat, perhaps it was just words. Others made a big show of taking the oath and there are reports of Lord Shaftesbury taking the Anglican sacrament, together with the King's eldest illegitimate son, the Duke of Monmouth. Some though, like the Duke of York—who by now was a heartbeat away from the throne—refused to take the oath or the sacrament in an Anglican church. They had to resign their office, soon after. King Charles II didn't have to take the oath—which is lucky, considering his secret Dover deal with King Louis XIV. On the other hand, it's unlikely he had converted by then (or ever).

In fact, the marriage between James and the Catholic Mary of Modena, which was announced around the same time, was widely condemned by parliament. I mention this rather touchy episode of extreme religious persecution against Catholics in the summer and fall of 1673 for one simple reason. Namely, Thomas Clifford—the person who first suggested and was the power behind the "stop"—also refused to take the oath and was forced to resign on June 19, 1673. In fact, four months later, the once powerful and outspoken "C" of the King's cabal was found dead. Some say it was suicide, perhaps it was accidental—and the historians are still debating his legacy. What we do know for certain is that the person who took over as Lord Treasurer (no more commission) after Clifford was gone in June 1673. His name is Thomas Osborne, aka (known later as) Earl of Danby. During that summer he was just beginning his long climb up the social hierarchy and was named Baron Osborne of Kiveton, which, recall, is (only) rank #1 on the ladder. And so in the early fall of 1673—the last protagonist in our financial tale—got to work.

Danby's ascent to power marked a turning point on a number of levels. First, there was the change in government personnel and power centers around the same time. A few months later, in November 1673, Shaftesbury was forced to relinquish "the seals" of power, and six months later, in May 1674 he was expelled from the privy council (and actually asked to leave London) as part of his transition to becoming the King's great nemesis. So the second "A" in the cabal was gone. He now leaves our story, but not the stage of history. Then in September 1674, Lord Arlington was forced to sell his place as Secretary of State and the first "A" in the cabal was now gone as well. Buckingham had his own (deep) financial troubles and the "B" would soon depart the stage.

By January and February 1674, most of the cabal[33] was on their way out. The Treaty of Westminster—which would formally end the third Anglo-Dutch war—was close to being finalized. But the temporary "stop" of the Exchequer had now become permanent because the underlying funds on which the CTOs were based and secured had been completely exhausted. The excise, customs and hearth revenues backing that particular debt had been used by the Exchequer for many other purposes. The time had finally come to think about a permanent resolution, and by June 1674, the (by now properly called) Earl of Danby sat down with the largest goldsmith-bankers and started to negotiate. He was operating on two fronts. He needed to reach some sort of agreement with the holders of the defaulted CTOs, but also needed to locate fresh[34] sources of revenue.

At that point—almost 36 months after the "stop" itself, the creditors had yet to receive a penny of interest and certainly none of their principal back, other than some of the side (swap) deals I described earlier. The total outstanding debt at the time of the "stop" was now thought to be in the range of £1,167,000 (the final tally was only £5000 higher). At a rate of 6% per year or 12% for two years (without compounding), the interest due on the date of January 1674 would have been (0.12) (1,167,000) = £140,000. A full listing of all creditors had not yet been publicly released, but individual bankers were trying to reach their own agreements. At last, during the summer of 1674 approval was given to pay the above-calculated £140,000 to the bankers in eight quarterly installments. The first payment would take place in late March or early April of the following year.

The Reopening of the Exchequer

And so, finally *after almost 40 months of waiting*, the first interest payment of £17,500 was distributed and paid directly to the goldsmith-bankers and holders of the CTOs in early April (or possibly late March) 1675. Those quarterly payments continued and the last one was (likely) made

---

[33] Shaftesbury's attention was now focused on giving anti-Catholic speeches in parliament and he was no longer part of the in-crowd at court.

[34] Danby arm-twisted the corporation of the City of London into lending money by threatening that otherwise he wouldn't disband the Army (which the City loathed and feared).

in early January 1677, which—to keep the clocks rolling—was 60 months after the "stop." It was then, in early February 1677 after the last quarterly payment had been made, that Danby published the first (and only) known list of all the people who were owed money—not all of whom were goldsmith-bankers. It was a creditor's *who's who*. He also tabled a most audacious proposal for a permanent solution for the Bankers' Debt—one that might serve as a lesson on how to "bail out" bankers in the twenty-first century.

I'll get to Danby's bold scheme in a moment, but I should be clear that it wasn't only Danby who was involved. There was a full parliamentary committee struck and Danby actually consulted with some of the (earlier, 1667) members of the Treasury commission. There is even reference to old George Downing, who was asked his opinion on the best way to compensate the bankers. In fact, Downing wanted the funds to reimburse the bankers to flow through the Exchequer itself, likely so that he could get a small fee in the process.

Anyway, enough gossip. Let's take a closer look at the list of creditors displayed in Table 6.1 which became available when the Exchequer was finally reopened[35] in 1677. Note that at the very top of the list is Sir Robert Viner, with the stunningly large sum owed of £416,725. This is the principal plus compound interest (not yet paid) due five years after the "stop" in February 1677. In modern-day terms, that would be over £40 million owed to one single person using the double-zero rule. Next on the list is Edward Backwell, which is another name that should be very familiar by now. He was owed £295,995 from the "stop" and was the second-largest creditor. The original list wasn't printed (in the official records) in alphabetical order or in the order of amount owed. Here, I listed the names verbatim. The third-largest creditor was Gilbert Whitehall, who was owed £248,867. Next is John Lindsay, with £85,833 owed, and he was the fourth-largest creditor. Note that (by 1677) John Lindsay had actually married the widow of another banker, John Colville, and had acquired some of the debt as a result of that family "merger." Rounding out the top five was John Portman, owed £76,761—all of these numbers were (marked to market) five years after the "stop" and were obviously net of any interest that had been paid to date.

In sum, the top five creditors were owed a total of £1,124,180, which is approximately 85% of the total debt (adding up the 25 names) of

[35] See Turnor (1677).

£1,314,941 itemized and listed on February 1677. The second column in the table created and presented by Danby listed the 6% interest that would be due to each of the 25 creditors, and that column adds up to £78,897. It would be due yearly until the principal of the debt was paid back or redeemed.

This list was made available and published in February (or perhaps March) 1677, which, recall, was just a few months after the bankers had received their final quarterly payment of £17,500 (equivalent to £70,000 per year) and were petitioning the House of Common for a permanent solution with the proper amount of interest. And sometime in April 1677, a permanent resolution was indeed reached, but one that the goldsmith-bankers might have not been expecting or even wanted. The Exchequer would soon be opened again in 1677—joyful news, proclaimed the pamphleteers—but the interest payments of £78,897 due to the 25 creditors would instead be redirected or *assigned* to their own creditors—if they were bankers and had their own depositors to satisfy.

The 25 people on the above list were given a year (from August 1677 to August 1678) to make those assignments, which then excused them from (individual) lawsuits and demands for payments from their depositors. The customers and depositors of the bankers—waiting for their own payments to flow—would now become creditors of the government (or the Crown). They were essentially swapping the goldsmith-bankers for the King.

This led to a fascinating social and legal process in which each banker had to create the paperwork and stipulate that the interest he was receiving was "in trust for such of his creditors ... who shall deliver their securities ... and accept the assignments." There are many contemporary accounts of this development, as well as pamphlets in which creditors and depositors debate the merits of accepting the assignments or whether they are better off having the goldsmith-bankers as their own creditor. The sociologist Bruce Carruthers, in his (1996) book *City of Capital*, documented the wide variety of people—their social rank, occupations and location—who took these assignments and became creditors of the Crown instead of the bankers themselves.

How did it work out for them? Well, the interests on the assignments were indeed paid for a few years—intermittently from 1677 to 1685—although there were quite a few delays in payments, as reported by certain individuals. Recall that at this point, the underlying CTOs and their Downing numbers no longer existed and the process of getting paid from the Exchequer was rather haphazard. The interest (never principal) payments trickled to a few drops after the death of King Charles II in 1685 and came to a complete "stop" (again) during the Revolution of 1688. In fact, no payments were made after that for almost 18 years!

Alas, I am forced to be brief, but one could fill an entire book with court documents and the lawsuits that were filed by the many assignees and their heirs attempting to get payment. Instead of 25 people clamoring for justice, there were now hundreds. Only a single one of them managed to get a bit of justice early in the year 1700 and received a few hundred pounds. See the column entitled "payment" in Table 6.2 (which I'll return to in a moment) for the sum total of the money that was dispersed in any given fiscal year.

Finally, exactly 34 years after the original "stop" in 1672 and 18 years since the last proper interest payment had been made, the entire principal of £1,173,353 simply disappeared in the year 1706. With one strike of the pen (or better described as a statute), the interest payments were reduced to 3% (from 6%) and the outstanding sum was rolled into (what is now called) the national debt. In other words, at that time, it became indistinguishable as a stand-alone budget item, distinct from the many other bills, notes, bonds, annuities and even tontines that had been issued since the Revolution of 1688. Moreover, the government now had the option at any time to make a lump-sum payment of only *half the original amount* and pay off all the creditors with a 50% haircut. So, from *time-value-of-money* perspective, you can consider this as finally getting 50% of your original money (or loan) back in the year 1706, except that you are paid with a government bond instead of cash. The other 50% of the principal is completely written off. It is gone.

Ah, yes, the bankers? Well, Danby's solution in 1677 was basically five years too late for them. Robert Viner held on for a while, but was declared bankrupt and his business failed in 1684. He died soon after that, in 1688. Edward Backwell managed to stave off his creditors for a few years and actually tried to propose some alternative schemes to Danby, *à la* John Banks. He then ran for and became a member of the House of Commons, which entitled him to (temporary) protection from debtors' prison. But he eventually failed in 1682, and his family was still trying to clean up the mess 15 years later.

The #3 person on the list, Gilbert Whitehall, failed or went bankrupt and ended up in debtors' prison by 1685. The next person (#4) on the list in terms of debt size was John Lindsey, who—according to the *Handbook of Goldsmith Bankers* published by Hilton Price—escaped to Europe (aka absconded, in the words of J. K. Horsefield)—and never returned to

Table 6.2 Cash flow from Bankers' Debt and Accrued Interest Over Time

Year	Fiscal time period	Total debt start of year	Paid to bakers	6% accrued interest
1	Apr 1672–Mar 1673	£1,173,353	£0	£70,401
2	Apr 1673–Mar 1674	£1,243,754	£0	£74,625
3	Apr 1674–Mar 1675	£1,318,379	£0	£79,103
4	Apr 1675–Mar 1676	£1,327,482	£70,000	£79,649
5	Apr 1676–Mar 1677	£1,309,882	£97,249	£78,593
6	Apr 1677–Mar 1678	£1,322,969	£65,506	£79,378
7	Apr 1678–Mar 1679	£1,336,841	£65,506	£80,210
8	Apr 1679–Mar 1680	£1,351,545	£65,506	£81,093
9	Apr 1680–Mar 1681	£1,398,937	£33,700	£83,936
10	Apr 1681–Mar 1682	£1,437,191	£45,683	£86,231
11	Apr 1682–Mar 1683	£1,480,450	£42,972	£88,827
12	Apr 1683–Mar 1684	£1,540,375	£28,902	£92,422
13	Apr 1684–Mar 1685	£1,600,536	£32,261	£96,032
14	Apr 1685–Mar 1686	£1,680,721	£15,848	£100,843
15	Apr 1686–Mar 1687	£1,768,393	£13,171	£106,104
16	Apr 1687–Mar 1688	£1,861,412	£13,084	£111,685
17	Apr 1688–Mar 1689	£1,973,097	£0	£118,386
18	Apr 1689–Mar 1690	£2,091,483	£0	£125,489
19	Apr 1690–Mar 1691	£2,216,972	£0	£133,018
20	Apr 1691–Mar 1692	£2,349,990	£0	£140,999
21	Apr 1692–Mar 1693	£2,490,990	£0	£149,459
22	Apr 1693–Mar 1694	£2,640,449	£0	£158,427
23	Apr 1694–Mar 1695	£2,798,876	£0	£167,933
24	Apr 1695–Mar 1696	£2,966,809	£0	£178,009
25	Apr 1696–Mar 1697	£3,144,817	£0	£188,689
26	Apr 1697–Mar 1698	£3,333,506	£0	£200,010
27	Apr 1698–Mar 1699	£3,533,517	£0	£212,011
28	Apr 1699–Mar 1700	£3,745,528	£0	£224,732
29	Apr 1700–Mar 1701	£3,970,116	£143	£238,207
30	Apr 1701–Mar 1702	£4,208,001	£322	£252,480
31	Apr 1702–Mar 1703	£4,460,481	£0	£267,629
32	Apr 1703–Mar 1704	£4,728,110	£0	£283,687
33	Apr 1704–Mar 1705	£5,011,797	£0	£300,708
34	Apr 1705–Mar 1706	£5,312,505	£0	£318,750
	Interest paid over 34 years		£589,854	

England. Next down on the list was John Portman (#5), who went bankrupt quite early in the saga, relative to his other four compatriots, likely because he actually refused to sign over the assignments to his creditors. He went bankrupt in 1678 and died in Fleet Prison (The Fleet) in 1683.

By now you get the point. Next on the list was Jeremiah Snow (#6), who was in debtors' prison by 1690; then, Joseph Hornby (#7), who was reported to have gone bankrupt in 1701; then Thomas Rowe (#8), who failed in 1683; then Robert Ryves (#9), one of the earliest to arrive in debtors' prison in 1677; and finally rounding out the top ten was Robert Welstead (#10), who failed in 1678. According to J. K. Horsefield, writing in 1982 and attempting to correct some of the earlier misconceptions about the social and financial implications of the default, "Disaster, more or less complete, overtook all those listed as Charles' principal creditors." In fact, the failure of the larger bankers—like Viner and Backwell—triggered yet another chain reaction of failures and crisis in the early 1680s. Other bankers and financiers like Thomas (not to be confused with William) Price and John Temple, who didn't have any direct exposure to the CTOs or the debt that was stopped in 1672, went bankrupt because of their secondary exposure to the Banker's Debt.

At the same time as one generation was leaving, another generation was coming or emerging from the ashes of the "stop." As indicated in the data collected by P. Temin and H. Voth in the book *Prometheus Shackled*, new goldsmith-bankers entered the industry to take the place vacated by Viner, Backwell and their colleagues. I'll end with a quote or verdict about this sordid financial affair by the historian G. Nichols (1971), "If the treasury had been content to limit the issue of these orders to a responsible level, the Exchequer might have become a bank." In fact, England had to wait for over 20 years after the "stop," until the year 1694, when it got its own central bank.

Visiting Debtors' Prison

Readers might be familiar with the institution of debtors' prison from Charles Dickens' famous novel *Little Dorrit*, which started as a collection of articles for a magazine and eventually was published as a complete book in 1857. It became one of his enduring classics and has spawned a number of movies and mini-series over the years. Dickens tells the story of William Dorrit, who is imprisoned for some obscure and complicated debt nobody can understand or explain, in the infamous Marshalsea prison in London, south of the River Thames. The conditions are horrid, but the tenants try to maintain pride, dignity and some semblance of family and social life. William Dorrit is held in the Marshalsea for so long that his three children essentially spend their (early) life imprisoned together with him. One of those children is young Amy, nicknamed

Little Dorrit, and the rather complicated storyline—it's Dickens after all—is built around her evolving life, attempts to help her family and eventual love interests. Ultimately, a lost fortune materializes, her dear father is released from prison and the story goes on in various directions from there.

Aficionados of literary history will know that Charles Dickens' father himself was in debtors' prison for many years—apparently, he owed a few pounds to the local baker—and the story of *Little Dorrit* contains thinly veiled criticisms of many aspects of his own young life and family circumstances. The imprisoned patriarch wasn't an isolated or unique setup for a fine Victorian novel. Apparently no less than half of the inhabitants of English prisons in the eighteenth century consisted of indigent debtors who simply couldn't pay their creditors. The other half of the prison population was petty or hardened criminals, mutinous sailors, pirates and seditious plotters, all mixed together in large cells.

The Marshalsea as well as The Fleet, yet another infamous prison, was eventually closed down in the year 1842, perhaps as a result of Dickens' early activism and the social awareness he raised of the conditions inside such places—although recall that *Little Dorrit* was published 15 years afterward. Indeed, when the desolate buildings were finally vacated, it turned out that some inhabitants had in fact been there for over 30 years. What was their crime? Owing someone a few pounds and shillings. Not to be outdone by the English, colonial America also had debtors' prison in places like Massachusetts and Pennsylvania.

It was only after the passing of the Bankruptcy Act (in 1869, in what was by then Great Britain) that the punishment of imprisonment for debt was eventually terminated in law, much to the dismay of creditors, who really liked the concept for obvious reasons and tried to keep it alive in spirit. Even today, one still hears of isolated cases of imprisonment, when a strong-willed or activist judge decides to take it upon himself to sentence someone to jail for failure to pay a government fine, or more likely for evading child support payments.

But despite its rarity in the twenty-first century, vivid descriptions and memories of the Marshalesea, Fleet, Clink and King's Bench Prison by Dickens, Defoe and others—and even by artists like William Hogarth in his series of paintings *A Rake's Progress*—have lingered in the public consciousness. One can't but help but imagine with horror the fear of missing a credit card or mortgage payment one month and being thrown into Alcatraz soon after.

But like all popular impressions, the truth of the matter—and exactly what took place inside—was subtler, complicated and very much dependent on one's *station in life*. More important to our story, although many of the unlucky and indebted goldsmith-bankers did end up being imprisoned for debt, it's unlikely that they experienced the more extreme squalid and fetid conditions described by the novelists. So here is how the business—and it really was a business—of debtors' prison really[36] worked.

First of all, government, penal authorities or police did not manage these prisons. None of those institutions really existed in their currently known form, in the seventeenth century. Prisons were mostly private for-profit (corporate) ventures, often described as extortion rackets preying on the unfortunate. Some of the prisons were owned by well-known peers, such as the Bishop of Ely or the Duke of Portland, and then subleased or rented (perhaps like an airbnb) to the warden, who "managed the business." The warden would extract rents from inmates by charging them for room and board and allowing other businesses—like bars and steakhouses—to set up concession stands in the prison.

Of course, if the prisoner (or their family) didn't have the money to pay the warden, their liabilities would continue to grow and the cycle of debt would continue. Either way, it would be more appropriate to think of these prisons in the seventeenth and eighteenth centuries as lodging houses with various levels of privilege—some inhabitants were allowed to leave during the day to work off their debts—in contrast to the image of a twenty-first-century prison. Entire communities sprouted around these prisons to house extended family members. It was certainly a very unique neighborhood.

This brings me to the second point, which is that the purpose of the prison or incarceration itself wasn't to punish the debtor or make them repent their biblical sins. Rather it is best to think of it as *coercive imprisonment* to induce debtors and their families to fulfill their contractual obligations. A young Charles Dickens at the age of 12 was forced to go to work in a gloomy factory to help pay his father's debts and eventually get him released from prison. In contrast, in the twenty-first century, a debtor in his father's situation would simply file for bankruptcy protection. The courts and judicial system would partition and divide his assets among the various creditors, discharge him and give him a fresh start. But

---

[36] The source for the material in this section about bankruptcy and debtors' prison is primarily from Cohen (1982) and partially from Jones (1979).

in the seventeenth and eighteenth centuries, these bankruptcy, or insolvency statutes—although they did exist in some limited form—weren't as lenient to the debtor as they are today. So although there was a growing awareness that individuals needed some way to obtain relief from their unfortunate debts—to help commerce and capitalism flourish—the discharge of liabilities was only limited to *traders*. These were merchants, who, according to the legal definition, were individuals making a living by buying and selling. The moral theory was that they had likely suffered some random loss, perhaps a sinking boat or a pirate attack, and couldn't pay back their debts through no fault of their own. Consumption debt was frowned upon and created a perpetual obligation (perhaps no different from student loans in the twenty-first century, which is becoming a growing problem).

The definition or classification of *who* was a trader and could make this claim was expanded over the years to include butchers, carpenters and brick masters—that is, they could be discharged from their debts—but excluded tailors and innkeepers, for some odd reason. The legality and definitions were all rather complicated and perhaps worthy of a Dickens' novel, but these refinements only took place over the eighteenth and nineteenth centuries, far too late for the goldsmith-bankers (of 1672) in our story.

But here is the key takeaway: even prisons such as the Marshalsea had different areas and sections for debtors depending on their stature and station in life. Some were only forced to spend their nights in prison and could wander and (attempt to) do business during the day. Many had their family with them or living in the near vicinity, and others continued a semblance of social life. It wasn't pleasant—and a marked contrast to their gilded life during the good-old banking years—but Alcatraz it wasn't.

1706: INTERNAL RATE OF RETURN AND RECOVERY

With the substance of the story behind us, in this final section, we are now ready to roll up our sleeves and perform "final rites" on the Banker' Debt. As I mentioned earlier, the entire sum was eventually rolled into the (soon-to-be-called) British national debt in early 1706, which was exactly 34 years after the "stop" was first announced. Of course, by then the original goldsmith-bankers like Viner, Backwell, Whitehall and Lindsay were dead, although some of their heirs were still struggling to settle their financial affairs decades later. Likewise, the plaintiffs in most of the legal actions against the government during the 1690s—since interest had been suspended during the reign of William III and Mary II after the Revolution of 1688—were in fact the descendants of the original holders of the bankers' assignments. All of that is known. The final question then is as follows: if we assume that the entire amount of stopped debt or CTOs in early January 1672 was indeed[37] correctly estimated at £1,211,065 on day zero, what then was the internal rate of return (IRR) in aggregate after 34 years of waiting? What was the economic recovery rate when the CTOs were merged into the national debt? How bad of an investment were these (defaulted) bonds? All these questions are now asked—with a 20/20 hindsight bias of course.

Well, there have been a few estimates of the yield or total return that have been provided over the years—and I'll get to those in a moment—but to be very blunt, most of them have ignored something very basic (to a financial economist), which is the *time value of money*. So, if we are to conclude with a final analysis of risk and return for CTOs, then we must employ the standard methodology used for bond and mortgage pricing in the twenty-first century, even if it wasn't understood or appreciated by historians in the seventeenth century.

To obtain the proper summary numbers, Table 6.2 lays out the timeline and estimated cash flows. The first meaningful column in the table lists the fiscal period starting in (early) April and ending in March. This is no different from how I reported revenue and expenses in Chap. 4, when I discussed the King's personal finances. In the second column of the table and for each of the 34 fiscal periods, I list the *value* of the Bankers' Debt at the beginning of the year. Now, I have emphasized the word value because it can differ from the reported or assumed figures, and I'll get back to that issue in a moment. Also to be very clear, technically I'm glossing over the interest that would have been due for first three months of 1672 and assuming that Danby's number or estimate of £1,173,353 applied to April 1, 1672. The third column in the table is a critical one and I have relied on the historians and their archival work for those numbers. It reports the total amount of interest that was paid (aka cash that was distributed) to the debt holders during each one of the 34 fiscal periods. For example, during the first two years until the end of March 1674, absolutely no interest was paid (to anyone) on the debt. Recall that Danby issued guidelines during the summer of 1674 to begin making payments that only commenced at the very end of the fiscal year 1675, or the first day of April 1675. That

---

[37] This is as per Danby's estimate reported in the *CTB* on February 8, 1677, and also reproduced by Horsefield (1982) in Table 1.

(first) year's payment was for £70,000 (in total) and is the first number in that column. The next year, another £97,249 was paid during the fiscal year 1676–1677 to bring the total payments until the end of March 1677 (i.e. the first five years) to £167,249. These particular cash flows or payments reported all the way to the year 1688 are based on the work of C. D. Chandaman[38] (1975), and from that point onward the numbers (or lack therefore) are based on J. K. Horsefield (1982). All in all, the entire quantity of interest that was paid to creditors over the 34 years' period, from early 1672 to early 1706, was £589,854 and is listed[39] at the very bottom of the third column in the table. Please note that the pattern and timing of cash flows are just as important as the total itself, which is why I have taken the trouble to display them in this manner.

Now, the fourth and final column in the table calculates the *hypothetical* interest that should have accrued on the debt, assuming an interest rate (was ticking) at a compounding 6% per year from the very beginning in April 1672. This 6% is based on the maximum allowable by law at the time, as well as the original promise by King Charles II in the announcement of the "stop" to compensate all treasury order holders at that 6% rate per year. Now, although the 6% figure was the basis for negotiations and discussion with the goldsmith-bankers, it obviously wasn't paid and never formally accrued in this manner. This is an important point and critical for the calculations that follow.

For example, the financial *value* of the debt for the start of fiscal year 1676–1677 is computed as being £1,309,882 (in a shaded box), and for the year 1677–1678, it is £1,322,969. Again, this is derived by first subtracting any payments made to the bankers (or via assignments) and then adding the 6% interest. For comparison and sanity check purposes, note that the official (Danby) records list the *capital sum* due to the bankers as being £1,314,940, approximately five years after the stop, in early 1677. That £1,314,940 number appears and is quoted in almost all serious discussions or analysis of the Bankers' Debt, for example, Carruthers (1996), Roseveare (1991) and Horsefield (1982). As far as our numbers are concerned, it is the mid-point value in between the two cells. In other words, the official *capital sum* reported in 1677 was properly accounting for time value of money at 6% per year from the very beginning, assuming the amount of debt at the point of default was £1,173,353. Danby wasn't making any math mistakes.

---

[38] Page 338.
[39] Horsefield (1982) on p. 523 claims that Chandaman's figures were missing £43,000 in interest payments, which is why I'll conduct a "sensitivity analysis" around these numbers.

Now all this discussion of accruals and compounding might seem like obscure methodological issues, but they do have a substantial impact on the principal owed as we move up the decades to the year 1706. When you are compounding interest, a few percentage points will make an enormous difference. If—and this is a big if—we allow interest to accrue at 6% every single year for 34 years while subtracting payments to the creditors as they were made and recorded, then we are left with a mortgage schedule of sorts. We can then employ conventional and well-established calculations for returns and yields.

Of course this is a mortgage in which the homeowner borrowed £1.2 million to purchase a house—at an interest rate of 6%—but started off by making no payments for 3 years (and instead growing the debt). After that, the so-called homeowner then made interest payments for 13 years, but never really enough to cover the interest that was accruing. These payments certainly didn't pay down any of the principal. So, in that case, the gap or deficit between the (small) mortgage payments and the (larger) interest is capitalized and then added to the principal. This is basic finance 101.

What is owed at the end of the 34 years of (mostly not) paying your mortgage in this odd and erratic manner? Well, the very last number in the second column of the table is £5,312,505. That is what the homeowner owes the bank at the end of 34 years—even though they had originally only borrowed £1,173,353. Just as a reminder, the over £5 million pounds (in the early years of the eighteenth century) would be close to £500 million pounds (in the early years of the twenty-first century) using the wobbly double-zero rule I described in Chap. 3.

Now—and this is the final key to the calculation and analysis—recall that early in the year 1706, the outstanding Bankers' Debt was added to the principal of the national debt and interest was finally resumed (after 18 years of effectively nothing) at 3% per year. Moreover, the government declared that it could redeem the principal at 50% of its original value at any time. So, using that logic, the creditors were still getting 6% interest (in perpetuity) but only on half of the original £1,173,353. In other words, from early 1706 onward the debt could be redeemed or called for as little as £586,677 at the pleasure of the Treasury. Ergo, the debt's market price in early 1706 was now approximately £586,677 in the secondary market (so to speak). This is not my estimate or assumption. Historians such as J. K. Horsefield (1982) thereafter account for the debt at that *book value*. But the *economic value* of the debt was £5,312,505 using the (mortgage schedule) methodology I described above. Now divide the small number

(£586,677) into the big number (£5,312,505) and you are left with an *economic recovery rate* of (58/531) or 11%. Stated differently, a total of 91% of the value of the bond was lost in the default.

We are now ready to perform the final calculation of the chapter (and the book), and that is to compute the IRR for the hypothetical holders of the debt from day zero in early 1672 all the way to the beginning of the year 1706, when the new regime begins and the debt becomes part of the larger national debt. The IRR is a number or yield that equates the initial investment with subsequent cash flows, properly taking account of the exact time or spacing between the cash flows. It's a relatively easy calculation that can be conducted in any spreadsheet in the twenty-first century, but would have been rather time consuming in the seventeenth century. To make a long story short, the answer is: 0.01% or an *investment return of exactly 1 basis point*. See Appendix B for a carefull analysis of the actual investment return (or recovery rate) using a discounted cash-flow methodology, but which obviously leads to the exact same numerical result.

Perhaps that is yet another way to summarize the entire story of the "stop" in one number: a single basis point per year for 34 years. So—here is a shocker—the Bankers' Debt clearly[40] wasn't a very good investment compared with the 6% interest rate that would have been available elsewhere.

I conclude with one final comment, and that is with regard to a (rather odd) statement made by the much-referenced J. K. Horsefield, who, recall, is one of the recent historians and experts on the "stop." Toward the very end of his article, he computed that the return or yield on the Bankers' Debt was actually positive and in the range of 1.5% per year, which is quite far from the single basis point that I am estimating. There are some differences in methodology which I'll clarify in a moment, but he actually concludes by saying: "One may think, without prejudice, that the owners of the debt whoever they are had been hardly done by." Well, that is quite the statement—even if he was speaking for the Whigs (which he wasn't)—and begs the question: why the discrepancy?

Well, the answer likely comes down to the difference between the perspective of an economic historian and that of a financial economist. You see, the way Horsefield (1982) generated the numbers, he essentially

---

[40] Horsefield (1982) claims that Chandaman's (1975) figures on p. 338 are missing some £43,000 in interest that was actually paid to the bankers prior to 1688. If we add it (evenly) to the cash flows in Table 6.2, the internal rate of return increases to 19 basis points, or 0.19%.

divided the total £589,854 in interest payments by the 34 years for an average payment of £17,350 per year to the bankers. That *average* number then divided into the original debt of £1,173,353 is indeed 1.48% per year—a positive number.

But alas, there are two points to make here. First and foremost that is *not* how the bank will allow you to compute or pay down the mortgage. *When* you make the payments, it is just as important as *how much* you actually pay. You certainly can't purchase the house and then wait 34 years to pay the bank by claiming that, on average, they are getting the interest they had charged. Indeed, if I might be so audacious, historians often play fast and loose with the *time value of money*, and this is a good example.

Second, and more importantly, when you account for the financial risk that the holders of the CTOs were incurring, a risk I discussed at length in Chap. 5, it is quite clear that these instruments should have earned much more than the (risk-free rate) of 6%, both ex ante and ex post. And, of course, I'm not even adjusting for all the stress incurred by the bankers and creditors over the 34 years. Finally—although this was a final blow long after the contours of our particular story—most of the British national debt, which was in the form of Exchequer annuities, was swapped into stock of the infamous South Sea Company in early 1720. And that didn't end well either.

So, with all due to respect (and yes, despite the 100% recovery rate) the goldsmith-bankers most certainly were *done by*.

References

Beresford, J. (1925). *The Godfather of Downing Street*. Boston: Houghton Mifflin.

Browning, A. (1966). Settlement of the Banker's Debt Created by the Stop of the Exchequer. *English Historical Documents, Volume VI c. 1660–1714.* Routledge.

Carruthers, B. G. (1996). *City of Capital: Politics and Markets in the English Financial Revolution*. Princeton: Princeton University Press.

Chandaman, C. (1975). *The English Public Revenue 1660–1688*. Oxford: Clarendon Press.

Cohen, J. (1982). The History of Imprisonment for Debt and Its Relation to the Development of Discharge in Bankruptcy. *Journal of Legal History, 3*, 153–171.

Coleman, D. C. (1963). *Sir John Banks Baronet and Businessman: A Study of Business, Politics and Society in Later Stuart England*. Oxford: Clarendon Press.

Diamond, D. W., & Dybvig, P. H. (1983). Bank Runs, Deposit Insurance and Liquidity. *Journal of Political Economy, 91*(3), 401–419.

Dibden, W. G. S. (1965). *Four Hundred Years of Anglo Dutch Mail*. The Hague: Postal Historical Society.

Goetzmann, W. N., & Jorion, P. (1999). Re-Emerging Markets. *Journal of Financial and Quantitative Analysis, 34*(1), 1–31.
Grayling, A. C. (2016). *The Age of Genius: The Seventeenth Century and the Birth of the Modern Mind.* London: Bloomsbury.
Haley, K. (1968). *The First Earl of Shaftsebury.* Oxford: Clarendon Press.
Horsefield, J. K. (1982). The Stop of the Exchequer Revisited. *The Economic History Review, 35*(4), 511–528.
Hutchsinson, R. (2016). *The Audacious Crimes of Colonel Blood: The Spy Who Stole the Crown Jewels and Became the King's Secret Agent.* London: Weidenfeld and Nicolson.
Hutton, R. (1986). The Making of the Secret Treaty of Dover. *The Historical Journal, 29*(2), 297–318.
Hutton, R. (1989). *Charles the Second: King of England, Scotland and Ireland.* Oxford: Clarendon Press.
Iddesleigh, S. H. (1887). The Closing of the Exchequer by Charles II in 1672. *Lectures and Essays of the Earl of Northcote,* 244–285.
Isenberg, N. (2016). *White Trash: The 400-Year Untold History of Class in America.* New York: Viking: Penguin Random House.
Jones, W. J. (1979). The Foundations of English Bankruptcy: Statutes and Commissions in the Early Modern Period. *Transactions of the American Philosophical Society, 69*(3), 1–63.
Koudijs, P. (2015). Those Who Know Most: Insider Trading in 18th Century Amsterdam. *Journal of Political Economy, 123*(6), 1356–1409.
Koudijs, P. (2016). The Boats that Did Not Sail: Asset Price Volatility in a Natural Experiment. *The Journal of Finance, 71*(3), 1185–1126.
Lee, M. (1965). *The CABAL.* Urbana: University of Illinois Press.
Lowndes, W., & Gill, M. D. (1931). The Treasury: 1660–1714. *The English Historical Review, 46*(184), 600–622.
Melton, F. T. (1986). *Sir Robert Clayton and the Origins of English Deposit Banking 1658–1685.* Cambridge University Press.
Nichols, G. O. (1971). English Government Borrowing: 1660–1688. *Journal of British Studies, 10*(2), 83–104.
Pepys, S. (1997). *The Concise Pepys.* (T. Griffith, Ed.) Hertfordshire: Wordsworth Classics of World Literature.
Petram, L. (2014). *The World's First Stock Exchange.* New York: Columbia University Press.
Roseveare, H. (1991). *The Financial Revolution 1660–1760.* London and New York: Longman.
Shin, H. S. (2009). Reflections on Northern Rock: The Bank Run that Heralded the Global Financial Crisis. *Journal of Economic Perspectives, 23*(1), 101–119.
Turnor, T. (1677). *The Joyful News of the Opening of the Exchequer to the Goldsmiths of Lombard Street and Their Creditors.* London, England: Grays Inn Gate.

CHAPTER 7

Concluding Thoughts for the Twenty-First Century

Although it might appear that lessons from *the Stop of the Exchequer* are confined to the field of financial history or only pertinent to aficionados of seventeenth-century England, I do believe the story told contains a number of insights about risk, return and debt management that are equally valid in the twenty-first century. And although I don't know whether or not seventeenth-century goldsmith-bankers had any notion of proper asset and liability management for their balance sheet, the deadly mismatch between the investments they were holding as "assets" and the "liabilities" owed to their depositors has been at the financial core of almost every banking crisis for the last 350 years.

Of course, the wrong conclusion to draw from this entire sordid episode is the other extreme, that somehow borrowing money or personal debt is wrong or sinful and that it will inevitably get you into trouble. I'll label this erroneous approach the "Puritan[1] view." Figure 7.1 provides a snapshot illustration of how to think about borrowing and introduces a concept I would like to call the *Point of Optimal Debt Level* (PoDeL).

In Fig. 7.1 the horizontal (x-axis) measures the amount of debt that someone has on his or her personal balance sheet and the vertical (y-axis)

---

[1] Yes, I know there is absolutely no evidence that a Puritan would be opposed to running up large credit card debts, but it just feels that way. In fact there is a legitimate claim that the Puritan work ethic or philosophy is at the core and foundation of modern capitalism. See, for example, the writing of sociologist Max Weber and so on.

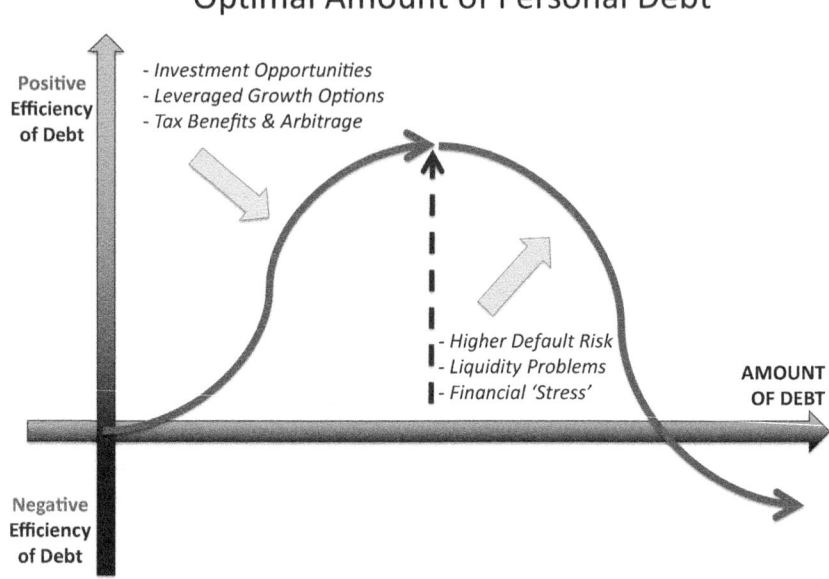

Fig. 7.1 Point of Optimal Debt Level (PoDeL)

denotes the efficiency or benefit of that debt, which might actually be negative and harming. And while there aren't any specific numbers or values on the *x*-axis—quite deliberately, since it really depends on personal circumstances—my main point here is that there is a unique mark or spot somewhere in the middle, after that you are indeed taking on "too much" debt. From there on, it's making your personal financial situation worse. In fact, if you go far right and well beyond your personal PoDeL, you might even fall into negative territory. In that negative region you really are harming your long-term financial prospects.

Now I admit this picture is a high-level abstraction. The shape of the curve in real life might not be as smooth or parabolic as the picture portrays and please don't ask me when it goes from being concave to convex and vice versa. But my message here is that the expected benefits of taking on more debt can't increase indefinitely. It has to peak at some point, which again I label your personal PoDeL. After you have reached the apex—whatever number that might be—more debt will not make you merrier (or a monarch).

7 CONCLUDING THOUGHTS FOR THE TWENTY-FIRST CENTURY   195

To the right of that point the benefits decline because you start to incur the risk of economic distress, liquidity difficulties and the general strain of constraints; all of which might be as psychological as they are financial. Stated bluntly, just because a bank or lender is offering you another hundred-thousand-dollar loan doesn't mean or imply that you should take the money and continue marching to the right.

In fact, you might already be to the right of the (goldilocks) point and getting dangerously close to negative territory. Instead, you should be veering to the left and reducing your debt. Why? Well, whether it is macroeconomic factors such as an increase in interest rates or the loss of a job, a family medical emergency or some other crisis, you might not end up in debtors' prison, but the consequences of default aren't pleasant.

On the other side of the PoDeL, one can make the opposite argument. Having too little debt deprives you of many valuable economic opportunities, such as investing in an education or buying a house or "smoothing" your consumption over your life cycle. Sometimes debt is simply inevitable. Moreover, recall that in many jurisdictions and depending on how the borrowed money is spent, the interest you pay is either tax deductible and/or subject to valuable tax credits. What all this means is that the taxpayer (i.e. your neighbor) is subsidizing part of the cost of the debt. Why not take advantage of that?

And speaking of income taxes, while I dare not give the figure the same gravitas as a so-called Philips curve, the efficiency of debt is (obviously) zero if you have no debt. The curve must converge to zero at the lower left-hand corner. Could there be multiple optimal points in between? Could the real debt efficiency curve be much more kinky? Personally, I don't think so. Like Newton's laws of gravity, I think there is some regularity and smoothness to these relationships.

More to the point, although I would like to avoid veering into tangential topics, there is some evidence[2] to suggest that the *personal equity*

---

[2] I have written and reported elsewhere (e.g. see my article in the *National Post* on April 5, 2016) that Canadian households with one additional dollar of debt on their personal balance sheet, relative to identical Canadians who do not have the extra dollar of liabilities, also have an additional 0.35 cents of equity or net worth. And this effect is actually more pronounced for households who rent as opposed to those who own their residence, so you can't chalk this all up (only) to increasing real estate prices. For example, households with debts over $200,000 have a median net worth of $377,000. But those with debts over $600,000 are at $1,172,000. Remember, this is net worth (E), not assets (A), in the basic $E = A - L$ relationship I alluded to in Chap. 1.

(aka net worth) of individuals does follow the semi-parabolic path displayed in Fig. 7.1. Households with very little debt on their personal balance—controlling for important factors such as age, gender, salary and geographic location—have lower net worth compared with (very similar) households who actually have debt. Moreover, as these households accumulate more debt (in a statistical sense), their net worth increases for a bit, but then peaks or reaches a maximum. After that point, households with "too much debt" relative to the optimum—although they have more assets on their balance sheet, likely because they have a bigger mortgage to buy a more expensive house—their comprehensive net worth isn't any greater.

So assuming this unique point exists and remains to be quantified, how do you decide upon or locate your PoDeL? How do you know if you are to the left or to the right? Well, here again, I believe there are some relevant insights from the story of the *Stop of the Exchequer* and specifically the collateralized treasury orders (CTOs), which got the King and his Exchequer into trouble.

In that vein here are four ideas.

IDEA #1: "**Borrow Against an Explicit Source of Regular Income. Tag It in Advance.**" There is some merit to the idea of *borrowing against income* instead of *borrowing against assets*, such as a house or a car. Sure, the bank or lender would never accept your salary or job as security—and slavery is obviously illegal—but nevertheless, this approach serves as an excellent benchmark for what you can afford without risking financial distress. Think about it this way, the next time you take on debt or a loan. What year's revenue (aka personal supply, in the lingo from Chap. 4) have you just spent? Will this house cost you your salary until the year 2050? Sure, you can afford the interest payments today and the house might be a good investment, but you have just spent 80% of the present value of—what economists call—your human capital on one single purchase. Is that smart? The CTOs were backed by tax revenues and the Exchequer or government could only borrow up to that minus an adjustment for interest. Perhaps individuals should add up the total amount they will earn—adjusted for interest—and use that as the baseline for borrowing.

IDEA #2: "**Live Within Your Lifecycle Means.**" One can debate—and historians certainly have—whether Charles could have avoided his financial difficulties if he had been more reasonable with his spending. It's unlikely that a few less jewels for his mistresses would have made a difference when he had the entire English Navy and Army to support out of his own royal pocket.

Nevertheless, I do think it's worth thinking of Sir George Downing and his committee of treasurers looking over your shoulder every time you open your wallet to spend. In the language of Fig. 7.1, you can move closer to your *personal optimal debt level* by cutting expenses instead of paying down debt.

IDEA #3: "**Don't Diversify Creditors. Keep Your Debts in One Basket with the Lowest Interest Rate.**" The goldsmith-bankers who lent money to Charles had themselves financed these loans and borrowed the money from many smaller depositors. When Charles and the Exchequer stopped interest payments, the bankers were left squeezed between one asset that defaulted and many liabilities that didn't. That is bad risk management on a number of levels. One of the principal reasons Sir John Banks didn't end up on the infamous list of creditors is that he didn't have his own bank customers (and creditors) to satisfy. But he also knew to diversify the assets on his balance sheet. So, think of Sir John's crafty maneuvers when managing your own personal finances.

Here, it is from another perspective. If you owe $100 on your home mortgage at an interest rate of 2.5% amortized over the next ten years, most financial experts would argue that it is relatively good debt. But if you owe $100 on your bank credit card or department store card and are paying 15% interest, then that is (a really) bad (idea and) debt. Oddly enough, these two types of debt—and everything in between—are tallied up in the officially reported consumer debt load; mortgages, lines of credit, cars, boats and even money owed to the local loan shark. The optimum amount of debt obviously depends on the interest rate you are paying. You can move closer to your PoDeL by rearranging your debts—even if you don't necessarily reduce the total amount you owe. In fact, I am always puzzled to learn of consumers who diversify their debts and owe money to different creditors at different interest rates. I don't mean to trivialize the advice or lesson here, but do go with the lowest interest rate or place those "eggs in one basket."

IDEA #4: "**Familiarize Yourself with the Cost of Financial Distress. It Can Be Enormous**." As you read in the previous pages, it took almost 34 years to resolve the mess created by the King's default—and in the end, the investors only got a small fraction of their original principal. You might think this is an historical anachronism that's been sorted out in the last 350 years—but make no mistake, these sorts of prolonged delays happen in the twenty-first century as well. If things blow up, be prepared for a very long wait while the dust settles. There have been many such examples recently. For example, the bankruptcy of Lehman Brothers—ten years later—is still being sorted out. These things will take longer than you think and you won't have Danby to help clear up the mess. My point is that the word "option to default" is often treated like other financial options that can be triggered with the flip of a mathematical switch, with little permanent trauma or scaring. The truth is that these events take on a life of their own.

Case Study for Business Ethics?

In conclusion—and on a much broader level—I would like to put on my proverbial professorial hat and suggest that many of the financial issues, decisions and even moral dilemmas that arose during the period surrounding the "stop" might be equally relevant and resonate in today's business environment. Indeed, perhaps the story I have just told can serve as the backdrop for a formal case study in a modern business school.

Here are some themes for discussion if you want to wander down this path.

What is the proper risk premium on novel fixed-income bonds or new methods of borrowing that are collateralized by uncertain cash flows? If you were a banker, how would you determine how much to discount (or what to pay for) a CTO? Yes, charging usurious interest rates might be unacceptable or illegal when it is imposed on risk-free loans, but what if there is a (substantial) risk that you will never get paid? The underlying cash flows might never materialize. Think of modern-day student loans as just one example. Considering that today there is over $1 trillion in US student loans outstanding—apparently more than what is owed on credit cards—it is prudent to carefully think about (and perhaps worry about) such matters. What rate should student borrowers be paying in the open market if there is uncertainty over whether they will earn enough to pay back the lender? In the event of default, would you sympathize with the borrower (student) or the lender (bank)? Should that sort of borrowing transaction be subjected to restrictions or limits? Moreover, if interest rates are capped, should risk premiums be capped as well?

Moving on to something even more controversial, is it appropriate to use private and confidential information—that is, news that only you know—to trade before the market learns or receives the information? It might have been perfectly acceptable and legal in the seventeenth century, but how is it looked upon today in the twenty-first century?

Be honest with yourself and acknowledge your prejudices. What are your thoughts and views about the fellow (Isaac) I described in Chap. 6 who tried to get to Amsterdam with his CTOs before the mail boat arrived? Would that be acceptable today? Or did he somehow have a moral obligation to suffer the unjust financial loss quietly and with dignity? What about the goldsmith-banker (Edward) and the attempt to seize Queen Catherine's dowry as recompense for frozen CTOs he was left holding after the default? I mentioned that the King and his privy council put an end to that idea, but would it be morally acceptable today? How about Lord Shaftesbury's bank withdrawals—and purchase of safe land as an alternative—in the months preceding the stop? Could anybody defend that sort of activity in the moral climate of the twenty-first century? And yet, in many countries and jurisdictions, politicians do stand to benefit economically (directly or indirectly) from policies they promote or advocate.

Why is it different?

Finally, back to the topic with which I started this chapter—or the indebted Charlie who motivated the story in the preface—what is a prudent or optimal amount of debt, be it for government, corporate or personal? More importantly, does its usage matter? Or is it only the magnitude or notional value that counts? Is money borrowed to fund wars or provision ships any more or less acceptable than borrowing money to finance the purchase of jewelry and housing for mistresses? Stated differently, would you have had more or less sympathy for the goldsmith-bankers if it were the Great Fire of London (natural disaster)—as opposed to the Treaty of Dover (political dealings)—that triggered or led to the default announcement?

Anyway, hopefully you get my point. These sorts of questions can provide food for thought, or fodder for conversation at the dinner table, the bar or perhaps even a book club. I like to think that these exact topics were debated in the taverns and coffee shops of the late seventeenth century—as they would be in the early twenty-first century.

If there is one final message from the *Stop of the Exchequer* that might resonate further, it is that although the financial solutions or economic *answers* have changed considerably during the last three centuries, the underlying *questions* haven't.

Appendix A: The Fate of a 2007 Banker

Table A.1

CEO or Chairman of the Board of Directors (BoD)	Bank or institution	Home country	2007 compensation ($M)	CEO charged? Prison? Jail? Company fined?
Fred A. Goodwin	Royal Bank of Scotland	UK	$8.38	Investigation. No charges. No prison.
Josef Ackerman	Deutsche Bank	Germany	$12.95	No charges. No prison.
Baudouin Prot	BNP Paribas	France	$4.88	No charges. No prison.
John Silvester Varley	Barclays Bank	UK	$3.84	No charges. No prison.
M. F. Geoghegan	HSBC Holdings	UK	$3.14	No charges. No prison.
Rene Carron	Credit Agricole	France	$0.80	No charges. No prison.
Charles Prince	Citigroup	USA	$15.62	No charges. No prison.
Marcel Rohner	UBS	Switzerland	$2.58	Investigation. No charges.

(continued)

Table A.1 (continued)

CEO or Chairman of the Board of Directors (BoD)	Bank or institution	Home country	2007 compensation ($M)	CEO charged? Prison? Jail? Company fined?
Kenneth D. Lewis	Bank of America	USA	$24.84	Investigation. Fine and three-year ban.
Daniel Boulton	Société Générale	France	$4.52	Investigation. Charges dropped.
James Dimon	JPMorgan Chase	USA	$27.80	No charges, but company paid $13B fine.
Dick Fuld	Lehman Brothers	USA	$73.10	No charges, amazingly....
Alessandro Profumo	UniCredit	Italy	$12.60	Investigation, but acquitted of tax fraud.
Michel Tilmant	ING Bank	Netherlands	$4.51	No charges. No prison.
Alfredo Saenz Abad	Santander	Spain	$7.65	No charges. Resigned and retired.
Brady Dougan	Credit Suisse	Switzerland	$2.90	No charges, but company paid $2.6B fine.
Jiang Jiangin (C)	ICBC	China	$0.24	No charges. No prison.
Lloyd Blankfein	Goldman Sachs	USA	$27.56	No charges, but company paid $5B fine.
Klaus-Peter Mueller	Commerzbank	Germany	$3.38	No charges. No prison.
Giovanni Bazoli	Intesa San Paolo	Italy	$1.64	No charges. No prison.
John Mack	Morgan Stanley	USA	$0.80	No charges. No prison.
Gang Xiao	Bank of China	China	$0.20	No charges. No prison.
G. K. Thompson	Wachovia Corp.	USA	$10.79	Investigated. No prison. Industry ban.
James Cayne	Bear Stearns	USA	$38.30	No charges. No prison.

Table A.1 (continued)

CEO or Chairman of the Board of Directors (BoD)	Bank or institution	Home country	2007 compensation ($M)	CEO charged? Prison? Jail? Company fined?
Victor Blank	Lloyds	UK	$1.32	No charges. No prison.
Peter Straarup	Danske Bank	Denmark	$2.46	No charges. No prison.
John Thain	Merrill Lynch	USA	$17.30	Investigation. No charges.
John Stumpf	Wells Fargo	USA	$12.60	No charges. No prison.
John McFarlane	ANZ Group	Australia	$6.36	No charges. No prison.
Martin Sullivan	AIG	UK	$10.20	AIG settled with shareholders for $970.5M.
Andy Hornby	HBOS	UK	$3.80	Investigations, but CEO cleared.
Ken Chenault	American Express	USA	$26.08	No charges. No prison.
Robert Kelly	BNY Mellon	USA	$20.12	No charges. No prison.
Richard Syron	FREDDIE MAC	USA	$18.18	Investigation and settlements. No prison.
Rick Waddell	Northern Trust	USA	$6.03	No charges. No prison.
James Rohr	PNC	USA	$18.45	Investigation. No charges.
Ronald Loque	State Street	USA	$28.30	Investigation. $660M settlement with company.
Richard K. Davis	US BANK	USA	$4.39	Investigation. $660M settlement with company.

Source: Collected from various public sources by the author, with special thanks to Daniel Tut at the Schulich School of Business.

Appendix B: Unpacking the IRR

In this section I'll explain in a bit more detail how exactly I computed the *internal rate of return* (IRR) of only 0.013%—which is *one basis point*—for the ex post yield from the bankers' debt over the 34-year period from 1672 to 1706. The table (at the end of this section) displays all the intermediate steps or components of that calculation.

To compute an IRR, which is a single summary number, one requires very accurate and assumed times for all cash flows as well as a precise starting point, sometimes referred to as the pivot date. My pivot date will be April 1, 1672, which I'll take as the beginning (roughly) of the fiscal year when the outstanding bankers' debt was valued at £1,173,353. Technically I am computing a recovery rate on defaulted debt, although I am positioning as the IRR on an investment of £1,173,353 at time zero. This was the exact number recorded by Danby himself and used by J. K. Horsefield (1982, p. 515) in his calculations, albeit related to early January 1672. Either way, it is a negative cash flow as far as the IRR calculation is concerned because the bankers paid out that money. Recall that in fiscal (starting in) April 1672, no interest was paid on the debt, nor was it paid in April 1673 or in April 1674. The bankers waited for at least 36 months. But then, for the year starting April 1675, a total of £70,000 interest was paid and distributed to the creditors. I'll assume that the entire payment was made on that one single date of April 1, 1675—since the formulas require this precision—and I'll return to any bias a lump-sum assumption might introduce at the end. Then again, on April 1, 1676 another

£97,249 was paid to the creditors, and so on and so forth. All of this is based on numbers collected by C. D. Chandaman (1975, p. 338) and then allocated by fiscal year. Finally, on April 1, 1706 (34 years later), the bankers' debt was reduced by 50% (from £1,173,353 to £586,677) and merged into the national debt. This is why the final entry in that column is £586,677.

Now, although the creditors never received this amount in actual cash on that date (and technically the settlement took place a few months prior), I assumed it was the market *value* of the bond from that point onward. The sum total of that column, 15 years (out of 34) of interest plus the final £586,677, is exactly £1,176,531. To be clear, that is the *sum* of the actual cash and not the *discounted* or economic value of the cash flows. Nevertheless, the fact that it's so (uncannily) near to the original debt of £1,173,353 should give an immediate indication that the IRR is close to zero. Recall, once again, that my analysis hinges on being able to assign a magnitude for that final action in early 1706 in which the bankers' debt was merged into the national debt at 50% of its original value.

Moving on, the next few columns in the table compute the discounted value of the individual component cash flows during those 34 years, at four different rates: 6%, 3%, 1.5% and 0.013%. The last number (which is a mere basis point, using the modern language of interest rates) wasn't selected arbitrarily but arrived at via a process of trial and error. Actually, I solved for the rate that would result in a present value of exactly £1,173,353 (the original debt). But, I am getting ahead of myself here. Let me explain the individual steps.

Begin with the numbers in the "6%" column. They represent the discounted (to April 1, 1672) values of the 15 interest payments and the final (market, assumed) value of the debt. For example, the £70,000 received on April 1, 1675 would only have been worth £58,773 (in present value terms) on April 1, 1672 using a discount rate of 6%. The mathematics is as follows. The discount *factor* for three years is: 1.06^{-3}, which is approximately 0.84. So, the nondiscounted cash of £70,000 leads to a properly discounted value of £58,773. Likewise, the final cash flow of £586,677 on April 1, 1706 has to be adjusted by a discount factor of $1.06^{-34} = 0.138$, for a discounted economic value of £80,909 on April 1, 1672 and so on. Finally, add up the 34 numbers (or the 15 nonzero numbers) and you arrive at a discounted value of £477,647 under an assumed 6% discount rate. This number is (much) less than the original bankers' debt of £1,173,353, which means that the IRR was (much) less than 6%. This is yet another (trial and error) way to obtain the IRR. The 6% is too high, so we reduce.

Hopefully, this process is clear. The next column does the same analysis for a discount rate of 3%, in which case all the values are naturally higher (£695,038 now vs. £477,647 before), but still nowhere near the £1,173,353 lent by the bankers. Again, what this means is that the IRR must be lower than 3% as well. Or, stated differently, had the bankers' original debt been (only) £695,038 *and* they would have then received the 15 interest payments as stated *and* then received another £586,677 at the end of the 34 year, then yes, the IRR would have been 3%. But the debt was £1,173,353. Perhaps I'm flogging a dead king's horse here. We must reduce again.

In sum—and to wrap this up—the only way to obtain a present discounted value of exactly £1,173,353 (i.e. present value of the cash flow equals the outlay) is with a discount rate of 0.013%.

Ergo, the IRR to the creditors over the entire 34 years is one basis point. And finally, as far as any biases are concerned, if the cash flows occurred later during the year (from April onward) as opposed to on April 1 itself, then the present values would be (even) lower and the IRR would also be (even) lower. However—and this is key—since the sum total of payments was (slightly) more than the original bankers' debt (£1,176,531 vs. £1,173,353), we do know that the IRR was positive.

We leave the reader with the following takeaway: unless the cash flows were made earlier—which the Exchequer data from C. D. Chandaman (1975) simply do not support or the value of the debt in 1706 was somehow higher—the IRR on the bankers' debt was between 1 and 0 basis points, end of story. As I mentioned earlier, it is *not* valid to add up the interest payments or £589,854 and then divide over 34 years. The £17,348 yearly average, which happens to be 1.48% of £1,173,353, does not result in a proper yield of 1.48%—at least not using twenty-first-century finance techniques. In fact, my own calculation is really an upper bound on the IRR when you consider the fact that no cash was actually paid-out in the year 1706. Again, the Bankers' Debt was merged with the national debt. And, as many readers know 15 years later the South Sea Bubble came along.

Table B.1

Banker's debt:		£1,173,353	PV=£477,647	PV=£695,038	PV=£884,877	PV=£1,173,353
			\multicolumn{4}{c}{Discount rate for cash flows, back to April 1672}
Cash flow to creditors			6%	3%	1.5%	0.013%
April	1672	£0	£0	£0	£0	£0
April	1673	£0	£0	£0	£0	£0
April	1674	£0	£0	£0	£0	£0
April	1675	£70,000	£58,773	£64,060	£66,942	£69,972
April	1676	£97,249	£77,030	£86,404	£91,626	£97,198
April	1677	£65,506	£48,950	£56,506	£60,807	£65,463
April	1678	£65,506	£46,179	£54,861	£59,908	£65,455
April	1679	£65,506	£43,565	£53,263	£59,023	£65,446
April	1680	£33,700	£21,144	£26,603	£29,916	£33,664
April	1681	£45,683	£27,040	£35,012	£39,954	£45,629
April	1682	£42,972	£23,995	£31,975	£37,028	£42,915
April	1683	£28,902	£15,225	£20,879	£24,536	£28,860
April	1684	£32,261	£16,033	£22,627	£26,983	£32,210
April	1685	£15,848	£7430	£10,792	£13,059	£15,821
April	1686	£13,171	£5826	£8708	£10,693	£13,147
April	1687	£13,084	£5459	£8398	£10,465	£13,058
April	1688	£0	£0	£0	£0	£0
April	1689	£0	£0	£0	£0	£0
April	1690	£0	£0	£0	£0	£0
April	1691	£0	£0	£0	£0	£0
April	1692	£0	£0	£0	£0	£0
April	1693	£0	£0	£0	£0	£0
April	1694	£0	£0	£0	£0	£0
April	1695	£0	£0	£0	£0	£0
April	1696	£0	£0	£0	£0	£0
April	1697	£0	£0	£0	£0	£0
April	1698	£0	£0	£0	£0	£0
April	1699	£0	£0	£0	£0	£0
April	1700	£143	£28	£63	£94	£142
April	1701	£322	£59	£137	£209	£321
April	1702	£0	£0	£0	£0	£0
April	1703	£0	£0	£0	£0	£0
April	1704	£0	£0	£0	£0	£0
April	1705	£0	£0	£0	£0	£0
April	1706	£586,677	£80,909	£214,750	£353,633	£584,052
	Sum:	£1,176,531				

Source: Calculations by the author.

BIBLIOGRAPHY

Acemoglu, D., & Robinson, J. A. (2012). *Why Nations Fail: The Origins of Power, Prosperity and Poverty*. New York: Crown Business, a division of Random House.
Admati, A., & Hellwig, M. (2013). *The Bankers' New Clothes: What's Wrong with Banking and What to Do About It*. Princeton: Princeton University Press.
Ahamed, L. (2009). *Lords of Finance: The Bankers Who Broke the World*. London: Penguin Books Ltd.
Atwood, M. (2008). *Payback: Debt and the Shadow Side of Wealth*. Toronto: House of Anansi Press.
Bagehot, W. (1999). *Lombard Street: A Description of the Money Market (1873)*. New York: John Wiley and Sons.
Balen, M. (2002). *The King, the Crook and the Gambler: The True Story of the South Sea Bubble and the Greatest Finacial Scandal in History*. New York: Harper Collins.
Beresford, J. (1925). *The Godfather of Downing Street*. Boston: Houghton Mifflin.
Bernstein, P. L. (1996). *Against the Gods*. New York: John Wiley and Sons.
Brewer, J. (1988). *The Sinews of Power*. Cambridge: Harvard University Press.
Browning, A. (1913). *Thomas Osborne: Earl of Danby and Duke of Leeds*. Oxford: Oxford University Press.
Browning, A. (1929). The Stop of the Exchequer. *History, 14*(56), 333–337.
Browning, A. (1966). Settlement of the Banker's Debt Created by the Stop of the Exchequer. *English Historical Documents, Volume VI c. 1660–1714*. Routledge.
Bruner, R. F., & Carr, S. D. (2007). *The Panic of 1907: Lessons Learned from the Market's Perfect Storm*. Hoboken, NJ: John Wiley & Sons, Inc.
Carruthers, B. G. (1996). *City of Capital: Politics and Markets in the English Financial Revolution*. Princeton: Princeton University Press.

Carswell, J. (1960). *The South Sea Bubble*. Stanford, CA: Stanford University Press.
Chamley, C. (2011). Interest Reductions in the Politico-Financial Nexus of Eighteenth-Century England. *The Journal of Economic History, 71*, 555–570.
Chancellor, E. (1999). *Devil Take the Hindmost: A History of Financial Speculation*. New York: Farrar, Straus and Giroux.
Chandaman, C. (1975). *The English Public Revenue 1660–1688*. Oxford: Clarendon Press.
Clark, D. (1938). Edward Backwell as a Royal Agent. *The Economic History Review, 9*(1), 45–55.
Cohen, J. (1982). The History of Imprisonment for Debt and Its Relation to the Development of Discharge in Bankruptcy. *Journal of Legal History, 3*, 153–171.
Coleman, D. C. (1963). *Sir John Banks Baronet and Businessman: A Study of Business, Politics and Society in Later Stuart England*. Oxford: Clarendon Press.
Coote, S. (1999). *Royal Survivor: The Life of Charles II*. London: Hodder and Stoughton.
Dale, R. (2004). *The First Crash: Lessons from the South Sea Bubble*. Princeton: Princeton University Press.
Desan, C. (2014). *Making Money: Coin, Currency and the Coming of Capitalism*. Oxford: Oxford University Press.
Diamond, D. W., & Dybvig, P. H. (1983). Bank Runs, Deposit Insurance and Liquidity. *Journal of Political Economy, 91*(3), 401–419.
Dickson, P. G. (1967). *The Financial Revolution in England*. London: Macmillan.
Drelichman, M., & Voth, H. J. (2014). *Lending to the Borrower from Hell: Debt, Taxes and Default in the Age of Philip II*. Princeton: Princeton University Press.
Evelyn, J. (1955). *The Diary of John Evelyn*. In E. de Beer (Ed.), *Six Volumes*. Oxford: The Clarendon Press.
Ferguson, N. (2008). *The Ascent of Money: A Financial History of the World*. New York: Penguin Books.
Fraser, A. (2002). *King Charles II*. London: Phoenix, Imprint of Orion Books Ltd.
Galbraith, J. K. (1997). *The Great Crash 1929*. New York: Houghton Mifflin Company.
Geist, C. R. (2013). *Beggar Thy Neighbour*. Philadelphia: University of Pennsylvania Press.
Glaeser, E. L., & Scheinkman, J. (1998). Neither a Borrower Nor a Lender Be: An Economic Analysis of Interest Restrictions and Usury Laws. *Journal of Law and Economics, 61*, 100–120.
Gleeson-White, J. (2013). *Double Entry: How the Merchants of Venice Created Modern Finance*. New York: W.W. Norton and Company.
Goetzmann, W. N. (2016). *Money Changes Everything: How Finance Made Civilization Possible*. Princeton: Princeton University Press.
Goetzmann, W. N., & Jorion, P. (1999). Re-Emerging Markets. *Journal of Financial and Quantitative Analysis, 34*(1), 1–31.

Goodare, J. (2009). The Debts of James VI of Scotland. *The Economic History Review, 62*(4), 926–952.
Graeber, D. (2011). *DEBT: The First 5,000 Years.* Brooklyn, NY: Melville House Publishing.
Grayling, A. C. (2016). *The Age of Genius: The Seventeenth Century and the Birth of the Modern Mind.* London: Bloomsbury.
Gregory, J., & Stevenson, J. (2007). *Britain in the Eighteenth Century: 1688–1820.* New York: Routledge.
Haley, K. (1968). *The First Earl of Shaftesbury.* Oxford: Clarendon Press.
Harris, T. (2006). *Restoration: Charles II and His Kingdoms.* London: Penguin Books.
Hobbes, T. (2013). *Leviathan.* New York: Oxford University Press.
Holmes, F. (2003). *The Sickly Stuarts.* Gloucestershire: Thrupp, Stroud and Sutton.
Homer, S., & Sylla, R. (2005). *A History of Interest Rates* (4th ed.). New York: John Wiley & Sons, Inc.
Hoppit, J. (1987). *Risk and Failure in English Business 1700–1800.* Cambridge: Cambridge University Press.
Hoppit, J. (2002). The Myths of the South Sea Bubble. *Transactions of the Royal Historical Society, 12,* 141–165.
Horsefield, J. K. (1949). The Cash Ratio in English Banks Before 1800. *Journal of Political Economy, 57*(1), 70–74.
Horsefield, J. K. (1982). The Stop of the Exchequer Revisited. *The Economic History Review, 35*(4), 511–528.
Hull, J. C. (2014). *Options, Futures and Other Derivatives* (9th ed.). New York: Pearson/FT.
Hume, D. (1778). *The History of England: From the Invasion of Julius Caesar to the Revolution in 1688.* Indianapolis, IN: Liberty Fund (1983).
Hutchsinson, R. (2016). *The Audacious Crimes of Colonel Blood: The Spy Who Stole the Crown Jewels and Became the King's Secret Agent.* London: Weidenfeld and Nicolson.
Hutton, R. (1986). The Making of the Secret Treaty of Dover. *The Historical Journal, 29*(2), 297–318.
Hutton, R. (1989). *Charles the Second: King of England, Scotland and Ireland.* Oxford: Clarendon Press.
Iddesleigh, S. H. (1887). The Closing of the Exchequer by Charles II in 1672. *Lectures and Essays of the Earl of Northcote,* 244–285.
Isenberg, N. (2016). *White Trash: The 400-Year Untold History of Class in America.* New York: Viking: Penguin Random House.
Jha, S. (2015). Financial Asset Holdings and Political Attitudes. *Quarterly Journal of Economics,* 1485–1545.
Johnson, N. D., & Koyama, M. (2014). Tax Farming and the Origin of State Capacity in England and France. *Explorations in Economic History, 51,* 1–20.

Jones, N. L. (1989). *God and the Moneylenders: Usury and Law in Early Modern England*. Oxford: Oxford University Press.

Jones, W. J. (1979). The Foundations of English Bankruptcy: Statutes and Commissions in the Early Modern Period. *Transactions of the American Philosophical Society, 69*(3), 1–63.

Keay, A. (2016). *The Last Royal Rebel: The Life and Death of James, Duke of Monmouth*. London: Bloomsbury.

Kerridge, E. (2003). *Usury, Interest and the Reformation*. London: Ashgate.

Kindleberger, C. P., & Aliber, R. (2005). *Manias, Panics and Crashes: A History of Financial Crises* (5th ed.). Hoboken, NJ: John, Wiley & Sons, Inc.

Koudijs, P. (2015). Those Who Know Most: Insider Trading in 18th Century Amsterdam. *Journal of Political Economy, 123*(6), 1356–1409.

Koudijs, P. (2016). The Boats that Did Not Sail: Asset Price Volatility in a Natural Experiment. *The Journal of Finance, 71*(3), 1185–1126.

Larman, A. (2016). *Restoration: The Year of the Great Fire*. London: Head of Zeus.

Lee, M. (1965). *The CABAL*. Urbana: University of Illinois Press.

Lehman, C. (2016). *The Money Cult: Capitalism, Christianity and the Unmaking of the American Dream*. Brooklyn, NY: Melville House Publishing.

Lewin, C. G. (2003). *Pensions and Insurance Before 1800: A Social History*. East Lothian, Scotland: Tuckwell Press Ltd.

Livingstone, N. (2015). *The Mistresses of Cliveden: Three Centuries of Scandal, Power and Intrigue in an English Stately*. Home: Ballantine Books.

Lowndes, W., & Gill, M. D. (1931). The Treasury: 1660–1714. *The English Historical Review, 46*(184), 600–622.

Melton, F. T. (1986). *Sir Robert Clayton and the Origins of English Deposit Banking 1658–1685*. Cambridge University Press.

Milevsky, M. A. (2015). *King Williams Tontine: Why the Retirement Annuity of the Future Should Resemble Its Past*. New York: Cambridge University Press.

Milevsky, M. A. (2017). Valuing the Debt that Stopped the Exchequer in 1672, Schulich School of Business, available at www.moshemilevsky.com

Miller, J. (1991). *Charles II*. London: George Weidenfeld and Nicolson Limited.

Murphy, A. (2009). *The Origins of English Financial Markets: Investment and Speculation Before the South See Bubble*. New York: Cambridge University Press.

Neal, L. (1990). *The Rise of Financial Capitalism*. Cambridge: Cambridge University Press.

Nichols, G. O. (1971). English Government Borrowing: 1660–1688. *Journal of British Studies, 10*(2), 83–104.

North, D. C., & Weingast, B. R. (1989). Constitutions and Commitment: Evolution of Institutions Governing Public Choice in 17th Century England. *Journal of Economic History, 49*, 803–832.

Oates, W. E., & Schwab, R. M. (2015). The Window Tax: A Case Study in Excess Burden. *Journal of Economic Perspectives, 29*(1), 163–180.
Pepys, S. (1997). *The Concise Pepys*. (T. Griffith, Ed.) Hertfordshire: Wordsworth Classics of World Literature.
Petram, L. (2014). *The World's First Stock Exchange*. New York: Columbia University Press.
Picard, L. (1997). *Restoration London: Everyday Life in London 1660–1670*. London: Weidenfeld and Nicolson.
Pincus, S. (2009). *1688: The First Modern Revolution*. New Haven: Yale University Press.
Plaidy, J. (2005). *The Loves of Charles II*. New York: Crown Publishing Group.
Poitras, G. (2000). *The Early History of Financial Economics: 1478–1776*. Cheltenham: Edward Elgar Publishing.
Price, F. G. (1970). *Handbook of Goldsmith Bankers*. New York: Burt Franklin.
Quinn, S. (1997). Goldsmith-Banking: Mutual Acceptance and Interbank Clearing in Restoration London. *Explorations in Economic History, 34*, 411–432.
Quinn, S. (2001). The Glorious Revolution's Effect on English Private Finance: A Microhistory 1680–1705. *The Journal of Economic History, 61*(3), 593–615.
Reinhart, C. M., & Rogoff, K. S. (2009). *This Time Is Different: Eight Centuries of Financial Folly*. Princeton: Princeton University Press.
Richards, R. D. (1927). The Evolution of Paper Money in England. *The Quarterly Journal of Economics, 41*(3), 361–404.
Richards, R. D. (1929). *The Early History of Banking in England*. London: P.S. King & Sons, Ltd.
Roseveare, H. (1973). *The Treasury 1660–1807: The Foundations of Control*. London: George Allen & Unwin Ltd.
Roseveare, H. (1991). *The Financial Revolution 1660–1760*. London and New York: Longman.
Schofield, E. A., & Wrigley, R. S. (1981). *The Population History of England: 1541–1871*. New York: Cambridge University Press.
Selgin, G. (2012). Those Dishonest Goldsmiths. *Financial History Review, 19*(3), 269–288.
Seymour, A. (2013). *Royalist Rebel*. Barnsley: Pen & Sword.
Shaw, W. (1904). *Introduction to the Calendar of Treasury Books*. London: His Majesty's Stationary Office.
Shin, H. S. (2009). Reflections on Northern Rock: The Bank Run that Heralded the Global Financial Crisis. *Journal of Economic Perspectives, 23*(1), 101–119.
Silber, W. L. (2007). *When Washington Shut Down Wall Street: The Great Financial Crisis of 1914 and the Origins of America's Monetary Supremacy*. Princeton: Princeton University Press.
Smith, A. (2000). *The Wealth of Nations*. Toronto: Random House, Inc.

Spurr, J. (2000). *England in the 1670s: The Masquerading Age*. Malden: Blackwell Publishers.
Steinmetz, G. (2015). *The Richest Man Who Ever Lived: The Life and Times of Jacob Fugger*. New York: Simon & Schuster.
Temin, P., & Voth, H.-J. (2013). *Prometheus Shackled: Goldsmith Banks and England's Financial Revolution After 1700*. New York: Oxford University Press.
Tinniswood, A. (2004). *By Permission of Heaven: The True Story of the Great Fire of London*. New York: Riverhead (Penguin).
Tomalin, C. (2002). *Samuel Pepys: The Unequalled Self*. New York: Vintage Books.
Trevelyan, M. G. (1960). *England Under the Stuarts*. Middlesex: Penguin Books.
Turner, A. (2016). *Between Debt and the Devil: Money, Credit and Fixing Global Finance*. Princeton: Princeton University Press.
Turnor, T. (1677). *The Joyful News of the Opening of the Exchequer to the Goldsmiths of Lombard Street and Their Creditors*. London, England: Grays Inn Gate.
Uglow, J. (2009). *A Gambling Man: Charles II and the Restoration*. London: Faber and Faber Ltd.
Wedgewood, C. V. (2011). *A King Condemned*. London: Tauris Parke.
Wennerlind, C. (2011). *Casualties of Credit: The English Financial Revolution 1620–1720*. Cambridge: Harvard University Press.
White, M. J. (2007). Bankruptcy Reform and Credit Cards. *Journal of Economic Perspectives, 21*(4), 175–199.
Wilson, J. H. (1954). *A Rake and His Times*. New York: Farrar, Straus and Young.
Wright, R. E. (2008). *One Nation Under Debt: Hamilton, Jefferson and the History of What We Owe*. New York: McGraw Hill.

Index

NUMBERS AND SYMBOLS
2007/2008 financial crisis (Great Recession), 2, 160

A
Absalom & Achitophel (poem), 26
Alvarez, Isaac, 166–70
American call option, 108
Anglo Dutch wars, 22, 28–30, 46, 58, 75, 76, 87, 132, 136, 142, 177
asset liability management, 193

B
Backwell, Edward (Banker), 30, 55–62, 69, 98, 114, 160–2, 166, 168, 169, 178, 180
Bagehot, Walter, 53n4, 144, 145
Banks, John, 62–5, 69, 98, 114, 126, 131, 166, 173–5, 180, 197

Bennet, Henry (Arlington), 33–5, 35n24, 172
British Navy, 127
Burnet, Gilbert, 44, 49, 148

C
cabal, 42, 43, 48, 49, 99, 115, 125, 130, 131, 133, 136, 139, 142, 148, 162–4, 166, 167, 172, 176, 177
Calendar of State Papers, Domestic (*CSPD*), 158, 171
Calendar of Treasury Books (*CTB*), 124, 125, 132, 133, 135, 145, 151, 158, 161–3, 166, 167, 186n37
Catholic *vs.* Protestant, 137, 139
Cavendish, Margaret, 123n3
central limit theorem (CLT), 116

---

[1] Note: Page numbers followed by "n" refer to notes

Chandaman, C.D., 15n32, 16, 74–6, 78, 87, 89, 91, 101n4, 119n16, 187, 187n39, 189n40, 205, 207
Charles I (King of England), 17, 24, 27, 33, 35, 36, 38, 51, 52, 54, 55, 73, 83, 123, 129, 137, 144
Charles II (King of England), 3, 4, 8–10, 12, 14, 15, 15n32, 17, 21, 23n4, 24–8, 30–5, 37, 38, 39n28, 40, 41, 43, 46–9, 56, 58, 59, 68, 73–81, 84–9, 91, 102, 103, 109, 118, 121, 129, 136–42, 144, 145, 147, 167, 172, 176, 180, 187
Chatham, 127–31, 142, 144, 159
Church of England, 47, 134, 137, 172
City of Bombay, 133, 137
Clifford, Thomas, 10, 31–5, 38, 41, 42, 123, 130, 138, 139, 141, 148, 149, 172, 174, 176
collateralized debt obligation (CDO), 95, 104, 108, 109, 115
collateralized treasury order (CTO), 104–14, 116, 117, 119, 122, 125, 126, 128–30, 141, 143, 145, 146, 154, 159, 162, 163, 166, 168–70, 172–4, 177, 179, 182, 186, 190, 196, 198, 199
Cooper, Anthony Ashley (Shaftesbury), 38–41
Cromwell, Oliver, 24, 28, 33, 36, 38, 43, 45, 46, 56, 69, 77, 102, 122, 137
CUSIP, 95, 105
customs (tax), 85–9, 105, 151, 154, 156, 174, 177

D
debtors' prison, 3, 5, 7, 49, 62, 69, 69n19, 167, 173, 180, 182–5, 195
Defoe, Daniel, 6, 69n19, 183

de Moivre, Abraham, 116
derivative security, 108, 108n10
Dickens, Charles, 3, 6, 42, 182–5
Downing, George, 44–7, 59, 78, 82, 98, 100, 101, 105, 109, 124, 126, 136, 141, 144, 147, 178, 197
dramatis personae, 9, 21–49, 115
Dryden, John, 26, 39, 121
Duke, Marquess, Earl, Viscount and Baron, 21–4

E
Earl of Rochester, 22, 37, 122n2
East India Company (EIC), 63, 64, 102, 133, 162, 171, 173, 174
Eleven Months Tax, 97, 98, 122
Elizabeth I (Tudor, Queen), 98, 102, 128, 137, 148
Elizabeth II, Queen, 73, 78, 92, 93
English civil war, 43, 52
Evelyn, John, 7, 7n15, 15, 27, 32, 33, 46, 49, 128, 149
Exchequer, 2, 3, 6, 8, 11, 15, 17, 30, 38, 41, 46, 58, 61, 74–80, 86–90, 92, 97–105, 109–15, 118, 119, 121–3, 125–30, 135, 141, 144–9, 152–8, 161, 162, 164, 166, 169–75, 177–80, 182, 190, 196, 197, 207
excise (tax), 85–9, 105, 154, 156, 174, 177

F
financial risk premium, 9, 111, 112, 114, 116, 117, 198
Five Books of Moses, 65
Fox, John, 69

G

General Monk (Albermarle), 28, 123, 128
goldsmith bankers, 4, 10, 35, 51–70, 83, 98, 101, 102, 104, 105, 108, 111, 112, 114, 116–19, 126–30, 133, 141–4, 149, 154, 156, 158–60, 166, 168, 170–4, 177–9, 182, 184, 185, 187, 190, 193, 197, 199
Gwyn, Nell, 17, 26, 139, 142, 146

H

hearth (tax), 85–9, 99, 105, 125, 146, 154, 156, 174, 177
Hornby, Joseph (Banker), 169, 182
Horsefield, J.K., 16, 16n35, 54n6, 98n2, 108n9, 145, 180, 182, 186n37, 187, 187n39, 188, 189, 189n40, 205
Hyde, Edward (Earl of Clarendon), 26, 130

I

internal rate of return (IRR), 186, 189, 189n40, 205–8

J

James, Duke of York, 9, 21, 27, 59, 81, 140
James I (King of England), 23n4, 40, 68, 73, 137
Jews & Sabbath, 162–71
Jews & usury, 65, 67, 69

L

Lehman Brothers (Lehman moment), 128, 158, 198, 202

liquor tax, 135
Locke, John, 41, 64, 115, 116, 128n7, 131, 150, 175
London fire in 1666, 57, 74
London Gazette, 11, 82, 99, 100, 105, 110, 122, 128, 130, 145, 146, 151, 158, 164, 175
London plague in 1665, 3, 74
Louis XIV (King), 27, 35, 56, 73, 86, 116, 116n15, 131, 136–43, 172

M

Maitland, John (Lauderdale), 41–4
Marshalsea prison, 182
Martin Luther, 67

N

New Testament, 65
Newton, Isaac, 98, 116, 136
nobility *vs.* gentry, 21–4

O

Osborne, Thomas (Danby), 47–9

P

Pepys, Samuel, 3, 7, 11, 11n21, 16, 24n5, 27, 31, 32, 43, 46, 46n33, 49, 57, 59, 61, 61n9, 62, 64, 64n12, 77, 83, 96, 121, 123, 126–30, 130n9, 132n10, 140
Philip II (King of Spain), 12
point of optimal debt & liability (PODeL), 193–7
Poisson model, 107, 109–15
Prince Rupert of the Rhine, 36, 59
Public Records Office (PRO), 74

Q
Queen Catherine of Braganza, 30–1, 133, 161, 174

R
The Rake's Progress (Hogarth, William), 37
restoration of monarchy, 46, 121

S
sale of Dunkirk, 56
Shakespeare, William, 5, 69
Shaw, W., 15, 16, 58n8, 145–7, 163
Shylock, 69
Snell, George (Banker), 61, 169
Snow, Jeremiah (Banker), 151, 160, 169, 182
South Sea Bubble, 8, 13, 70
Spain (default), 12
Standard & Poors, Moodys, 112

T
tally sticks, 103, 142–3
Temple, John, 182
Tests Act, 175
Tower of London, 22, 37, 43, 49, 52, 53, 81, 83, 130, 144

Treaty of Dover, 35, 139, 140, 142, 147, 199
Triple Alliance, 131, 137
Turner, Bernard (Banker), 61, 169

U
usury and interest, 35, 66

V
Villiers, George (Buckingham), 35–8, 131
Viner, Robert (Banker), 55, 59–62, 69, 98, 114, 133, 142, 151, 160, 166, 168, 169, 178, 180

W
Westminster, House of Commons, parliament, 2, 6, 11, 12, 14, 27, 28, 31, 32, 34–6, 38–40, 44, 49, 52, 68, 84–9, 92, 93, 103, 123, 130, 131, 134–6, 140, 156, 171, 175–7, 179, 180
Whigs & Tories, 17, 145
Whitehall, Gilbert (Banker), 160, 169, 178, 180, 185
Williamson, Joseph, 99, 163, 165, 166
Wren, Christopher, 61, 83

The manufacturer's authorised representative in the EU is Springer Nature Customer Service Centre GmbH, Europaplatz 3, 69115 Heidelberg, Germany. If you have any concerns regarding our products, please contact ProductSafety@springernature.com

Printed and bound by CPI Group (UK) Ltd, Croydon, CR0 4YY
23/03/2026
02076735-0006